Bloom's Modern Critical Interpretations

Edward FitzGerald's
THE RUBÁIYÁT OF OMAR KHAYYÁM

Edited and with an introduction by
Harold Bloom
Sterling Professor of the Humanities
Yale University

CHELSEA HOUSE
P U B L I S H E R S
A Haights Cross Communications ◆ Company

Philadelphia

©2004 by Chelsea House Publishers, a subsidiary of
Haights Cross Communications.

A Haights Cross Communications ✦ Company

Introduction © 2004 by Harold Bloom.

Printed and bound in the United States of America.

10 9 8 7 6 5 4 3 2 1

Library of Congress Cataloging-in-Publication Data
The Rubait of Omar Khayyam / edited and with introduction by
Harold Bloom.
        p. cm — (Bloom's modern critical interpretations)
Includes bibliographical references and index.
   ISBN 0-7910-7583-4
  1. Omar Khayyam. Rubáiyát. 2. FitzGerald, Edward, 1809–1883—
Criticism and interpretation. I. Bloom, Harold. II. Series
  PK6525.R83 2003
  891'.5511—dc21

                                                    2003006918

Contributing editor: Janyce Marson

Cover design by Terry Mallon

Cover: © Stapleton Collection/CORBIS

Layout by EJB Publishing Services

Chelsea House Publishers
1974 Sproul Road, Suite 400
Broomall, PA 19008-0914

www.chelseahouse.com

Contents

Editor's Note

My Introduction ponders the perpetual popularity of the *Rubáiyát*, and celebrates the authentic aesthetic achievement of Edward FitzGerald's marvelous poem.

John D. Yohannan examines the literary cult of the *Rubáiyát* down to 1909, the fiftieth anniversary of the poem's first publication, while Iran B. Hassani Jewett learnedly traces the history of FitzGerald's "translation" (to call it that) and offers a summary of it.

In another introduction to the *Rubáiyát*, Daniel Schenker addresses our current "inability to talk about the poem," after which Robert Bernard Martin gives us the biographical details as to just how FitzGerald "discovered" the *Rubáiyát*.

Frederick A. de Armas widens our sense of FitzGerald by describing his translation of Calderón's drama, *Life Is a Dream*, while Vinni Marie D'Ambrosio traces T.S. Eliot's early obsession with the *Rubáiyát*.

In a contrast between Tennyson and FitzGerald (who were close friends), Norman Page emphasizes some common patterns shared by *In Memoriam* and the *Rubáiyát*, after which Arthur Freeman tells the story of the crucial involvement of the publisher Bernard Quaritch in the availability of the *Rubáiyát*.

The poet-critic John Hollander illuminatingly reviews the best recent critical edition of the poem, while Tracia Leacock-Seghatolislami traces both the good and the bad effects upon our knowledge of Persian poetry brought about by FitzGerald's very free version of the *Rubáiyát*.

In this volume's final essay, Erik Gray traces the common pattern of benign "forgetting" that links *In Memoriam* and the *Rubáiyát*.

HAROLD BLOOM

Introduction

John Hollander, in his review-essay on the best critical edition of the *Rubáiyát*, interestingly compares Edward FitzGerald's poem to Thomas Gray's "Elegy Written in a Country Churchyard." The two poems have absolutely nothing in common except their perpetual popularity with both intellectuals and middlebrows. Each refuses to dwindle into a Period Piece.

Rubáiyát simply means "quatrains" of a particular kind, rhymed *a a x a* (there are some variants). The historical Omar Khayyám (1048–1131), a Persian mathematician, is hardly one of the great poets of the Persian tradition. His four-line epigrams might now be forgotten except for Edward FitzGerald's transposition and indeed transmogrification of the *materia poetica* that Omar provided.

FitzGerald's first *Rubáiyát* appeared in 1859, and would have vanished, unread and forgotten, except that a copy reached Dante Gabriel Rossetti, poet-painter and leader of the circle of Pre-Raphaelites. Rossetti indubitably must have recognized and enjoyed the Tennysonian coloring of the poem. Even as Keats was grandfather of the Pre-Raphaelite poets, and the father of Tennyson, so the early Tennyson of "The Lady of Shalott," "Mariana," and "Recollections of the Arabian Nights" can be said to have sired Rossetti, William Morris, and one aspect of Swinburne, who joined George Meredith and the painter Burne-Jones in circulating the *Rubáiyát*.

Lightning struck Edward FitzGerald, in a proverbial sense, since only

1

his *Rubáiyát* lives; his translations from Calderón and of Greek tragedy are not good. An amiable but strange man, FitzGerald had suffered through a belated marriage and hasty separation, and found solace for his spirit in *his Rubáiyát*. I cannot read Persian, but those who can agree that FitzGerald greatly improves upon his original.

I have just reread the *Rubáiyát* in its definitive fifth edition for the first time in seven years or so, and find it to be even better than I remembered. It holds together as a poem of one-hundred-and-one quatrains from sunrise to the rising of the moon. A magical eloquence and delight informs it at virtually every quatrain, a curiously negative joy that affirms Epicureanism and implicitly evades or rejects both Christianity and Islam. Had FitzGerald been a recent Iranian, the Ayatollah would have proclaimed a *fatwa* against him.

Writing in 1859, FitzGerald inevitably takes as precursor poem his close friend Tennyson's *In Memoriam A.H.H.* (composed from 1833 to 1850, and then published in that year). Tennyson elegizes Arthur Henry Hallam, his dearest friend and comrade who died in 1833, at twenty-two. FitzGerald was shrewd enough to see that Tennyson's Christian faith was less persuasive than his doubt, and the *Rubáiyát* honors only the Tennysonian doubt.

In Memoriam also is written in quatrains, but in a strict rhyme-scheme of *abba*. No one, not FitzGerald himself, nor the Pre-Raphaelites, nor any recent critic, could argue that *Rubáiyát* as poetic achievement eclipses *In Memoriam*. Tennyson was not a thinker, but he was a poetic artist comparable in accomplishment to John Milton and Alexander Pope, or to James Merrill in our era. FitzGerald genially follows Tennyson at a pragmatic distance, not trying so much to overgo *In Memoriam* as to isolate its doubts, and then develop them with charming abandon.

I think readers of all ages respond equally to the *Rubáiyát*, but I find it particularly poignant now, when I am halfway between seventy-two and seventy-three, and am just recovering fully from a long aftermath to a serious operation. Any recent reminder of mortality helps sharpen the experience of rereading FitzGerald's poem, though I am saddened as I encounter his perpetual celebration of wine, forever forbidden to me by my physicians. In praise of the *Rubáiyát*, its enthusiasm for wine is imaginatively contaminating.

Omar's epigrams were independent of one another, but FitzGerald shows a grand skill at arranging his one-hundred-and-one quatrains so that each has its own point, and yet the procession has continuity and appears to move towards a cumulative stance.

Tavern replaces temple, a gesture that eschews argument. There is a subtle avoidance of sexuality in this celebration of wine and song; presumably

FitzGerald would have preferred boys to women, but in the year 1859 thought better of saying so. The lip pressed throughout seems to be the rim of the wine-cup, yet FitzGerald makes this ambiguous.

Essentially the *Rubáiyát* tells us that we go from Nothing to Nothing, defying all spirituality:

> And this I know: whether the one True Light
> Kindle to Love, or Wrath-consume me quite,
>   One Flash of It within the Tavern caught
> Better than in the Temple lost outright.

> What! out of senseless Nothing to provoke
> A conscious Something to resent the yoke
>   Of unpermitted Pleasure, under pain
> Of Everlasting Penalties, if broke!

So much for Christianity and Islam alike: does FitzGerald offer only wine in their place? Does the hint of Eros serve to go beyond this?

> And much as Wine has play'd the Infidel,
> And robb'd me of my Robe of Honour—Well,
>   I wonder often what the Vinters buy
> One half so precious as the stuff they sell.

The answer presumably comes in the three final quatrains:

> Ah, Love! could you and I with him conspire
> To grasp the sorry Scheme of Things entire,
>   Would not we shatter it to bits—and then
> Re-mould it nearer to the Heart's Desire!

> Yon rising Moon that looks for us again—
> How oft hereafter we shall wax and wane;
>   How oft hereafter rising look for us
> Through this same Garden—and for *one* in vain!

> An d when like her, oh, Sákí, you shall pass
> Among the Guests Star-scatter'd on the Grass,
>   And in your joyous errand reach the spot
> Where I made One—turn down an empty Glass!

Sákí, the male server of wine, is a steady presence in the poem, but the unnamed "Love" is a female absence, even when evoked here at the end. If there is an imaginative eminence in the poem, it comes here:

> The Moving Finger writes; and, having writ,
> Moves on: nor all your Piety nor Wit
>   Shall lure it back to cancel half a Line,
> Nor all your Tears wash out a Word of it.

> And that inverted Bowl they call the Sky,
> Whereunder crawling coop'd we live and die,
>   Lift not your hands to *It* for help—for It
> As impotently moves as you and I.

> With Earth's first Clay They did the Last Man knead,
> And there of the Last Harvest sow'd the Seed:
>   And the first Morning of Creation wrote
> What the Last Dawn of Reckoning shall read.

> YESTERDAY *This* Day's Madness did prepare;
> TO-MORROW'S Silence, Triumph, or Despair:
>   Drink! for you know not whence you came, nor why:
> Drink! for you know not why you go, nor where.

"That inverted Bowl they call the Sky" is alluded to in Wallace Stevens' superb "The Poems of Our Climate." FitzGerald's nihilistic extended lyric can be found in many unlikely contexts, for that is the force of a universally popular poem. It is a kind of mystery, at least to me, just how FitzGerald, an indifferent man-of-letters, could so touch multitudes, but his incessant revisions of his *Rubáiyát* may provide the clue. At heart, he was a revisionist, and of more than his own work, or even that of Tennyson. The allegiance, however strained, between religion and poetry was broken by John Keats. Like Rossetti and his circle, FitzGerald employed Tennyson in order to get back to Keats, though hardly in a finer tone.

JOHN D. YOHANNAN

The Fin de Siècle Cult of
FitzGerald's "Rubaiyat" of Omar Khayyam

A translated Persian poem, which was Edward FitzGerald's consolation against a melancholy life, became—even in his own lifetime—a literary fad in both England and America. After FitzGerald's death in 1883, it was to become a cult and indeed to produce its own anticult.

Some critics remained content to explain the extraordinary success of the poem in purely aesthetic terms: John Ruskin, for instance, thought it "glorious" to read;[1] Holbrook Jackson saw it as part of the maturing "Renaissance" of English poetry that had begun with Blake and passed through Keats to arrive at Dante Gabriel Rossetti;[2] Theodore Watts-Dutton judged it generically—with the entire *fin de siècle* preoccupation with Persian poetry, in Justin McCarthy, John Payne, and Richard LeGallienne—as merely another species of Romanticism.[3]

But such a view could hardly explain the excessively strong feelings the *Rubaiyat* engendered in both proponents and opponents—feelings which lay at the levels of psychological bent or philosophical bias considerably below the level of purely aesthetic need. More to the point was the explanation of Elizabeth Alden Curtis, herself a translator of the *Rubaiyat*. For her, Omar was the "stern materialist front mystic skies," who, by combining Horatian hedonism with Old Testament fatalistic pessimism, had produced a fundamental human cry [that] had no nationality."[4] For Richard

From *Review of National Literatures* 2, no. 1. © 1971 by *Review of National Literatures*.

LeGallienne, too, there was more to the poem than its poetry, which he had successfully adapted as he had that of Hafiz. To be sure, the Khayyam-FitzGerald *Rubaiyat* was "one of the finest pieces of literary art in the English language"; but, he added, "this small handful of strangely scented rose-leaves have been dynamic as a disintegrating spiritual force in England and America during the last 25 years."[5] A few years later, LeGallienne wrote *Omar Repentant*, a book of original verses in the rubaiyat stanza in which he advised the young:

> Boy, do you know that since the world began
> No man hath writ a deadlier book for man?
> The grape!—the vine! oh what an evil wit
> Have words to gild the blackness of the pit!
> Said so, how fair it sounds—The Vine! The Grape!
> Oh call it Whiskey—and be done with it![6]

Whether the *Rubaiyat* was a "disintegrating" force would depend on one's spiritual view—whether of religion or temperance: but at any rate, the poem seemed to have much more relevance to the age than most native contemporary poetry. A. C. Benson, looking back at that time, later wrote:

> It heightened the charm to readers, living in a season of outworn
> faith and restless dissatisfaction, to find that eight hundred years
> before, far across the centuries, in the dim and remote East, the
> same problem had pressed sadly on the mind of an ancient and
> accomplished sage.[7]

The question, of course, was: Precisely what in the contemporary intellectual climate corresponded to precisely what in the philosophical quatrains of Omar Khayyam? Alfred North Whitehead has somewhere spoken of the inability of the nineteenth century to make up its mind as to what sort of cosmogony it wished to believe in. This is certainly demonstrated in the variety of coteries that either adored or despised the *Rubaiyat*. It was the shibboleth for such various and often conflicting dogmas as theosophy, aestheticism, eroticism, determinism, socialism, materialism, and numerous types of occultism. It would not be unfair to classify some of these in the lunatic fringe.

In light of the subsequent furor over the profound implications of the poem, there is a charming innocence in James Thomson's interest in it as an excuse for a good smoke. As early as 1877 Thomson, who wrote under the initials "B.V." (for Bysshe Vanolis, an allusion to his two favorite poets,

Shelley and Novalis), contributed an article on Omar Khayyam to a trade journal called *Tobacco Plant*. Despite his admiration for the poet's intellectual fearlessness and daring love of wine, it is obvious that what chiefly interested Thomson was tobacco. Believing that "in default of the weed, [Omar] celebrates the rose," Thomson imagined "What a smoker our bard would have made had the weed flourished in the Orient in his time! Hear him address his Beloved in the very mood of the *narghile* [water-pipe]...." There followed the familiar quatrain beginning "A Book of Verses underneath the Bough."[8] (Twenty years later, Edwin Arlington Robinson, discovering the same poem, was to have the same fantasy!)

More serious challenges in the poem were sensed by translators, editors, reviewers, and readers—both in England and America—to whom it increasingly appealed in the last years of the nineteenth century. John Leslie Garner of Milwaukee, who made his own translation of the *Rubaiyat* in 1888, refused (as had FitzGerald) to accept the Sufistic or mystical interpretation of Omar Khayyam. For him, Omar was a pantheist-fatalist (and a precursor of Schopenhauer), whom the Sufis had taken over after his death, as Huxley had said theologicans craftily are apt to do.[9] That was one view.

Talcott Williams, editing FitzGerald's translation ten years later, was impressed with the power of race rather than religion. Omar's Aryanism as a Persian was more important than the Semitic Islamic faith which he had to accept:

> Watered by his desires, rather than his convictions, the dry branch of semitic monotheism puts forth the white flower of mysticism and sets in that strange fruitage which is perpetually reminding us that under all skies and for both sexes religious fervor and sensuous passion may be legal tender for the same emotions.[10]

If pantheism and fatalism can be bedfellows, why not sex and religion? It was perhaps good Pre-Raphaelite doctrine.

A dominant note in the interpretation of the *Rubaiyat* was struck by a Harvard undergraduate who, along with George Santayana, edited the *Harvard Monthly*. A. B. Houghton announced with surprising urbanity in the mid-eighties that the philosophy of despair Omar passed on to the present generation was equally a refutation of those who believed in a "far off divine event towards which the whole creation moves" and of those who would rebel against "Him." The "He" was not God, but the force of the universe—a pantheistic-materialist force. If this did not make perfect sense, there was little ambiguity about the decadent accents that rang out of the following:

Omar's thought is thoroughly in accord with the essence of the
thought of this century. We are no longer a younger race ... our
faces are no longer turned towards the sunrise: they look towards
the sunset ... today we are given over to introspection. We have
lost our healthy out of door life ... our religious faith is
disappearing.[11]

At a later date, confessing his love of the *Rubaiyat*, the Hon. John
Hay, Ambassador to the Court of St. James, reechoed these sentiments.
He marveled at the "jocund despair" which the twelfth century Persian
had felt in the face of life's bafflements. "Was this Weltschmerz," he
asked, "which we thought a malady of our day, endemic in Persia in
1100?"[12]

The initial impact of the *Rubaiyat* had been as a statement of religious
skepticism. It appeared, after all, in 1859, the same year as *The Origin of
Species*, a book which Bernard Shaw said abolished not only God but also the
Thirty-nine Articles of the Anglican faith. There had been a natural
hesitancy on the part of the translator in offering it to a mid-Victorian public,
especially as he had had the benefit of a pious clergyman's help in discovering
it. After the death of FitzGerald in 1883, however, the poem spoke to a
generation who were the products, not of the milieu which had produced the
translation, but of the milieu which the translation had helped produce. Its
advocates were a bit more aggressive. To these younger devotees (whom
perhaps Shaw had in mind when he spoke of "Anacreontic writers [who] put
vine leaves in their hair and drank or drugged themselves to death"),[13] the
epicureanism of Omar Khayyam was of equal importance with his
skepticism. Moreover, the translator was of equal importance with the
Persian poet. Out of these two ingredients came the Omar Khayyam Clubs
of England and America.

Veneration of the translator tended to surpass worship of the poet.
FitzGerald came to be thought of as the author of a poem called *The Rubaiyat
of Omar Khayyam* rather than as the man who rendered into English Omar
Khayyam's *Rubaiyat*. Theodore Watts-Dunton recalls his excitement in the
presence of a man who, as a child of eight, had actually talked with
FitzGerald and "been patted on the head by him." In an obituary notice of
F. H. Groome, he wrote:

We, a handful of Omarians of those ante-deluvian days, were
perhaps all the more intense in our cult because we believed it to
be esoteric. And here was a guest who had been brought into
actual personal contact with the wonderful old "Fitz."[14]

One of these early "Omarians" actually depicted himself and his group in the words that Shaw had applied to the unidentified "Anacreontic writers." Sharply distinguishing between two possible interpretations of the *Rubaiyat*, Justin H. McCarthy said that "to some, the head of Omar is circled with the halo of mysticism, while others see only the vine-leaves in his hair."[15] The phrase was repeated in a *Blackwoods* article that described members of the Omar Khayyam Club with vine leaves in their hair drinking cheap Chianti wine and fixing a keen eye on posterity.[16]

The British, or parent, organization of the Omar Khayyam Club came into being in 1892 with Edmund Gosse as President. He was playfully referred to by the members as "Firdausi," in part no doubt in allusion to that poet's preeminence among Persian authors, but probably also because Gosse had written a lengthy poem about Firdausi's legendary exile at the hands of the conqueror Mahmound.[17] There are differing accounts of the number of founding members, who included McCarthy, Clement Shorter (a later president), and Edward Clodd, whose *Memories* in 1916 embalmed some of the Club's earlier activities.[18] It was apparently agreed that membership should never exceed fifty-nine, the year of the appearance of FitzGerald's first edition. The Club's purpose was primarily social, not literary. Its quarterly dinners began at Pagani's Restaurant, then moved to the Florence, and on to Frascati's; still later, when omnibuses showed up on Oxford Street, they returned to Pagani's. The official table cloth bore the insignia of a flagon, the sun, and a total of fifty-nine apples; five apples, denoting the original founders, were always to the right of the cloth.

In 1895, Meredith, Hardy, and Gissing attended one of the dinners; at another were J. M. Barrie, Andrew Lang, Augustine Birrell, and, from the United States, Charles Scribner. An occasional visitor was Henry James. It was humorously reported that the Shah of Persia, during one of his trips to England, was asked to dine at the Omar Khayyam Club, to which he supposedly replied, "Who is Omar Khayyam?"[19] At the March 25, 1897, dinner, Austin Dobson read some verses challenging the supremacy of Horace as the poet of good fellows:

> *Persicas odi*—Horace said
> And therefore is no longer read.
> Since when, for every youth or miss
> That knows *Quis multa gracilis*,
> There are a hundred who can tell
> What Omar thought of Heaven or Hell ...
> In short, without a break can quote
> Most of what Omar ever wrote.[20]

In the following year, without prejudice to Horace, a fellow at Magdalen College, Oxford, rendered FitzGerald's quatrains into Latin verse "as a breviary for those who make a sort of cult of the Rubaiyat."[21] There is an amusing account of the cultists in a satirical skit of the time in which a bright child asks his elder some pointed questions.

Q.   Who is this Omar, anyhow?
A.   Omar was a Persian.
Q.   And these Omarians, as the members of the Omar Khayyam Club call themselves, I suppose they go in for love and paganism, and roses and wine, too?
A.   A little; as much as their wives will let them.
Q.   But they know Persian, of course?
A.   No; they use translations.
Q.   Are there many translations?
A.   Heaps. A new one every day.[22]

True, there were numerous new translations of the *Rubaiyat*, and some by Club members. But it was common knowledge that "the Club recognizes one and only one translation of Omar Khayyam—that it is concerned with FitzGerald's poem and none other."[23] The figure of the Squire of Sussex was easier for Englishmen to identify with than that of the distant poet of Nishapur.

When John Hay addressed the English Club in 1897, he was able to report that a similar movement was afoot in America, where "in the Eastern states [Omar's] adepts have formed an esoteric sect...." (He had himself heard a Western frontiersman reciting "'Tis but a tent," etc.)[24] In fact, the American Club was formed in 1900, on the ninety-first anniversary of FitzGerald's birth. No doubt the idea had been given encouragement by Moncure Daniel Conway's detailed account, in the *Nation*, of the activities of the English organization—how the British had tried in vain to persuade the Persian Shah to repair the tomb of Omar Khayyam in Nishapur, how the artist William Simpson, visiting the site with the Afghan Boundary Commission in 1884, had brought back seeds of the roses growing at the old tomb, and how he had had them grafted to the roses in Kew Garden.[25]

Thus, what started as a barely audible voice of dissent in 1859 had become by the end of the century, and on both sides of the Atlantic, an articulate caucus of dissidence that threatened to win majority support. Inevitably, the opposition was galvanized into action. Scholars, amateur philosophers, and poetasters took part in an interesting game. The new culture hero, Omar-Fitz, was made to confront some worthy antagonist, who might be a rival philosophy or a large figure in human thought—ancient or modern—designed to serve as foil. But since even the opposition seemed to have a soft spot in its heart for the *Rubaiyat*, the foil often turned out to be a fellow.

An anonymous reply to Khayyam came out in 1899 as *An Old Philosophy*. The rebuttal to the Islamic hedonism of the *Rubaiyat* took the form of one-hundred one quatrains inspired by a sort of liberal Christianity much in the spirit of Tennyson. Altering the typography of FitzGerald's quatrains so that the third line, instead of being indented, was extended, the author rather weakly argued:

> The Moslem still expects an earthly bliss,
> The Huri's winning smile, the martyr's kiss,
> And with fair Ganymedes dispensing wine,
> No future lot, thinks he, can vie with this.

> There shall no Huris be to please the eye;
> No happy hunting grounds shall round thee lie.
> Of sensual pleasures there shall be no need:
> Shall not the Great Eternal be thee nigh?[26]

It was not likely that such doggerel would persuade many to shed the vine leaves from their hair.

There was more challenge in a confrontation arranged by Paul Elmer More, the American humanist. For More, the chief intellectual struggle of the time was symbolized in the persons of its two most popular poets: Omar Khayyam and Rudyard Kipling. Kipling advocated the energetic, forward-looking life (perhaps the out-of-door life earlier mentioned by A. B. Houghton?); Omar stood for defeatism and ennui. More observed that for many people, the "virility and out-of-door freedom" of Kipling was a much-needed tonic to the fin *de siècle* mood and entertained the thought that the rising star of Kipling's imperialism—which extolled the "restless energy impelling the race, by fair means or foul, to overrun and subdue the globe"—might signal the decline of the dilletantish and effeminate Omar worship.[27]

For W. H. Mallock, the polarity was between Christianity and the philosophy of Omar Khayyam and Lucretius.

> In Christ, originated that great spiritual avid intellectual movement which succeeded, for so many ages, in rendering the Lucretian philosophy at once useless and incredible to the progressive races of mankind; but now, after a lapse of nearly two thousand years, the conditions which evoked that philosophy are once more reappearing.

Those conditions were not indicated exactly, but obviously the new representative of the Lucretian view was Omar Khayyam in his contemporary vogue. Not that he and Lucretius were of identical mind, but a strong enough resemblance existed to warrant offering the ideas of the classical poet in the meter of the *Rubaiyat*. And so the famous opening passage of *De Rerum Natura* comes hobbling out thus:

> When storms blow loud, 'tis sweet to watch at ease,
> From shore, the sailor labouring with the seas:
>   Because the sense, not that such pains are his,
> But that they are not ours, must always please.[28]

Mallock found Lucretius more relevant to the science of the time than Omar Khayyam; and, though he did not believe that Christianity was still the superstition Lucretius attacked, he urged a second look at the great materialist.

In the opinion of John F. Genung, a rhetorician who wrote and lectured on religious subjects, the proper pendant for the *Rubaiyat* was Ecclesiastes.[29] He did not view Omar with particular alarm. Indeed, he found in him no pessimism, but rather a gaiety that boded well for the future. People were less morose (in 1904) than in the time of Clough and Arnold. Genung could cite no less an activist than Robert L. Stevenson to the effect that

> ... old Omar Khayyam is living anew, not so much from his agnosticism and his disposition to say audacious things to God, as from his truce to theological subtleties and his hearty acceptance of the present life and its good cheer.[30]

But for all that, Ecclesiastes offered the better alternative.

> We think again of the Epicurean man, the loafer of Omar Khayyam's rose-garden, and our Koheleth ideal looks no more paltry but strong and comely. There is not enough of Omar's man to build a structure of grace and truth upon.[31]

It has been asserted that Robert Browning wrote "Rabbi ben Ezra" as a retort to the "fool's philosophy" of the *Rubaiyat*. It remained for Frederick L. Sargent to stage the debate formally. With a fairness that betrays a real ambivalence in the author's thinking, Sargent matches the seductive pessimism of Omar with the bracing optimism of the Rabbi, giving the polemical advantage to the latter, but gladly permitting the former to continue with his pagan revels—to the satisfaction, no doubt, of an equally ambivalent reader.[32]

So potent was the appeal of the lovely quatrains that some were determined to save Omar Khayyam from the perdition to which his blasphemous ideas assigned him. A way out was provided in the legend that the poet had indeed made a deathbed retraction. Thus there appeared in 1907 a so-called *Testament of Omar Khayyam*, whose author, Louis C. Alexander, announced in his prefatory "Note":

> To those who conceive of Omar Khayyam only as a sot and Agnostic—if not the despairing Materialist and Infidel—of the *Rubaiyat*, these poems will come as a surprise and a revelation ... For Omar Khayyam was a man of lofty yet humble piety ... and the majestic figure of the *real* Omar Khayyam—the Astronomer, Poet, Philosopher, and Saint—stands revealed.

The *Wassiyat*, or Testament, consisted of eighty-five quatrains in a job-like dialogue with God, who *justifies* himself in rather Browningesque terms:

> For God is the end for which the universe
> Travails by Knowledge and Love and Pain entwined;
> And joy is its music, and Death, ah! no curse—
> For the enlarged Soul, through it, itself doth find.

The book added as a bonus some odes, presumably composed by the disciples of Omar Khayyam, lauding his piety in stanzas reminiscent of Arnold's "Empedocles." One disciple points out that the Master did teach "in sense / of metaphor and parable and "feign discontent and doubt," and that one day "lands thou never knewest will proclaim thy fame." Another disciple pleads:

> Hast thou a word, Oh, Master,
> For thy faithful band,
> Who knew thy face unmasked, thy tears beneath thy laugh,
> And the devotion
> Of thy Soul's most secret strand,
> And that the wine ne'er flowed thou didst pretend to quaff.[33]

This was, of course, a return to the persistent idea that the sensuous imagery of the *Rubaiyat* is but a cloak to cover the mystical Sufi thought beneath.

H. Justus Williams would not allow this backsliding from the old paganism. His sixty-three quatrains purported to be *The Last Rubaiyat of Omar Khayyam*. These, he maintained, gave proof that the story of the poet's repentance had been exaggerated. Omar was never converted; he only temporarily changed his ways, as is apparent from the following:

> At last! At last! freed from the cowl and hood,
> I stand again where once before I stood,
> And view the world unblinded by a Creed
> That caught me in a short repentant mood.[34]

Obviously, the best, the most effective opposition to Omar Khayyam would have to come from one of his compatriots—a sort of homeopathic treatment for what so many called the sickly *Rubaiyat* malaise. The Reverend William Hastie, a Scottish student of Hegelian idealism, thought he had the cure:

> We confess ... that we have hated this new-patched Omar Khayyam of Mr. FitzGerald, and have at times been tempted to scorn the miserable self-deluded, unhealthy fanatics of his Cult. But when we have looked again into the shining face and glad eyes of Jelalleddin, "the glory of religion," our hate has passed into pity and our scorn into compassion.

These words were part of an *obiter dictum* on Omar that Hastie permitted himself in a book of adaptations (from the German of Rückert) of some mystical poems of Jelalleddin Rumi.[35] If Christian orthodoxy could not fight off the virus of the *Rubaiyat*, perhaps Islamic mysticism, in the work of a great Sufi poet of Persia, could.

The leading Persian scholar in England, Edward G. Browne, showed sympathy for the spiritual legacy Persia had passed to the world. In *Religious Systems of the World: A Contribution to the Study of Comparative Religion*, he dealt specifically with Sufism and with Bahaism, a new offshoot of Islam, both of which he regarded as pantheistic systems of thought occupying a middle ground between religion and philosophy, and therefore as applicable in England as in Persia."[36] Another scholar in this area, Claud Field, prophesied that the Bahais would improve the quality of both Islam and Christianity. In an article for *The Expository Times* (an Edinburgh religious publication emphasizing the higher criticism), he asserted that, with so much mysticism in the air of late, it behoved Englishmen to know the Master Mystic, Jelalleddin Rumi. It was a pity, be thought, that Rumi did not have his FitzGerald.[37]

That was the difficulty. FitzGerald himself, in deference to the Reverend E. B. Cowell, Omar's true begetter, had expressed the wish that Cowell would translate Rumi, who would constitute a more potent polar force to Omar than did Jami, whose *Salaman and Absal* was FitzGerald's first translation from Persian (published anonymously, 1856). But Cowell never brought himself to deal any more fully with Rumi than with the other Persian poets. When Rumi found a soulmate in the superb Arabic and Persian scholar Reynold A. Nicholson, things looked promising for the anti-Omarians.

Nicholson had begun as a student of classical literature, and some of his early attempts at rendering the Persian poets show that orientation. In a poem on "The Rose and Her Lovers," he was clearly dealing with the familiar Persian theme of the *gul* and the *bulbul*, the rose and the nightingale, but he chose to call the bird Philomel. Very much in the spirit of the late nineteenth century, he allowed himself a parody of the *Rubaiyat* called "Omar's Philosophy of Golf." He experimented with the Persian verse form, the ghazal or lyrical ode, and made the usual translations from Hafiz and the other classical poets of Persia. In an original poem addressed to Hafiz, he both imitated and paraphrased the poet:

> Nightingale of old Iran,
> Haunt'st thou yet Ruknabad's vale,
> Dumbly marveling that man
> Now unqueens the nightingale?
> Zuhra, mid the starry quire,
> Hangs her head and breaks her lyre.[38]

But he came into his element with the translation of some of Rumi's passionate but mystical love poems. Convinced that Rumi was "the greatest mystical poet of any age," he devoted the remainder of his life as scholar and popularizer to the translation, publication, and elucidation of that poet's work.

His absorption with Sufism led him to the belief that many of the popular stories of Islamic literature—the romance of Yusuf and Zulaikha (Joseph and Potiphar's Wife), the legend of the moth and the flame, of the *gul* and the *bulbul*, were but "shadow pictures of the soul's passionate longing to be reunited with God."[39] But he would not join those who wished to make Omar a Sufi. He contented himself with asking "What should they know of Persia who only Omar know?" It was his belief that

> to find the soul of Persia, we must say good-bye to her skeptics
> and hedonists—charming people, though sometimes (like the
> world) they are too much with us—and join the company of

mystics led by three great poets, Jelalledin Rumi, Sadi and Hafiz,
who represent the deepest aspirations of the race.[40]

Not all students of religion and mysticism in England, however, were
prepared to accept the aid of Jelalleddin Rumi and the Sufis. The gloomy
Dean Inge, a serious student of the subject, in a course of lectures in the late
nineteenth century, spoke with some acerbity of the loose (as he conceived
it) mysticism of the Persian Sufis. He held that, in regarding God as both
immanent and transcendent, they denied the existence of evil and threw the
door open to immorality, lack of purpose, and pessimism. The tendency to
self-deification he found in both the Sufis and Ralph Waldo Emerson; where
a predecessor of his had accepted both, he now rejected both. "The Sufis or
Mohammedan mystics," he said, "use erotic language freely, and appear, like
true Asiatics, to have attempted to give a sacramental or symbolical character
to the indulgence of their passions."[41] At the High Church level, at any rate,
ecumenism was a dubious possibility.

The sum of it was that, whether cultivated as flower or attacked as
weed, the *Rubaiyat* continued to thrive. Especially after 1909, when the
fiftieth anniversary of the first edition of FitzGerald was celebrated (and the
copyright lifted), editions multiplied. Even Nicholson, in that memorable
year, edited a reissue of FitzGerald's translation.[42] The explanation of the
extraordinary appeal of the poem to readers of all sorts may be found in an
area bounded on one side by high art, on another by pop culture, but on the
other two sides trailing off into a no-man's-land of unsolved anthropological
problems. Andrew Lang found the diagnosis for "Omaritis" (in America, at
least) in a condition of middle-browism. "Omar is the business man's poet....
To quote Omar is to be cultured." There was so little of him, you could take
him everywhere and read him hurriedly as you rushed about your business.
The Americans were throwing out Browning and Rossetti and reading Omar
along with *David Harum* and *The Virginian*.[43] For the Reverend John
Kelman, Omar was not an influenza, but a kind of plague. Calling for a
quarantine, he warned that "if you naturalize him, he will become deadly in
the West." It would be wiser, he advised, to take the poem as simply a
fascinating example of exotic Eastern fatalism.[44] But by 1912 it was probably
already too late.

Even more sober commentators, attempting to answer the question,
tended to leave it in ambiguity or to raise new and more difficult questions.
It helped little for Arnold Smith to tell readers of his book on Victorian
poetry in 1907 that the *Rubaiyat* appealed to doubters, atheists, and
Christians alike, and that it counseled Epicurean asceticism.[45] Equally

unsatisfactory was the commentary of Edward M. Chapman, a historian of religious ideas. It seemed to him that Omar's translator mixed the zest and the satiety of the third quarter of the century. The new discoveries in science, he said, had left the heart clamant, but the deeper feelings did not find utterance; "their burden, therefore, [was] increased by a school of thinkers who would, if they could, have denied them utterance at all." When the new science told people to deny these feelings, when they thought about religion but weren't sure they had a right to, they fell into Omar's mood of jovial cynicism. The "humorous perversity," of the poem, Chapman believed, led directly to the *reductio ad absurdum* of W. E. Henley's verses:

> Let us be drunk, and for a while forget,
> Forget, and ceasing even from regret,
> Live without reason and in spite of rhyme.[46]

Warren B. Blake turned his attention, with more interesting results, to the translator. FitzGerald, after all, was both a symptom of the condition that had produced his poem and a cause of the malady that came out of it. Fascinated by the valetudinarian habits of FitzGerald, Blake said darkly that "the curse of the nineteenth century lay upon him," as it did upon Flaubert, who was also an incomplete man wanting to be either an atheist or a mystic.

> We are waiting to be told what it was that doomed these men, these Flauberts and FitzGeralds, to an incompleteness that seems almost failure. Does the expression "atrophy of the will" help explain the riddle?[47]

The answer is of course not given, but the implied premises of the question say much about the age that made a cult of the *Rubaiyat*. What constitutes success? Are success in art and in life identical? Whatever FitzGerald might have given to life, would it have been more or better than he gave to art?

NOTES

1. Quoted in Alfred M. Terhune, *The Life of Edward FitzGerald, Translator of the Rubaiyat of Omar Khayyam* (New Haven, Conn.: Yale University Press, 1947), p. 212.

2. Holbrook Jackson, *Edward FitzGerald and Omar Khayyam, an Essay* (London: David Nutt, 1899), section IV.

3. Theodore Watts-Dutton, *Poetry and the Renascence of Wonder* (London: Herbert Jenkins, 1916), "Poetry."

4. Elizabeth Alden Curtis, *One Hundred Quatrains from the Rubaiyat of Omar Khayyam* (New York: Brothers of the Book, 1899), p. 11.

5. Richard LeGallienne, "The Eternal Omar," in *The Book of Omar and Rubaiyat* (New York: Riverside Press, 1900), pp. 16, 21.

6. Idem., *Omar Repentant* (New York: Mitchell Kennerley, 1908). unpaged.

7. Quoted by John T. Winterich in *Books and the Man* (New York: Greenberg, 1929), p. 332.

8. "B. V.," *Selections from Original Contributions by James Thomson to Cope's Tobacco Plant* (Liverpool, 1889), p. 60 ff.

9. John Leslie Garner, *The Strophes of Omar Khayyam* (Milwaukee: The Corbett and Skidmore Co., 1888).

10. Edward FitzGerald, *The Rubaiyat of Omar Khayyam*, ed. Talcott Williams (Philadelphia: Henry T. Coates & Co., 1898), "Foreword."

11. A. B. Houghton, "A Study in Despair," *Harvard Monthly*, I (Oct. 1885–Feb. 1886), p. 102 ff.

12. John Hay, *In Praise of Omar Khayyam, an Address before the Omar Khayyam Club* (Portland, Maine: Mosher, 1898).

13. Bernard Shaw, "Preface," in Richard Wilson, *The Miraculous Birth of Language* (New York: Philosophical Library, 1948).

14. James Douglas, *Theodore Watts-Dunton, Poet, Novelist, Critic* (New York: John Lane, 1907), p. 79.

15. Justin H. McCarthy, *The Quatrains of Omar Khayyam in English Prose* (New York: Brentano's 1898), "Note on Omar."

16. Cited in *The Book of Omar and Rubaiyat*, p. 47.

17. Edmund Gosse, "Firdausi in Exile," in Helen Zimmern, *Epic of Kings, Stories Retold from Firdausi* (London: T. Fischer Unwin, 1883).

18. Edward Clodd, *Memories* (London: Chapman and Hall, 1916), esp. pp. 89, 98, 161.

19. John Morgan, *Omar Khayyam, an Essay* (Aberdeen: Aberdeen University Press, 1901), "Introduction."

20. Austin Dobson, *Verses Read at a Dinner of the Omar Khayyam Club* (London: Chiswick Press, 1897). "Persian garlands I detest" is William Cowper's rendering of "Persicos odi" from Horace's Odes, I, 38. John Milton's version of "Quis multa gracilis" (Odes, I, 5) is "What slender youth, bedew'd with liquid odors, / courts thee on roses in some pleasant cave, / Pyrrha?" The two odes are among Horace's best known.

21. Herbert W. Greene, *Rubaiyat of Omar Khayyam rendered into English Verse by Edward FitzGerald and into Latin by* ... (Boston: Privately printed, 1898).

22. *The Book of Omar and Rubaiyat*, p. 47 ff.

23. *Ibid.*, 37.

24. Hay, *In Praise of Omar Khayyam*.

25. Moncure Daniel Conway, "The Omar Khayyam Cult in England," *Nation*, Vol. LVII, No. 1478 (Oct. 26, 1893), 304.

26. *An Old Philosophy in 101 Quatrains, by the Modern Umar Kayam* (Ormskirk: T. Hutton, 1899).

27. "Kipling and FitzGerald," *Shelburne Essays*, 2d ser. (Boston: Houghton Mifflin, 1905), pp. 106, 117.

28. W. H. Mallock, *Lucretius on Life and Death, in the Metre of Omar Khayyam* (London: Adam and Charles Black, 1900), p. xix and stanza 1.

29. John F. Genung, *Ecclesiastes, Words of Koheleth, Son of David, King of Jerusalem* (Boston: Houghton Mifflin, 1904), p. 167.

30. John F. Genung, *Stevenson's Attitude to Life* (New York: Thomas Y. Crowell, 1901), pp. 16–17.

31. Genung, *Ecclesiastes*, p. 156.

32. Frederick L. Sargent, *Omar and the Rabbi* (Cambridge: Harvard Cooperative Society, 1909).

33. Louis C. Alexander, *The Testament of Omar Khayyam [the Wassiyat] Comprising His Testament (or Last Words), a Song, Hymn of Prayer, The Word in the Desert, Hymn of Praise, also the Marathi or Odes of the Disciples* (London; John Long, 1907), "Note," stanza LXXVI, and "The Marathi."

34. H. Justus Williams, *The Last Rubaiyat of Omar Khayyam* (London: Sisley's Ltd., n.d.), stanza I.

35. William Hastie, *Festival of Spring, from the Divan of Jelalleddin* (Glasgow: James MacLehose & Sons, 1903),. p. xxxiii.

36. Edward G. Browne, "Sufism" and "Babism" in *Religious Systems of the World* (London: Swan Sonenshein & Co., 1902), pp. 314 ff., 333 ff.

37. Claud Field, "The Master Mystic," *The Expository Times*, XVII (Oct. 1905–Sept. 1906), 452 ff. Field also wrote *Mystics and Saints of Islam* (London: F. Griffiths, 1910).

38. R. A. Nicholson, *The Don and the Dervish, a Book of Verses Original and Translated* (London: J. M. Dent, 1911), pp. 62, 70 ff.

39. Nicholson, *Mystics of Islam* (London: C. Bell, 1914), pp. 116–17.

40. Nicholson, *Persian Lyrics* (London: Ernest Benn, 1931), "Preface."

41. William Ralph Inge, *Christian Mysticism* (New York: Scribner's, 1899), pp. 118, 321, 371.

42. *Rubaiyat of Omar Khayyam*, translated by Edward FitzGerald, edited with an Introduction and Notes by H. A. Nicholson (London: A. & C. Black, 1909).

43. Andrew Lang, "At the Sign of the Ship," *Longman's Magazine*, July 1904, p. 264.

44. John Kelman, *Among Famous Books* (London: Hodder and Stoughton, 1912), p. 89 ff.

45. Arnold Smith, *The Main Tendencies of Victorian Poetry* (Cournville, Birmingham: St. George Press, 1907), pp. xii, 135 ff.

46. Edward M. Chapman, *English Literature in Account with Religion, 1800–1900* (Boston: Houghton Mifflin, 1910), pp. 457–59.

47. Warren B. Blake, "Poetry, Time and Edward FitzGerald," *The Dial* (Chicago: 1909), XLVI, 177–80.

IRAN B. HASSANI JEWETT

The Rubáiyát of Omar Khayyám

I FitzGerald's Marriage

The most important literary event of 1856 for FitzGerald was his introduction to Omar Khayyam. While working in the Bodleian library, Cowell had found a copy of the quatrains of the eleventh-century Persian poet, Khayyam. The manuscript was a fourteenth-century one, and it belonged to the Ouseley collection. Cowell, who had never seen a manuscript of Khayyam's quatrains, was pleased with his find, and made a copy of it for his own use. He showed the quatrains to FitzGerald, and that summer, when FitzGerald visited the Cowells at Rushmere, they read Omar Khayyam together and discussed his philosophy. Omar undoubtedly made an impression on FitzGerald, who must have found his humor and his ironic jests at man's helplessness quite different from the solemn tones of *Salámán and Absál*. He wrote to Alfred Tennyson about his Persian studies on July 26, 1856: "I have been the last Fortnight with the Cowells. We read some curious Infidel and Epicurean Tetrastichs by a Persian of the Eleventh Century—as Savage against Destiny &c as Manfred—but mostly of Epicurean Pathos of this kind—'Drink—for the Moon will often come round to look for us in this Garden and find us not.'"

That summer's visit with the Cowells was FitzGerald's last for a long time. The Cowells left for India in August, and as a parting gift, Cowell gave

From *Edward FitzGerald.* © 1977 by G.K. Hall & Co.

FitzGerald a transcript of Omar Khayyam's quatrains similar to the one that he had made for himself. In Calcutta, Cowell remembered to look in the library of the Royal Asiatic Society for copies of Omar Khayyam's poetry; and he found one—a "dingy little manuscript," with the last page or two missing—that contained several hundred more tetrastichs than the Ouseley manuscript. In Cowell's letter to FitzGerald announcing his discovery, he wrote a Persian passage from the Calcutta manuscript that related a story about Omar Khayyam on the authority of Nizami of Samarkand. Cowell included a translation of this passage in his article on Omar Khayyam published in the *Calcutta Review* of 1858. Later, in his introduction to the *Rubáiyát of Omar Khayyám*, FitzGerald quoted Cowell's translation of the account.

In the meantime, FitzGerald was occupied with matters of a personal nature. On November 4, 1856, after a long engagement lasting seven years, FitzGerald married Lucy Barton, the daughter of his Quaker friend, Bernard Barton. The marriage held little promise of success. FitzGerald's close friends, who knew his idiosyncrasies as well as his sterling qualities, realized that he was making a mistake; and the more outspoken ones tried to dissuade him. Although FitzGerald himself had misgivings about his marriage, his sense of honor would not let him withdraw from the contract unless Lucy signified her willingness to break the engagement. But to a woman as strong minded as Lucy, FitzGerald's hesitation seemed like the behavior of a man inclined to look on the worst side of things; as for herself, she had no fears for the future.

How the engagement between two such strongly contrasting personalities had come about no one knows for certain, but close friends and relatives of both FitzGerald and Lucy shared the view that FitzGerald had become unwittingly involved in the contract and found it impossible to withdraw honorably. Perhaps his promise to Bernard Barton to watch over Lucy's interests and protect her from harm had occasioned his proposal. FitzGerald's grandniece, Mary Eleanor FitzGerald Kerrich, suggests that Bernard Barton had placed Lucy's hand in FitzGerald's as they both stood at the poet's bedside in his last moments, and FitzGerald had acquiesced helplessly in this implied promise of marriage which a more worldly man would have immediately disclaimed.[1]

Undoubtedly, the future welfare of the daughter of a very dear friend must have been an important consideration to FitzGerald, since Barton had suffered financial loss in the last year of his life and had left his daughter virtually penniless.

After Barton's death, FitzGerald had assisted Lucy in editing the letters and poems of her father and had published them with a memoir about

Bernard Barton, thus perpetuating the memory of the Quaker poet, as well as helping Lucy financially. F. R. Barton, in his edition of FitzGerald's letters to Bernard Barton, holds the view that FitzGerald proposed to Lucy during the time they were preparing the edition of her father's poems. "Nothing definite is known as to what impelled FitzGerald to take this step," he writes. "They had both passed their fortieth year: she a few months the senior. In point of intellect, culture, benevolence, and address, Lucy Barton was doubtless attractive, but she lacked physical charms. Her features were heavy, she was tall and big of bone, and her voice was loud and deep. The key of the puzzle is probably to be found in FitzGerald's quixotic temperament."[2]

Reading between the lines of the fragmentary records available, F. R. Barton reconstructs a series of events leading to the marriage. Starting with Barton's uneasiness about the future of his daughter and FitzGerald's assurance to him to help her, F. R. Barton concludes that after Barton's death, FitzGerald had made an impetuous offer to make up the deficiency in her income from his own; but her sense of propriety forbade her to accept such an offer. "One can imagine the effect of her refusal upon a temperament so sensitive as FitzGerald's," F. R. Barton writes. "He accused himself of having committed an indelicacy—a breach of good taste. His disordered fancy prompted him to believe that he had grossly outraged the feelings of his old companion's daughter by offering her money. The thought was intolerable to him. He must make amends at any cost. And so, heedless of the consequences, he proposed marriage, and she—blind to the distraction of mind that had impelled him—accepted his offer."[3] Whatever the circumstances surrounding the engagement, FitzGerald was obviously acting from a purely altruistic motive, for there had never been any romantic attachment between the two. In none of his published letters pertaining to this period is there a hint of any romantic feeling toward Lucy.

If FitzGerald did propose to Lucy Barton after her father's death, he was not able to carry out his promise of marriage for several years. His father's bankruptcy, occasioned by unwise commercial ventures, had also reduced FitzGerald's income by a considerable amount. Not until the death of his mother in 1855 was FitzGerald able to establish a home. As for Lucy Barton, following the death of her father, she had become companion to the two grandnieces of a wealthy Quaker, Hudson Gurney, and had lived at Keswick Hall in Norwich very much like one of the family. Her exposure to high society had apparently changed her considerably by giving her a taste for fine living; she looked forward to the time when, as the wife of a gentleman of means, she would be able to take part in the round of parties and dances that were the chief amusement of the local gentry.

FitzGerald, too, had changed in the seven years. Always of a retiring nature, he had become more of a recluse; he spent his time reading or taking walks, and visited only a few close friends. He had no use for the fashionable gentry and their conventions, and he cared little for what they said about him. His attire varied little from day to day; he always wore an old black coat with a crumpled collar and a tall slouch hat which he secured around his head with a handkerchief on windy days. In winter, an old shawl was his constant companion. Abstemious in habit, he lived very simply; he ate sparingly, mostly bread and fruit; but he never imposed his own way of life on others. His table was loaded with meat and game when guests were present, and he often sent presents of the local delicacies to his friends. In the mode of life that he had adopted, he had freed himself from convention; and he had no wish to impose restrictions on others.

In contemplating marriage with Lucy, FitzGerald was undoubtedly aware of the differences in their habits and attitudes. But he apparently hoped that, as he was fulfilling an obligation of friendship by giving her security and status, she, on her part, would respect his way of life and leave him alone. He had known her when she had lived a simple life with her father, and he evidently thought that it would not be difficult for her to adjust to a quiet, uneventful life with him. If FitzGerald had expected such an accommodation on Lucy's part, he was soon to be disappointed. She had her own ideas about how a gentleman should live, and she tried to make FitzGerald conform to them, which he would not do. Both were strong minded, neither would yield, and FitzGerald was very unhappy. They separated for a time, then tried to live together again; but their differences were irreconcilable. After less than a year of marriage, the two parted. Though they were never divorced, they did not live together again. FitzGerald blamed himself for all that had gone wrong; he made a handsome settlement on Lucy and returned to his old ways. Lucy FitzGerald lived until 1898, dying at the age of ninety.

The months of married life were perhaps among the unhappiest of FitzGerald's life. The two friends who had been closest to him and might have provided solace were thousands of miles away in India. His letters to the Cowells during this period show how sorely he missed them and how miserable he was. "I believe there are new Channels fretted in my Cheeks with many unmanly Tears since then," he wrote to Cowell on January 22, 1857, "'remembering the Days that are no more,' in which you two are so mixt up." For comfort, FitzGerald turned to Persian, which he associated with his friends and with the happy times he had spent in their company.

He started reading *Mantic uttair* of the Persian mystic Farid uddin Attar with the help of an analysis of the poem published by the French Orientalist Garcin de Tassy. Learning that de Tassy was printing a Persian text of the *Mantic*, FitzGerald wrote to him to ask where he could obtain a copy; at the same time, he sent de Tassy a copy of his *Salámán and Absál*. In his reply, de Tassy mentioned his intention of translating the *Mantic* into prose; his French translation was published in 1863. Though FitzGerald used de Tassy's Persian text of *Mantic*, he did not consult de Tassy's translation for his own version which is in verse, and which he had completed before the publication of the French translation.

By the end of March, 1857, FitzGerald had finished a rough draft of *Mantic uttair*, which he called *Bird-Parliament*. He put it away, hoping to come on it one day with fresh eyes, as he said, and to trim it with some natural impulse.

II   *Translation of the* Rubáiyát

FitzGerald next turned his attention to the *Rubáiyát of Omar Khayyám*. He was working with Cowell's transcript of the quatrains; and, wishing to find out if there were any other manuscripts extant, he wrote a letter to Garcin de Tassy. Since De Tassy had not heard of Omar Khayyam, FitzGerald copied the quatrains and sent them to him. De Tassy was so taken with the stanzas that he wrote a paper, "Note sur les rubâ'iyât de 'Omar Khaïyâm," which he read before the Persian ambassador at a meeting of the Oriental Society. When the article was published in the *Journal Asiatique* of 1857, he wished to acknowledge his debt to FitzGerald and Cowell in his article; but he was urged by FitzGerald not to do so. As FitzGerald later explained to Elizabeth Cowell, "he did not wish E. B. C. to be made answerable for errors which E. F. G. (the '*copist*') may have made: and that E. F. G. neither merits nor desires any honourable mention as a Persian Scholar: being none."[4]

FitzGerald continued his Persian studies with Cowell by mail. His letters to the Cowells in the spring and summer of 1857 resemble his diarylike letters to Thackeray during the Larksbeare period. FitzGerald added to his missives from day to day, keeping them for as long as two months; he described his progress in reading the *Rubáiyát*, wrote down his comments, and sought clarification of words and lines he could not understand. In his note of June 5 to a very lengthy letter which he had started on May 7, 1857, laid aside, and resumed a month later during a visit to his friend W. K. Browne, FitzGerald mentions working on a Latin translation of Omar:

> When in Bedfordshire I put away almost all Books except—Omar Khayyám!—which I could not help looking over in a Paddock

covered with Buttercups & brushed by a delicious Breeze, while
a dainty racing Filly of W. Browne's came startling up to wonder
and snuff about me. "Tempus est quo Orientis Aurâ mundus
renovatur, Quo de fonte pluviali dulcis Imber reseratur; *Musi-
manus* undecumque ramos insuper splendescit; Jesu-spiritusque
Salustaris terram pervagatur." Which is to be read as Monkish
Latin, like "Dies Irae," etc., retaining the Italian Value of the
Vowels, not the Classical. You will think me a perfectly
Aristophanic Old Man when I tell you how many of Omar I could
not help running into such bad Latin. I should not confide such
follies to you who won't think them so, and who will be pleased
at least with my still harping on our old Studies. You would be
sorry, too, to think that Omar breathes a sort of Consolation to
me! Poor Fellow; I think of him, and Oliver Basselin, and
Anacreon; lighter Shadows among the Shades, perhaps, over
which Lucretius presides so grimly.

The transcript of the Calcutta manuscript of the *Rubáiyát* that Cowell had
sent from India reached FitzGerald in June, 1857. The copy was in such
inferior script that it was indecipherable in places, and it must have taxed
FitzGerald's eyes and his knowledge of Persian to read it. But he studied it,
collated it with the Ouseley manuscript, and made annotations as he
progressed. He noted the differences in the two manuscripts in his long
letter to Cowell, suggesting what might be the correct reading of a word or
line, and received Cowell's reply by mail. By July 13, 1857, he had
accomplished enough to write to Cowell, "By tomorrow I shall have finisht
my first Physiognomy of Omar, whom I decidedly prefer to any Persian I
have yet seen, unless perhaps Salámán...."[5] As he read the transcript of the
Calcutta manuscript and compared it with that of Ouseley's, he was
constantly thinking of the Rushmere days: "Here is the Anniversary of our
Adieu at Rushmere," he added to the July 13 letter on July 14. "And I have
been (rather hastily) getting to an end of my first survey of the Calcutta
Omar, by way of counterpart to our joint survey of the Ouseley MS. then. I
suppose we spoke of it this day year; probably had a final look at it together
before I went off, in some Gig, I think, to Crabbe's." He ends the letter with
his translation of one of Omar's quatrains:

I long for wine! oh Sáki of my Soul,
Prepare thy Song and fill the morning Bowl;
For this first Summer month that brings the Rose
Takes many a Sultan with it as it goes.

He later changed the stanza to:

> And look—a thousand Blossoms with the Day
> Woke—and a thousand scatter'd into Clay:
>   And this first Summer Month that brings the Rose
> Shall take Jamshýd and Kaikobád away.

By August 6, FitzGerald had a rough plan for a translation of the *Rubáiyát*. "I see how a very pretty *Eclogue* might be tesselated out of his scattered Quatrains," he wrote to Cowell; then, remembering Cowell's religious scruples, he added, "but you would not like the Moral of it. Alas!"[6] Cowell himself was at this time planning to submit an article on Omar Khayyam to *Fraser's Magazine* which had already published three articles by Cowell, including one on Jami, but which had rejected FitzGerald's *Salámán and Absál*. On December 8, 1857, FitzGerald wrote to Cowell of his intentions regarding the Omar quatrains that he had translated:

> You talked of sending a Paper about him to Fraser, and I told you, if you did, I would stop it till I had made my Comments. I suppose you have not had time to do what you proposed, or are you overcome with the Flood of bad Latin I poured upon you? Well: don't be surprised (*vext*, you won't be) if I solicit Fraser for room for a few Quatrains in English Verse, however—with only such an Introduction as you and Sprenger give me—very short— so as to leave you to say all that is Scholarly if you will. I hope this is not very Cavalier of me. But in truth I take old Omar rather more as my property than yours: he and I are more akin, are we not? You see all his Beauty, but you don't feel *with* him in some respects as I do. I think you would almost feel obliged to leave out the part of Hamlet in representing him to your Audience: for fear of Mischief. Now I do not wish to show Hamlet at his maddest: but mad he must be shown, or he is no Hamlet at all. G. de Tassy eluded all that was dangerous, and all that was characteristic. I think these *free* opinions are less dangerous in an old Mahometan, or an old Roman (like Lucretius) than when they are returned to by those who have lived on happier Food. I don't know what you will say to all this. However I dare say it won't matter whether I do the Paper or not, for I don't believe they'll put it in.

How correct FitzGerald was in his estimate of Cowell's approach— "you don't feel *with* him ... as I do"—can be seen from Cowell's article on the

Persian poet that was published in the *Calcutta Review* of March, 1858. Entitled, "Omar Khayyam, the Astronomer-Poet of Persia," it was a review of two works on Khayyam—of K. Woepke's 1851 Paris edition of Omar's *Algebra* and of the article "Khayyám" from A. Sprenger's catalog of the Oude collection of manuscripts. In Cowell's account of Omar, he included his translation of a number of the quatrains; his literal rendering of one of the stanzas reads

> Wheresoever is rose or tulip-bed,
> Its redness comes from the blood of kings;
> Every violet stalk that springs from the earth,
> Was once a mole on a loved one's cheek.

FitzGerald's version of the same quatrain illustrates dramatically the difference between translation and creation:

> I sometimes think that never blows so red
> The rose as where some buried Caesar bled;
>   That every Hyacinth the Garden wears
> Dropt in its Lap from some once lovely Head.

Cowell's article on Omar Khayyam is interesting for two reasons. First, he was FitzGerald's teacher in Persian, but his views about Omar were not shared by FitzGerald. Second, his article represents the attitude of a Victorian Orientalist who is not untypical of his times when he expresses a distaste for all things not Christian and not English. He judges Khayyam not as a poet but as a heathen. In his opinion, Omar was not a mystic; his knowledge of the exact sciences "kept him from the vague dreams of his contemporaries." But Cowell thinks that Omar would have been better off had he been a mystic: "The mysticism, in which the better spirits of Persia loved to lose themselves, was a higher thing, after all, than his keen worldliness, because this was of the earth, and bounded by the earth's narrow span, while that, albeit an error, was a groping after the divine."

Cowell sees a deep gloom in Omar's poetry and offers his reason for it:

> He lived in an age and country of religious darkness, and the very
> men around him who most felt their wants and misery, had no
> power to satisfy or remove them. Amidst the religious feeling
> which might be at work, acting in various and arbitrary
> directions, hypocrisy and worldliness widely mingled; and every
> where pressed the unrecognised but yet over-mastering reality—

that the national creed was itself not based on the eternal relations of things as fixed by the Creator. The religious fervour, therefore, when it betook itself to its natural channel to flow in— the religion of the people—found nothing to give it sure satisfaction; the internal void remained unfilled.

Cowell compares Omar to Lucretius, but he thinks that "Omar Khayyam builds no system,—he contents himself with doubts and conjectures,—he loves to balance antitheses of belief, and settle himself in the equipoise of the sceptic." In Cowell's view, "Fate and free will, with all their infinite ramifications, and practical consequences,—the origins of evil,—the difficulties of evidence—the immortality of the soul—future retribution,—all these questions recur again and again. Not that he throws any new light upon these world-old problems, he only puts them in a tangible form, condensing all the bitterness in an epigram." From this group of philosophical verses, Cowell selects what he calls "two of the more harmless"; for he thinks that some of the "most daring" are better left in the Persian:

> I am not the man to fear annihilation;
> That half forsooth is sweeter than this half which we have;
> This life of mine is entrusted as a loan,
> And when pay-day comes, I will give it back.

> Heaven derived no profit from my coming hither,
> And its glory is not increased by my going hence;
> Nor hath mine ear ever heard from mortal man,—
> This coming and going—why they are at all?

Cowell's second stanza would be more familiar to readers in FitzGerald's version:

> Into this Universe, and *why* not knowing,
> Nor *whence*, like Water willy-nilly flowing:
>   And out of it, as Wind along the Waste,
> I know not *whither*, willy-nilly blowing.

Cowell's description of Omar's verses as "most daring" may seem strange to present-day readers, but Omar's "impiety" was shocking to many Victorians, and FitzGerald himself was aware of this reaction. Thomas Wright records in his biography an anecdote showing FitzGerald's respect for the religious scruples of others. In 1882, when he visited his childhood friend Mary Lynn, he gave her copies of his *Sea Words and Phrases*, *Euphranor*, and other publications. "Aware that Miss Lynn had no sympathy with the agnosticism in his great poem, he said to her, 'I shall not give you a copy of *Omar Khayyam*, you would not like it,' to which she said simply, 'I should not like it.' 'He was very careful,' commented Miss Lynn, 'not to unsettle the religious opinions of others.'"[7]

Cowell's article on Omar Khayyam perhaps reveals more about Cowell himself and the mores of his times than about Omar. The deadly seriousness of Cowell's approach shows no comprehension of Omar's humor and his light-heartedness—both so important to an understanding of his poetry. FitzGerald, however, did appreciate the humor in Omar and seems to have captured to a small extent his tongue-in-cheek ridicule of convention. He did not regard Khayyam as a mystic, as some other Orientalists did; and the many translators who have tried to follow in FitzGerald's footsteps have adopted one view or the other, depending on their own background. The wrangle over what philosophical label to attach to Omar Khayyam continues to this day. In 1858, Cowell summarized the reason for Omar Khayyam's skepticism:

> That Omar in his impiety was false to his better knowledge, we may readily admit, while at the same time we may find some excuse for his errors, if we remember the state of the world at that time. His clear strong sense revolted from the prevailing mysticism where all the earnest spirits of his age found their refuge, and his honest independence was equally shocked by the hypocrites who aped their fervour and enthusiasm; and at that dark hour of man's history, whither, out of Islam, was the thoughtful Mohammedan to repair? No missionary's step, bringing good tidings, had appeared on the mountains of Persia....

More than a hundred years after Cowell, a Soviet writer on Omar has found an entirely different reason for what he terms the "negativism" of Omar's philosophy. In his work *Khayyam*, A. Bolotnikov thinks that Omar, though a rebel, was unable to revolutionize the social conscience through his writings. Bolotnikov states that, since the world of commerce and finance to which Omar looked for support was unable to combat the feudal system, this defeat created the despairing skepticism in Omar that merges into a pessimism without hope. Cowell had sought an answer in religion, but the Soviet writer finds it in class struggle and in the failure of revolution. The only truth that emerges is the immortality of the genius of two men—Omar and FitzGerald—whose poems continue to hold the attention of readers and critics while times change and ideologies alter.

Even before the publication of Cowell's article in the *Calcutta Review*, FitzGerald had completed his translation of Omar's quatrains. In January, 1858, he gave it to J. W. Parker of *Fraser's Magazine*, who told him the magazine would publish thirty-five of the "less wicked" stanzas; but be told Parker that he might find them "rather dangerous among his Divines." *Fraser* kept the *Rubáiyát* for almost a year; but FitzGerald, who had gloomily predicted that the magazine would not print them, was not surprised. He wrote to Cowell that he supposed "they don't care about it: and may be quite right." He thought that, if the magazine did not publish his quatrains, he would copy them and send them to Cowell, adding, "My Translation will interest you from its *Form*, and also in many respects in its *Detail*: very unliteral as it is. Many Quatrains are mashed together: and something lost, I doubt, of Omar's Simplicity, which is so much a Virtue in him."[8]

By November, FitzGerald was sure that *Fraser's Magazine* had no intention of publishing his quatrains. "I really think I shall take it back," he wrote to Cowell on November 2, "add some Stanzas which I kept out for fear of being too strong; print fifty copies and give away; one to you, who won't like it neither. Yet it is most ingeniously tesselated into a sort of Epicurean Eclogue in a Persian Garden." FitzGerald added forty more quatrains to the thirty-five he took back from the magazine, and he had the *Rubáiyát* printed and bound in brown paper. Of the two hundred and fifty copies of the small volume he had printed, FitzGerald kept forty for himself: sent copies to Cowell, Donne, and George Borrow, the author of *The Romany Rye*; and turned over the remainder to Bernard Quaritch, the bookseller, from whom FitzGerald bought Oriental and other works. He instructed Quaritch to advertise Omar Khayyam in the *Athenaeum*, in any other paper he thought good, and to send copies to the *Spectator* and others. Enclosing payment for the advertisement and "any other incidental Expenses regarding Omar," FitzGerald wrote to Quaritch, "I wish him to do you as little harm as possible, if he does no good."[9]

Any satisfaction FitzGerald may have felt in the completion of his self-appointed task was soon marred by the death of his dear friend, W. K. Browne, who had been the model for Phidippus in *Euphranor*. Browne, who had been badly injured in a riding accident, lingered in great pain for several weeks. FitzGerald visited him and burst into tears when he heard Browne's familiar greeting, "My dear Fitz—old fellow" uttered in slow, painful syllables. I went to see him before he died," FitzGerald wrote to Cowell on April 27, 1859, "the comely spirited Boy I had known first seven and twenty years ago lying all shattered and Death in his Face and Voice.... Well, this is so: and there is no more to be said about it. It is one of the things that reconcile me to my own stupid Decline of Life—to the crazy state of the world—Well—no more about it." Referring to the volume of the *Rubáiyát* that had been printed, he added:

> I sent you poor old Omar who has his kind of Consolation for all these Things. I doubt you will regret you ever introduced him to me. And yet you would have me print the original, with many worse things than I have translated. The Bird Epic might be finished at once: but "cui bono?" No one cares for such things: and there are doubtless so many better things to care about. I hardly know why I print any of these things, which nobody buys; and I scarce now see the few I give them to. But when one has done one's best, and is sure that that best is better than so many will take pains to do, though far from the best that *might be done*, one likes to make an end of the matter by Print. I suppose very few People have ever taken such Pains in Translation as I have: though certainly not to be literal. But at all Cost, a Thing must *live*: with a transfusion of one's own worst Life if one can't retain the Original's better. Better a live Sparrow than a stuffed Eagle.

Here, in his own words, is FitzGerald's guiding philosophy in all his translations—a thing must live. He was slighted for not adopting a scholarly approach, and he was attacked for taking liberties with his originals. FitzGerald himself placed little value on his own works; whenever he referred to Omar, he included a little apology for the Persian's "wickedness." But his awareness of the opinions of others did not deter him from undertaking those tasks that he considered worthwhile. Even Cowell's lukewarm attitude towards the translations did not discourage FitzGerald greatly. Fortunately for English literature, FitzGerald adhered to his principle of "making an end of the matter by print." Though he always severely underrated his own efforts, and talked in 1859 of shutting up shop in the poetic line, he did continue his translations by rendering two more plays from Calderon into English, by adapting *Agamemnon* and the Oedipus dramas of Sophocles, and by putting the finishing touches to the *Bird-Parliament*, which he had hoped to print, but never did.

The story of the first edition of the *Rubáiyát* has been told many times. The small volumes stayed forgotten on Quaritch's shelves for a long time, and several were lost when the bookseller moved to new quarters. The copies that remained were marked down in price repeatedly, and they finally appeared in the penny box outside the shop. There they caught the eye of a contributing editor of the *Saturday Review*, believed to be Whitley Stokes, who purchased several copies at a penny each and distributed them among his friends. Someone, perhaps Stokes himself, mentioned the unusual quatrains to Gabriel Rosetti who told Algernon Swinburne about them. They bought copies for themselves; and, fascinated by what they read, returned to buy more copies. They found that the unexpected demand for the book had raised its, price. The fame of the *Rubáiyát* soon spread among the Pre-Raphaelite brotherhood. Swinburne, Rosetti, and William Morris praised the book and distributed it among their friends. Swinburne gave a copy to Edward Burne-Jones, who showed it to John Ruskin in 1863. Ruskin was so impressed by the quatrains that he sat down immediately and wrote a note addressed to the translator of the *Rubáiyát of Omar Khayyám*, to be delivered when the identity of the poet should become known. This note remained with Burne-Jones for nearly ten years, for not until 1872, when the third edition of the *Rubáiyát* appeared, was FitzGerald identified as the translator of the *Rubáiyát*.

III   *The Editions of the* Rubáiyát

The enthusiastic reception of the *Rubáiyát* by the Pre-Raphaelites stimulated demand, and by 1865 Quaritch was asking FitzGerald to consider a new edition. But FitzGerald, who had no financial interest in the venture and little hope of any literary success, could not make up his mind. His indecision seems to have been finally ended by praise from a dear friend. Mrs. Tennyson, who corresponded with FitzGerald, usually answering letters on her husband's behalf as well, wrote to him that Alfred Tennyson had expressed admiration for the *Rubáiyát*. FitzGerald was greatly pleased, and he embarked upon the task of preparing a second edition of the poem. To the seventy-five quatrains of the first edition, he added thirty-five more which increased the number of stanzas to one hundred and ten. He revised and altered many of the quatrains, and in some places changed their sequence.

In the preface to his first edition, FitzGerald had set forth the view that Omar Khayyam was not a Sufi and that his *Rubáiyát* did not propound mystical allegories. In 1867, J. B. Nicolas published the text of a lithograph copy of Khayyam's' quatrains that he had found in Tehran, as well as a prose translation in French in which he stated his conviction that Omar was a Sufi whose songs of wine and pleasure carried hidden mystical meanings. FitzGerald studied Nicolas' volume while preparing his second edition; and though he found inspiration in it for some new stanzas, he discovered no justification for the Frenchman's views, and no reason to alter his own opinion that Omar Khayyam was above all things a philosopher, as

FitzGerald had stated in his preface to the first edition:

> It has been seen that his Worldly Desires, however, were not
> exorbitant; and he very likely takes a humourous pleasure in
> exaggerating them above that Intellect in whose exercise he must
> have found great pleasure, though not in a Theological direction.
> However this may be, his Worldly Pleasures are what they
> profess to be without any Pretense at divine Allegory: his Wine is
> the veritable juice of the Grape: his Tavern, where it was to be
> had: his Sáki, the Flesh and Blood that poured it out for him: all
> which, and where the Roses were in Bloom, was all he profess'd
> to want of this World or to expect of Paradise.

The second edition of the *Rubáiyát*, consisting of two hundred copies, was printed and put on sale in 1868. FitzGerald kept a few copies for himself to give to friends. FitzGerald's agreement of sale with Quaritch showed FitzGerald's lack of interest in any financial gain. The bookseller was empowered to fix a salable price for the books; to take his own profit; and, after fifty copies were sold, to give the translator his share of the profits. FitzGerald would have handed the whole edition over to Quaritch to do with as he pleased had he not thought that he would "look more of a Fool by doing so." He did not expect even fifty copies to sell during his lifetime, and he remarked jokingly that his ghost would have to call upon Bernard Quaritch to collect his share of the profit.

The second edition of the *Rubáiyát*, with a hundred and ten stanzas, was the largest of all the five editions. In the third edition, FitzGerald cut back the *Rubáiyát* to a hundred and one stanzas; and he kept the fourth edition, the last one published in his lifetime, to the same length. Some of the stanzas that FitzGerald added to the second edition are as fine as the best of the first edition, as for example stanza 71, which does not appear in the first edition:

> I sent my Soul through the Invisible,
> Some letter of that After-life to spell:
>   And after many days my Soul return'd
> And said, "Behold, Myself am Heav'n and Hell:"

and stanza 72:

> Heav'n but the Vision of fulfill'd Desire,
> And Hell the Shadow of a Soul on fire,
>   Cast on the Darkness into which Ourselves,
> So late emerg'd from, shall so soon expire.

FitzGerald revised many of the stanzas of the first edition and changed the sequence of some of them. In each of the four editions and in the fifth one as well, which was published after his death, there are alterations and revisions, sometimes only a word or two in a stanza. FitzGerald did not refer to the original in making these changes, for his objective was not to bring his version closer to the Persian but to please his own fastidious literary judgment. The famous "Book of Verses" in the stanza that is the eleventh in the first edition, twelfth in the second, and the twelfth in the subsequent three editions—shows his method of revision:

1859

Here with a Loaf of Bread Beneath the Bough,
A Flask of Wine, a Book of Verse—and Thou
    Beside me singing in the Wilderness—
And Wilderness is Paradise enow.

1868

Here with a little Bread beneath the Bough
A Flask of Wine, a Book of Verse—and Thou
    Beside me singing in the Wilderness—
Oh, Wilderness were Paradise enow!

1872

A Book of Verses underneath the Bough,
A Jug of Wine, a Loaf of Bread—and Thou
    Beside me singing in the Wilderness—
Oh, Wilderness were Paradise enow!

1879 and 1889

A Book of Verses underneath the Bough,
A Jug of Wine, a Loaf of Bread—and Thou
    Beside me singing in the Wilderness—
Oh, Wilderness were Paradise enow!

FitzGerald's later revisions did not please many of those who had admired the first edition, among them A. C. Swinburne, who thought that the first edition was the only one worth having since FitzGerald had deleted from the later editions the first stanza which Swinburne considered the crowning stanza, the core or kernel of the whole work. In the first stanza in the first edition, FitzGerald is closer to the original than in the subsequent editions; he employs in it Omar's images of the emperor of day who is casting the pebble into the cup to signal the start of the chase, and the sun is throwing the noose of morning upon the rooftops:

> Awake! for Morning in the Bowl of Night
> Has flung the Stone that puts the Stars to Flight;
>   And Lo! the Hunter of the East has caught
> The Sultán's Turret in a Noose of Light.

In the second edition of 1868 FitzGerald altered this stanza to read:

> Wake! For the Sun behind yon Eastern height
> Has chased the Session of the Stars from Night;
>   And, to the field of Heav'n ascending strikes
> The Sultan's Turret with a Shaft of Light.

In the 1872 edition he changed it again:

> Wake! For the Sun who scatter'd into flight
> The Stars before him from the Field of Night,
>   Drives Night along with them from Heav'n, and strikes
> The Sultán's Turret with a Shaft of Light.

In the fourth and fifth editions, he left the stanza in its 1872 form and only added a comma after "Sun" in the first line. FitzGerald obviously preferred the later version, but many a reader would agree with Swinburne that the first version is the best.

The second edition of 1868 also did not bear the translator's name, but Quaritch seems on occasion, to have conveniently forgotten FitzGerald's wish for anonymity. In Quaritch's catalog of books that was issued in the autumn of 1868, E. FitzGerald, Esq., was listed as the translator of Omar Khayyam. The advertisement did not escape FitzGerald's notice, for he wrote to Quaritch that the price of three shillings and six pence for a copy of the *Rubáiyát* made him blush.

Meanwhile, the fame of the *Rubáiyát* had spread to the United States. In 1868, Charles Eliot Norton, an American critic and writer, who was a frequent visitor to England, was shown the *Rubáiyát* by his friend Burne-Jones, who also told Norton about John Ruskin's note addressed to the anonymous translator. Norton carried back to the United States a copy of the second edition of the *Rubáiyát* as well as the translation in French by J. B. Nicolas. Using the two versions as the basis of his review, Norton published an article in the *North American Review* of October, 1869, in which he was enthusiastic in his praise of FitzGerald's *Rubáiyát*; he considered FitzGerald's work not so much a translation as a literary masterpiece in its own right:

> He is to be called "translator" only in default of a better word, one which should express the poetic transfusion of a poetic spirit from one language to another, and the re-presentation of the ideas and images of the original in a form not altogether diverse from their own, but perfectly adapted to the new conditions of time, place, custom, and habit of mind in which they reappear. In the whole range of our literature there is hardly to be found a more admirable example of the most skilful poetic rendering of remote foreign poetry than this work of an anonymous author affords. It has all the merit of a remarkable original production, and its excellence is the highest testimony that could be given, to the essential impressiveness and worth of the Persian poet. It is the work of a poet inspired by the work of a poet; not a copy, but a reproduction, not a translation, but the redelivery of a poetic inspiration.

At the end of the review, Norton quoted seventy-six of FitzGerald's quatrains. Norton's article, the first review of the *Rubáiyát* to appear in any periodical, firmly established the reputation of the poem in the United States. The number of readers increased steadily, much to FitzGerald's surprise, who had predicted an "immortality" of a dozen years for his book. It was mostly to satisfy the demand of admirers in the United States that the third and fourth editions of the *Rubáiyát* were published.

In England, however, FitzGerald's *Rubáiyát* continued to be ignored by the critics until 1870 when *Fraser's Magazine* at last took notice of the poem. In the June issue of that year, an unsigned review of the *Rubáiyát* was published by the periodical. The reviewer, who later identified himself in a letter to Quaritch as Thomas W. Hinchliff, took notice of the difference in approach between the French version of the *Rubáiyát* by Nicolas and the English version. The reviewer, who congratulated the anonymous English translator on the "excellence and elegance of his performance," declared that "it would be difficult to find a more complete example of terse and vigorous English, free from all words of weakness or superfluity." The reviewer devoted eight pages to the poem in which he retraced the historical background of Omar and quoted Norton's tribute to the *Rubáiyát* in the

North American Review. In a comparison which seems forced, the British reviewer tried to establish a similarity between Tennyson and Omar by quoting lines from *In Memoriam* and *The Two Voices* to prove his point. He maintained that the lines from *The Two Voices*—

> To Which he answered scoffingly;
> Good Soul! suppose I grant it thee,
> Who'll weep for *thy* deficiency?

> Or will one beam be less intense,
> When thy peculiar difference
> Is cancelled in the world of sense?

—expressed sentiments akin to Omar's:

> And fear not lest existence closing *your*
> Account, should lose, or know the type no more;
>   The eternal Saki from that bowl has poured
> Millions of bubbles like us, and will pour.

> When you and I behind the veil are past,
> Oh but the long long while the world shall last,
>   Which of our coming and departure heeds
> As much as ocean of a pebble-cast.

The writer's conclusion was in favor of Tennyson's philosophy as opposed to Omar's:

> It is the scepticism of a man, who, after working through all the fields of science open to him, finds himself disposed to weep despairingly over the unsatisfactory result of human knowledge. Tennyson, in the masterly poem alluded to, was as unable as Omar to untie the knot in a logical manner; but, with the better light of modern thought to guide him, he cut it by an assertion of faith in the beauty and life and happiness of the world around him. To the old Persian sage such a lofty stage of thought was perhaps impossible: he knew the difficulty equally well, but he was not prepared with such a happy solution of it. We must be content to admire his verses for their intrinsic beauty. The vigour of his thought and expression, and their harmony with much that is now going on around us, inspire us with a strange feeling of

sympathy for him who in the darkest ages of Europe filled himself with all knowledge accessible to him before he went to his last sleep under the roses of Naishápúr.

Though FitzGerald was pleased with the favorable review, he still did not think that the *Rubáiyát* would attract many readers. He wrote to Quaritch on July 8, 1870:

> Thank you for your note about poor old Omar's first "fiasco"—I suppose he does not fare much better now, in spite of all those Gentlemen's good opinions; which might not have been the case had one of them given him a good word years ago. But I never ask anyone to do such a job for me, as someone I hear has now done in Fraser's Magazine. However Omar does not take up much room on your shelves, & will go off one day—when probably I shall be out of reach of a third Edition of 150 copies. Meanwhile I console myself with my little ship, & am
>
> Yours truly, Edward FitzOmar.

FitzGerald, of course, could not have been more wrong. Not only was the fame of his *Rubáiyát* becoming well-established across the Atlantic, but the name of the translator as well, largely unknown in England, was no secret to a circle of Omarians in the vicinity of Philadelphia. Mrs. Sarah Wister, the daughter of FitzGerald's old friend Fanny Kemble, was acquainted with FitzGerald's writings; and she was certain that FitzGerald was the translator of the *Rubáiyát*. She wrote to him, and was pleased to learn that she had guessed correctly. Thus, while *Fraser's Magazine* was paying tribute to the anonymous English translator of Omar Khayyam, Horace H. Furness, the Shakespeare scholar, was writing to Quaritch from Philadelphia in December, 1870: "If you ever communicate with Mr. Edward FitzGerald, I wish you would express to him, if he care to learn it, the keen delight with which his translation has been read by quite a circle of my friends here in this city; and I must confess so exquisite is the English and rhythmical is the verse that we all, ignorant as we are of the original, mistrust that the beauties of Omar are largely due to the genius of the translator."[10]

Owing largely to the purchases of admirers such as Furness, who bought ten copies of the *Rubáiyát*, the second edition of 1868 was almost completely sold. Quaritch, who did not wish to lose this modestly lucrative business with customers across the Atlantic, was trying to persuade FitzGerald to prepare a new edition by dovetailing the first and second editions. But FitzGerald's eyes were bothering him, and he was reluctant to undertake any extensive alterations. Moreover, he did not like Quaritch's suggestion of "reconciling two in one"; he thought that "such a scheme, with brackets &c. *would be* making too much of the thing: and you and I might both be laughed at for treating my Omar as if it were some precious fragment of Antiquity." His own plan was to have the second edition republished, "with some Whole Stanzas which may be 'de trop' cut out, & some of the old readings replaced." He added the following note to the letter, which is dated March 31, 1872: "By the by, Cowell wrote me some months ago that Ed[n]1 had been reprinted by someone in India. So I have lived not in vain, if I have lived to be *Pirated!*" The date of the letter, March 31, coincided with FitzGerald's birthday; and FitzGerald notes it: "Easter Sunday my own Birthday (64). I wonder how it is with Omar but I think I know."

After the third edition of the *Rubáiyát* was published in 1872, FitzGerald wrote to Quaritch on August 24: "I found Omar on my return home yesterday. I can only say that I doubt you have put him into a finer Dress than he deserves—and that some other Critics will have their Bile raised to say so—if they take any notice now of the old Offender. I only hope you have not overestimated your Transatlantic friends who I fancy are our chief Patrons—the Americans (as I found from Mrs. Wister—a daughter of Mrs. Kemble's) taking up a little *Craze* of this sort now and then." As for FitzGerald's share of the profit from the second edition, he instructed Quaritch to give it to some charity, public or private: "If the Persian *Famine Fund* still subsists, the money might properly be added to that—as I daresay old Omar would have done had he translated the Works of yours truly." From the third edition, FitzGerald asked for a dozen copies for himself; and bound copies were sent to Cowell and to Alfred Tennyson. His own copies FitzGerald wanted "*not* bound, as I would do them up with a Revision of Salámán, which I amused myself with two years ago. So I can stitch up the Saint & the Sinner together, for better or for worse." Obviously, FitzGerald had not forgotten *Salámán*, Cowell's favorite and his own: and remembered it again when the time came for a fourth edition of the *Rubáiyát*.

Just as the second edition with its revisions and additions had displeased some admirers of the first edition, the third edition with its alterations drew protest from at least one admirer of the second edition. Thomas Hinchliff wrote a letter to Quaritch dated January 28, 1876, in which he not only identified himself as the writer of the review in *Fraser's Magazine* but also expressed his disappointment with the changes in the third edition and the increase in price:

> When I sent for the copy of Omar Khayyám for which I am sorry
> to see that I have forgotten to pay, it was for the purpose of

sending it to a friend whose acquaintance I made when in Japan, & one I knew would appreciate it. I am honest enough to tell you that when I found it had grown at a jump from half a crown to 7s 6d I looked over it to see what changes there might be in the text, in company with my friend Mr. Simpson, the artist of the Illustrated News now in India, who is another worshipper of Omar: but we were grieved to find that Mr FitzGerald, in altering the text here and there, had grievously injured the Original. So much so that we agreed to send our friend in Japan an old copy which I had to spare, instead of the new and smarter edition. In quatrain 12 and in the last few of the poem I think the changes have been peculiarly for the worse, and regret it deeply. The old edition was so good that I should have liked to see "well let alone." Authors however will have their own fancies on such points.

Though the third edition was published mainly for the American market, the *Rubáiyát* was gaining readers in England, and curiosity about its authorship was increasing. Norton, who was visiting England in 1872, heard it rumored that the translator of the *Rubáiyát* was a certain Reverend Edward FitzGerald who lived somewhere in Norfolk and was fond of boating. The following spring, while walking with his friend Thomas Carlyle, Norton mentioned the *Rubáiyát* and expressed his admiration for it. Carlyle remarked that he had never heard of the poem, and asked whose work it was; Norton repeated to him what he had heard—that the translation was by a Reverend Edward FitzGerald who lived in Norfolk and who spent much time in his boat. Norton relates Carlyle's reaction:

"The Reverend Edward FitzGerald?" said he in reply. "Why, he's no more Reverend than I am! He's a very old friend of mine.... I'm surprised, if the book be as good as you tell me it is, that my old friend has never mentioned it to me"; and then he went on to give me a further account of FitzGerald. I told him I would send him the book, and did so the next day. Two or three days later, when we were walking together again, he said: "I've read that little book which you sent to me, and I think my old friend FitzGerald might have spent his time to much better purpose than in busying himself with the verses of that old Mohammedan blackguard." I could not prevail on Carlyle even to do credit to the noble English in which FitzGerald had rendered the audacious quatrains of the Persian poet; he held the whole thing as worse than a mere waste of labour.[11]

Norton remarks in another place that Carlyle had not taken to Omar Khayyam because he had found Omar's skepticism too blank and his solution of life in drink too mean. To Norton, "Carlyle's talk about Omar ... was the Philistinism. of a man of genius."[12]

When Norton informed Burne-Jones about his discovery of the translator's identity, he was sent Ruskin's letter with the request that it be given to the author of the *Rubáiyát*. Norton enclosed the letter in a note to Carlyle, saying that, "if he would not object to giving FitzGerald pleasure, on the score of his translation of the verses of the 'old Mohammedan blackguard,'" he was to put the right address on the letter and forward it to the translator. Carlyle sent both the note and Ruskin's letter to FitzGerald; and, in spite of his strictures against Omar, he added a handsome tribute of his own. He called FitzGerald's translation "excellent," and "the Book itself a kind of jewel in its way." FitzGerald wrote his thanks to Norton in a letter of April 17, 1873:

> Two days ago Mr. Carlyle sent me your Note, enclosing one from Mr. Ruskin "to the Translator of Omar Khayyam." You will be a little surprized to hear that Mr. Ruskin's note is dated September 1863: all but ten years ago! I dare say he had forgotten all about it long before this: however, I write him a Note of Thanks for the good, too good, messages he sent me; better late than never; supposing that he will not be startled and bored by my Acknowledgments of a forgotten Favor rather than gratified. It is really a funny little Episode in the Ten years' Dream.

FitzGerald's letter was the beginning of an epistolary friendship with Norton which lasted until FitzGerald's death.

Ruskin's letter, which was dated September 2, 1863, read as follows:

> My dear and very dear Sir,
>
> I do not know in the least who you are, but I do with all my soul pray you to find and translate some more of Omar Khayyam for us: I never did—till this day—read anything so glorious, to my mind as this poem—(10th. 11th. 12th pages if one were to choose)—and that, and this, is all I can say about it—More—more—please more—and that I am ever gratefully and respectfully yours.
>
> J. Ruskin.[13]

The popularity of the *Rubáiyát*, especially among the Americans, "Omar's best Friends," as FitzGerald called them, was increasing the sales of the book; and by 1875 Quaritch was hinting about another edition. But FitzGerald did not think that there would be enough demand to justify a fourth edition. He did concede, however, that Omar had done better than he had expected: "As to old Omar—I think he has done well, considering that he began his English Life as an 'Enfant Trouvé';—or rather 'perdu' in Castle Street 15 years ago. I only wonder he has survived up to this time. We will leave at present to smoulder away what Life is in him—perhaps as much as in myself. I had once wished to associate him with the Jámi—which I altered, but which I suppose no one would care for with all my alterations—"14 While Quaritch was still discussing the feasibility of another edition, Boston publisher James Osgood issued a reprint of the third edition in 1878. FitzGerald, who was sent a copy of the volume, wrote to Quaritch about it on January 25, 1878: "I know not if I am in any way indebted to you for a handsome—too handsome—Edition of Omar which came here a week ago; Messrs. Osgood, I see, Publishers. I wish that, at any rate, they would have let me know of their intention, as I have a few alterations, & an additional Note."

FitzGerald wrote again to Quaritch two days later about the Osgood reprint: "I think Messrs. Osgood who are, I believe, respectable Publishers, might have apprized me before they brought out their Edition. It is such a Curiosity of spinning out that I will send it to you to look at. But I think I will, as I said, leave Omar for the present; there has been Enough of him here, & now will be more in America. One day I may bring him out in better Company." The better company was *Salámán and Absál* which FitzGerald hoped to rescue from obscurity. He had hinted at this long-cherished wish when the second edition of the *Rubáiyát* was published; and he had even bound the third edition of the *Rubáiyát* with the revised edition of *Salámán*, a few copies of which FitzGerald had had printed at Ipswich. But Quaritch chose not to take the hint.

When the American reprint of the *Rubáiyát* appeared, Quaritch urged the necessity of another edition; but FitzGerald, whose *Agamemnon* had been printed in 1876, had no wish to undertake another revision of the *Rubáiyát*. He had, however, set his heart on introducing *Salámán* to Omar's ever-increasing readers; and he told Quaritch that the only condition upon which he would agree to a fourth edition of Omar was that *Salámán* be included with the *Rubáiyát*. He did not wish *Salámán* to be printed separately, as Quaritch proposed to do. "Salámán however would be much longer, & not half so welcome," he wrote to Quaritch on August 19, 1878, "& that is why

I did not think he w^{d} do alone. Besides, I really could not bear another of my things to be separately published, & recommended by Advertisement, so close upon the other two: whereas, *alongwith* Omar for Trumpeter, Salámán might come modestly forth: *both*, at a moderate price. You, however, may wish to keep the two separate; and that much you can tell me about if you care to do so; and I will then decide what shall be done in this very important matter." Quaritch had no desire to saddle the popular favorite with the unknown *Salámán*. But FitzGerald remained adamant. He did say, however, that he would consult with Cowell on the subject and let Quaritch know his decision. "If Omar be reprinted, Cowell wishes Salámán to go along with him," FitzGerald announced in his next letter of December 9, 1878; and Quaritch had to surrender.

The fourth edition of the *Rubáiyát*, in company with the revised *Salámán and Absál*—my "Persian Siamese" as FitzGerald called them—was published in 1879. The book was to have been dedicated to Cowell, but it finally appeared without any dedication. Cowell, according to FitzGerald, was "frightened at last from the two which he taught me being dedicated to him, as he had once agreed to: & even wished for." FitzGerald took an unusual amount of interest in the form and size of the volume, and he lavished a great deal of care on the printing of *Salámán*. Convinced that this edition would be the last one in his lifetime, FitzGerald made certain stipulations, the first of which was that "Omar, who is to stand *first*, be never printed separate from Jami."[15] He hoped in this way to ensure that *Salámán* would not be forgotten as long as the *Rubáiyát* was remembered. FitzGerald's affection for *Salámán and Absál*, if misplaced, is still understandable. *Salámán* was associated with his friend Cowell and a pleasant era in FitzGerald's life, as he himself admitted. FitzGerald also had great respect for Cowell's scholarship; and, modest and unassuming as FitzGerald was, he must have felt pride in Cowell's approval of his translation of *Salámán and Absál*.

But personal reasons alone cannot account, for FitzGerald's preference for *Salámán*. He was too meticulous an artist to have included *Salámán* with the *Rubáiyát* if he had had any doubts about the literary quality of the former. His reasons for insisting upon having both published together must have been literary as well as personal. From the moral point of view, Omar would appear, especially to a contemporary of FitzGerald, as a debauched spokesman for cynicism and godlessness. FitzGerald himself leaned towards agnosticism, but he was not a professed atheist. He did not regard Omar as a heathen wandering in the outer darkness; and, though he included quotations from Cowell in his preface, he did not agree with Cowell's "apology" for Omar. Nor did he consider Omar's praises of wine an indication of the poet's debauchery. He might have realized, however, that many of his readers would not agree with him; for, not having read the Persian, they would not only consider Omar an advocate of immorality, but would identify FitzGerald with this attitude. *Salámán*, on the other hand, represents a higher, spiritual view of life. Its allegory attaches a deeper meaning to life than the "eat, drink, and be merry" philosophy of the English *Rubáiyát*. The presence of the moral *Salámán* would nullify, therefore, the effect of the epicurean Omar.

Placing *Salámán and Absál* side by side with the *Rubáiyát* may also have been FitzGerald's way of answering those Orientalists who maintained that Omar Khayyam was a Sufi. Jami's mysticism is undisputed and his *Salámán and Absál* is regarded as a true mystical allegory. By reading both *Salámán* and the *Rubáiyát*, it would be possible to see not only what true mysticism was, but also how different from it was the imagery of the *Rubáiyát*. Philosophically and artistically, *Salámán* offers a perfect balance to the *Rubáiyát*. The latter ends on a note of resignation; whatever religion may have to say about the immortality of the soul, there could be no rebirth for man as far as observation and reason tell the poet. In *Salámán*, the ending is a glorious justification of faith. In the *Rubáiyát*, man descends into earth to become a part of it; in *Salámán*, man ascends to heaven to become one with the Deity. The shining light in the concluding lines of *Salámán* is in direct contrast to the "night" quatrains of the *Rubáiyát*. The *Rubáiyát* sings of the body; *Salámán* of the soul. FitzGerald knew that Omar spoke for him and for all mankind, but he may not have wished to leave Omar as his only spokesman. When the reader judged him, the mystic was to be there with the skeptic. Whether or not FitzGerald had all these objectives in view, he obviously failed in his effort to raise *Salámán* to the eminence that the *Rubáiyát* was soon to occupy in the hearts of millions all over the world. FitzGerald's emphatic stipulation that Omar never be published without *Salámán* was apparently disregarded after his death. His wish that "perhaps Persian, Greek, and Spanish might one day all gather into one little Volume" did not materialize in his own lifetime. Nor did he live to see the "little Craze" of the *Rubáiyát* grow into a worldwide popularity that has outlasted the works of contemporaries FitzGerald himself regarded as towering geniuses.

IV *FitzGerald's Version of the* Rubáiyát

FitzGerald's *Rubáiyát*—the "Epicurean Eclogue" as FitzGerald once described it—follows a pattern that is lacking in the original. By their very genre, Omar Khayyam's quatrains are individual entities that formulate and present a complete idea in each stanza and follow no set arrangement. The

Persian manuscripts that FitzGerald used for his translation had the quatrains arranged in an alphabetical order, a method often used for the convenience of both the copyist and the reader. The *rubai*, the Persian word for the quatrain, is regarded as a typically Iranian innovation. According to a popular story, the rhythm of the *rubai* was discovered by a Persian poet in the ninth or tenth century who used as his metrical model a phrase sung by a boy at play. The lyrical swing of the *rubai* and its short and epigrammatic form soon made it a popular vehicle of poetic expression among both the common folk and the literati. To compose a *rubai* on the spur of the moment became a skill worthy of respect and a pastime indulged in by the quick witted and the fluent.

The *rubai* consists of four hemistichs of up to thirteen syllables each, and a rhyme scheme of *a a b a* or *a a a a*. Traditionally, the first three hemistichs are regarded as the prelude to the fourth, which should be sublime, subtle, or epigrammatic. The range of subject matter and the variation of thought and mood in the *rubai* are unlimited; masters of the poetic art as well as anonymous composers of folk poetry have used the form. Sometimes, the masters have indulged in the ribald as well as in the sublime the contrast one finds in the quatrains of Omar Khayyam. The obscene jests in some of his stanzas greatly perplexed and troubled Omar's French translator J. B. Nicolas, who nevertheless stoutly maintained that Omar was a Sufi who employed only mystical imagery in his quatrains.

As regards the authenticity of the stanzas attributed to Omar in the manuscripts that have come under scholarly scrutiny, including the two manuscripts that FitzGerald used as his sources, no consensus exists among Orientalists. Some scholars, mostly in the West, have questioned the authorship of many of the quatrains and have attributed them to anonymous poets, but others have seen no reason to doubt that Khayyam composed the stanzas bearing his name. The process of authentication has been rendered difficult by the fact that no manuscripts of the *Rubáiyát* are to be found either in Khayyam's own hand or with his signature. The fact that no manuscripts survive from Omar's own lifetime, or from the period after his death is undoubtedly the result of the havoc wrought by the Mongol invasion which destroyed a large part of the cultural wealth of Iran.

Selections from Khayyam's *Rubáiyát*, however, have appeared in Persian anthologies, one of which goes as far back as 1611. These anthologies attest to the popularity of Omar's *Rubáiyát* and the existence of a large number of his quatrains at one time. No one who has read Omar's *Rubáiyát* in Persian can deny their merit. Khayyam may not be in the first rank of Persian poets, but he is not among the least. Persian scholars regard him as a liberal agnostic in the tradition of Avicenna and as a forerunner of

Hafez in whose poetry Omar's earthly wine assumes a mystical significance. Omar's place in the hierarchy of poets is expressed best in a statement attributed to the Moghul Emperor of India, Akbar, who said that each of Hafez's *ghazals* ("lyrics") should be accompanied by a *rubai* from Omar Khayyam, for reading Hafez without Omar was like wine without relish.

As for the philosophical content of FitzGerald's *Rubáiyát*, the diversity of thought in the Persian original far outstrips that of the English version. Omar's quatrains are not confined to the themes of doubt of a future life and the advocacy of enjoyment in this one. The freedom of the *rubai* form allowed Omar to indulge in satire, parody, veiled jokes sometimes taken as serious observations by critics, and in piety as well as skepticism. His changes of mood are one reason for his popularity, for every man can find a corroboration of his own state of mind in Omar.

The paradoxes of life that Omar points out in his *Rubáiyát* have puzzled men for centuries. Sufism was one attempt to answer these questions. The Sufi movement started in the early years of Islam, perhaps in the seventh or eighth century, and gained many adherents. The word Sufi is derived from the Arabic word *suf* and denotes an individual who prefers to wear a garment of simple woollen cloth rather than the silks and brocades fashionable among the wealthy. The Sufis renounced worldly goods and physical comforts, and devoted their lives to seeking reunion with the Creator. In its heyday in Iran, Sufism inspired some of the finest poems in the Persian language. The movement, however, fell into disrepute, and some of its practices drew sharp criticism not only from orthodox Muslims who regarded Sufism as dangerously close to heresy, but also from intellectuals in general.

Some of Omar's *rubais* enunciate thoughts found in Sufism, thus leading to the theory that Omar was a Sufi. Those who hold this view, however, disregard Omar's attacks on the hypocrisy of the Sufis and his jokes at their expense. His works show him to have been a liberal philosopher who tried to examine questions in the light of reason and logic. If his musings sometimes sound like mysticism or Sufism, it may be because mysticism also tries to find reasons for ostensibly unreasonable phenomena; and in its attempts to do so, it sometimes resorts to logical absurdities. As a creed, Sufism has rigidities that an independent thinker like Omar would have found hard to accept; nor is it possible to believe that a rationalist like Omar could have subscribed to the extremes of thought and behavior practiced by the Sufis in general.

FitzGerald himself described Omar in his preface to the *Rubáiyát* as a man "of such moderate worldly Ambition as becomes a Philosopher, and such moderate wants as rarely satisfy a Debauchee," who bragged more than he drank of the wine that he celebrates. If FitzGerald had been better acquainted with the conventions of Persian poetry, he might have pointed out as well that the wine mentioned with such frequency in Omar's poetry could be regarded as one of these conventions. Since wine was forbidden by Islam, it came to be used as a symbol of many things, such as rebellion against fate, the forbidden fruit, the hope of future happiness—since holy wine is one of the joys provided in paradise—and the mystical love of God. Persian poets have used wine in innumerable contexts; and, if they have praised it not symbolically but for its earthly effects, they have refrained from saying so openly, perhaps hoping that the nondrinker would interpret their wine as a symbolic one, and the wine-drinker embrace them as a comrade in sin. The wisdom of this course is illustrated by Omar's *Rubáiyát*, which is accepted by one group as mystical and by another as a celebration of inebriety.

Omar uses wine in many contexts, sometimes as a device to illustrate the absurdities in human concepts of sin and virtue. Khayyam is always critical of convention, but his attitude is not that of an indignant social reformer, but that of a scholar with a sense of humor. His approach is a tongue-in-cheek one, and his verses are lighthearted. He cannot resist applying the principles of logic and mathematics to all conventional beliefs, including the poetic and religious. In one quatrain, he examines addiction to wine in the light of the belief in divine omniscience. God knew, he says, since the beginning of time, that Omar would drink wine. If Omar should not drink wine, would it not turn God's omniscience to ignorance? Obviously an impossibility!

In another *rubai*, Omar propounds a joke in logic. His opponents told him, he says, not to drink, because wine is the enemy of faith. Realizing this, Omar declares, I swore by God that I would drink the blood of the enemy; for killing the enemies of God is a forgivable act. Drinking then, by Omar's calculation, becomes a doubly meritorious action. He is not above poking fun at the Deity; and, in one quatrain that is popular among the Persians, he complains that God had broken his jug of wine and ruined his pleasure. Dear God, he asks, could it be that you are drunk? Omar may or may not have written this stanza himself, but this irreverent humor is so typical of his quatrains that one can easily believe that Omar wrote it.

Little of Khayyam's humor survives in the English version. Perhaps FitzGerald did not understand or could not capture in English the subtle jokes, and the ribald and irreverent ones he left alone. He did notice the concepts of logic, mathematics, and physics that Omar employs in his *rubais*. In a note to stanza fifty-six in the third and fourth editions, he points out that the lines were a jest at his studies. He says that Omar has a mathematical quatrain comparing himself and his beloved to a pair of compasses, a metaphor made famous in English poetry by John Donne.

Omar's observations on life that have earned him the reputation of skeptic can be reduced to a few essential points. He advocates that man make the most of this life; for, whatever sages and saints may say, no one has verified the existence of another world beyond this one. He poses the question of sin and evil; if God created the world and everything in it, he also created evil. The responsibility for the existence of evil in this world thus lies at Gods own door. Since only good emanates from God, wine and sin cannot be evil, for these are also God's creations.

V *FitzGerald's Innovations*

In regard to FitzGerald's *Rubáiyát*, the reader who is unacquainted with the Persian may still find it hard to decide whether FitzGerald's poem is a translation or mostly his own creation. Persian words such as "Máh" and "Máhi" and the names of Persian monarchs that are deliberately used by FitzGerald to give an Oriental color to his poem tend to confuse the student, who begins to search for abstruse Eastern allusions in quatrains that proclaim their meaning in plain English. To look for obscurity in FitzGerald's *Rubáiyát* is to defeat the poet's main objective in not only the quatrains but in all his poems: the presentation of a foreign or difficult concept in a form familiar to the English reader. As FitzGerald repeatedly said in his letters, he was trying to achieve literary excellence rather than fidelity to the original. In this pursuit of excellence, he achieved in the *Rubáiyát* a lyrical beauty that in places outstrips the Persian.

Since FitzGerald conceived of the *Rubáiyát* as an "Epicurean Eclogue," he chose from Khayyam only those quatrains that fitted this pattern. He discarded all those stanzas that expressed piety or religious sentiment, though he was well aware of them; for in a letter to George Borrow of June, 1857, he copied the Persian and translated one of Khayyam's quatrains expressing repentance:

> Alas, that life is gone in vain!
> My every mouthful is unlawful, every breath is tainted;
> Commands not fulfilled have disgraced me;
> And alas for my unlawful deeds!

In choosing to translate only the "epicurean" quatrains, FitzGerald gave the *Rubáiyát* a superficiality and a one-sidedness not found in the original. On the other hand, FitzGerald's English version sparkles with a sustained light and color found only occasionally in the Persian. FitzGerald seems to have captured in his *Rubáiyát* the sunlight and spring flowers of his beloved Suffolk, all the more precious because so fragile and transient. Like the paradox of life itself, the poem evokes visions of beauty while constantly reminding one of its evanescence; FitzGerald's quatrains cluster around the single theme of the shortness of life and the uncertainty of the future. As he said many times, his poem is intended for those who are not acquainted with the Persian; for such a reader does not then miss the many subtle meanings and allusions in Khayyam's quatrains, and he does not resent FitzGerald's treatment of the Persian. To appreciate the *Rubáiyát*, one should regard it, therefore, as an English poem inspired by a Persian poet.[16]

FitzGerald's contribution to the shaping of the *Rubáiyát* is evident in the form of the English version. In the Persian, each independent quatrain expresses a thought and a mood perhaps quite different from the preceding or the succeeding one. In composing his version, FitzGerald had to find a unifying element which would connect the stanzas to each other and form a continuous whole. He solved the problem by introducing the element of drama and by giving his poem the unity of time—one day; the unity of character—the poet himself; and the unity of action—the poet's musings.

FitzGerald explained his approach in the *Rubáiyát* in a letter he wrote to Quaritch on March 31, 1872, in which he was defending the alterations and additions in the second edition which had displeased some readers:

> I daresay Ed[n] 1 is better in some respects than 2, but I think not altogether. Surely, several good things were added—perhaps too much of them which also gave Omar's thoughts room to turn in, as also the Day which the Poem occupies. He begins with Dawn pretty sober and contemplative: then as he thinks & drinks, grows savage, blasphemous &c., and then again sobers down into melancholy at nightfall. All which wanted rather more expansion than the first Ed[n] gave. I dare say Ed[n] 1 best pleased those who read it first: as first Impressions are apt to be strongest.

The introduction of action in a poem which deals essentially with philosophical concepts was a difficult task that FitzGerald accomplished successfully. He chose as his opening stanza a quatrain which does not appear as the first one in either of the two sources that he used. The quatrain conveys a sense of urgency and propels the reader into the dramatic action:

> Awake! for Morning in the Bowl of Night
> Has flung the Stone that puts the Stars to Flight:
>   And Lo! the Hunter of the East has caught
> The Sultán's Turret in a Noose of Light.

The journey of the sun across the sky, of man in this life, and of Omar through the realm of philosophy is on its way. The second and third stanzas maintain the hurried, breathless pace set by the first quatrain, and they convey the basic concept of the poem—that, in this life, there is no time to postpone pleasure. In the fourth edition, FitzGerald specified that the first three stanzas, which he called the "Lever de Rideau," should appear on the first page.

The start of day also heralds the advent of springtime in the fourth stanza:

> Now the New Year reviving old Desires,
> The thoughtful Soul to Solitude retires,
>   Where the WHITE HAND OF MOSES on the Bough
> Puts out, and Jesus from the Ground suspires.

For the poet, spring is the time of youth and pleasure; "The Nightingale cries to the Rose," and the poet calls out for more wine (Seventh stanza):

> Come, fill the Cup, and in the Fire of Spring
> The Winter Garment of Repentance fling:
>   The Bird of Time has but a little way
> To fly—and Lo! the Bird is on the Wing.

The three succeeding stanzas all continue the imagery of spring. Stanza eight introduces summer:

> And look—a thousand Blossoms with the Day
> Woke—and a thousand scatter'd into Clay:
>   And this first Summer Month that brings the Rose
> Shall take Jamshýd and Kaikobád away.

Stanzas nine to thirteen continue the images of early summer—green herbage, red rose, blossoms of a thousand hue. The twelfth stanza is the famous "Here with a Loaf of Bread beneath the Bough," and the quatrains of early summer culminate in the exquisite thirteenth:

> Look to the Rose that blows about us—"Lo,
> "Laughing," she says, "into the World I blow:
>   "At once the silken Tassel of my Purse
> "Tear, and its Treasure on the Garden throw."

The fourteenth stanza creates an abrupt change with its "Ashes" and its "Snow upon the Desert's dusty Face." The fifteenth stanza, however, returns to the summer images of golden grain, rain, wind, and aureate earth. FitzGerald apparently did not like the break in continuity, for in the second edition he inserted the "Golden grain" stanza after that of "the blowing Rose"; and he also made the "Ashes" quatrain number seventeen and the prelude to stanzas suggesting a change in mood, season, and the time of day.

In the first edition, stanzas sixteen to twenty-two indicate a change from early summer. The absence of color in these quatrains, the repeated use of "day," the description of Bahram sleeping, and the loveliest and the best drinking a round or two and creeping silently to rest—all evoke a quiet and somnolent atmosphere such as prevails at high noon in midsummer. Stanza twenty-two, which mentions summer's dressing in new bloom, gives an indication of the season of the year the poet is still describing. The section seems to end with the twenty-third stanza, which introduces a series decrying abstract theorizing. Even in quatrains that deal with abstract concepts, FitzGerald maintains the lively and energetic pace by using active metaphors, as in stanza twenty-eight:

> With them the seed of Wisdom did I sow,
> And with my own hand labour'd it to grow:
>   And this was all the Harvest that I reap'd—
> "I came like Water, and like Wind I go."

Images that occur most frequently in the *Rubáiyát* are the rose, the nightingale, and the green of spring and summer, all of which are favorite topics of Persian poetry. FitzGerald also uses light and color to indicate the time of day and the change of seasons, as well as to evoke a mood. Stanzas twenty-three, twenty-four, and twenty-five, which describe the futility of conjectures about the future, emphasize darkness and dust:

> Ah, make the most of what we yet may spend,
> Before we too into the Dust descend;
>   Dust into Dust, and under Dust, to lie,
> Sans Wine, sans Song, sans Singer, and—sans End!

> Alike for those who for To-Day prepare,
> And those that after a TO-MORROW stare,
>   A Muezzin from the Tower of Darkness cries
> "Fools! your Reward is neither Here nor There!"

Why, all the Saints and Sages who discuss'd
Of the Two Worlds so learnedly, are thrust
   Like foolish Prophets forth; their Words to Scorn
Are scatter'd, and their Mouths are stopt with Dust.

Stanzas twenty-nine and thirty ask the reason for man's creation in lines that flow with the sharpness of a clear, mountain spring:

Into this Universe, and *why* not knowing,
Nor *whence*, like Water willy-nilly flowing:
   And out of it, as Wind along the
Waste, I know not *whither*, willy-nilly blowing.

What, without asking, hither hurried *whence?*
And, without asking, *whither* hurried hence!
   Another and another Cup to drown
The Memory of this Impertinence!

Because these stanzas are as colorless as water, the brilliant flash of stanza thirty-one comes as a surprise:

Up from Earth's Centre through the Seventh Gate
I rose, and on the Throne of Saturn sate,
   And many Knots unravel'd by the Road;
But not the Knot of Human Death and Fate.

The seventeen stanzas that follow concentrate primarily on the play of light and shadow: Destiny's Lamp and "little Children stumbling in the Dark" (stanza 33); "Dusk of Day" in the marketplace (36); the stars setting and the caravan starting for the "Dawn of Nothing" (38); "The Angel Shape" stealing through the dusk (42); the "black Horde" contrasted with the polish of the "enchanted Sword"(44); and the "Magic Shadow-show / Play'd in a Box whose Candle is the Sun" (46). The only touches of color in these stanzas are gold, rose, and ruby vintage; and each is mentioned only once. The tempo of the poem quickens suddenly in stanza forty-nine, and is heightened in stanza fifty by the metaphor of the player striking the ball. The action reaches a peak in stanzas fifty-four and fifty-five, which together form a complete sentence:

I tell Thee this—When, starting from the Goal,
Over the shoulders of the flaming Foal

> Of Heav'n Parwin and Mushtara they flung,
> In my predestin'd Plot of Dust and Soul
>
> The Vine had struck a Fibre; which about
> If clings my Being—let the Súfi flout;
>   Of my Base Metal may be filed a Key,
> That shall unlock the Door he howls without.

These two stanzas, and stanza fifty-six, all of which contain words of light, heat, and suddenness, suggest to the mind's eye the last brilliant light cast by a sinking sun. Stanza fifty-eight with its direct address to the Deity—

> Oh, Thou, who Man of baser Earth didst make,
> And who with Eden didst devise the Snake;
>   For all the Sin wherewith the Face of Man
> Is blacken'd, Man's Forgiveness give—and take!

—provides a fitting end to the day and to the start of night which, as FitzGerald may or may not have known, is observed by Omar's countrymen with a prayer.

Stanza fifty-nine, which in the first edition is the beginning of the "Kúza-Náma" or the episode of the pots, uses the storyteller's device of attracting his audience's attention, "Listen again," in order to set the stage for the dramatic narrative of the pots. The episode occupies that part of the evening when the sun has set, but the moon has not as yet risen. The haze of twilight which surrounds the stanzas is skillfully suggested by "the surly Tapster," his visage daubed with the "smoke of Hell." The greyness of twilight is matched, as it were, with the aridity of abstract speculation in stanza sixty-five:

> Then said another with a long-drawn Sigh,
> "My Clay with long oblivion is gone dry:
>   "But, fill me with the old familiar juice,
> "Methinks I might recover by-and-by!"

The advent of "the little Crescent" ends the episode and ushers in a mood of calm cheerfulness. The garden is alive again; perfume is in the air; spring has come; and nature has renewed herself. But, for the poet, there is no return. His farewell is sad, but not bitter:

Ah, with the Grape my fading Life provide,
And wash my Body whence the Life has died,
    And in a Windingsheet of Vine-leaf wrapt
So bury me by some sweet Garden-side.

That ev'n my buried Ashes such a Snare
Of Perfume shall fling up into the Air,
    As not a True Believer passing by
But shall be overtaken unaware.

Though the poet is no more, he lives on in nature, having merged with it.

The end of the poem returns to the beginning: the garden, spring, and wine. But, in place of the hubbub of dawn, there is the peaceful quiet of a moonlit night. The last two stanzas of the *Rubáiyát* shine with a lyrical beauty seldom matched in English literature:

Ah, Moon of my Delight who know'st no wane,
The Moon of Heav'n is rising once again:
    How oft hereafter rising shall she look
Through this same Garden after me—in vain!

And when Thyself with shining Foot shall pass
Among the Guests Star-scatter'd on the Grass,
    And in thy joyous Errand reach the Spot
Where I made one—turn down an empty Glass!

VI   *Kúza-Náma*

In the episode of the pots, FitzGerald retained the paradoxes formulated by Omar. FitzGerald arranged the speculative stanzas consecutively in the form of questions. In the 1872 edition, he revised one of the stanzas to indicate the Sufistic nature of the questions raised. In the first edition, he had written the stanza thus:

And, strange to tell, among that Earthen Lot
Some could articulate, while others not:
    And suddenly one more impatient cried—
"Who *is* the Potter, pray, and who the Pot?"

                                         (stanza 60)

In the second edition he revised the stanza:

> Thus with the Dead as with the Living, *What?*
> And *Why?* so ready, but the *Wherefor* not,
>   One on a sudden peevishly exclaim'd,
> "Which is the Potter, pray, and which the Pot?"
>
>   (stanza 94)

This version did not please FitzGerald, for in the third edition he changed it, adding the word "Súfi" as well:

> Whereat some one of the loquacious Lot—
> I think a Súfi pipkin—waxing hot—
>   "All this of Pot and Potter—Tell me, then,
> Who makes—Who sells—Who buys—Who is the Pot?"
>
>   (stanza 87)

In the fourth edition, he restored the last line to its original form, but left the first three lines intact:

> Whereat some one of the loquacious Lot—
> I think a Súfi pipkin—waxing hot—
>   "All this of Pot and Potter—Tell me, then,
> "Who is the Potter, pray, and who the Pot?"
>
>   (stanza 87)

In the first edition, the questions appear under "Kúza-Náma," beginning with stanza sixty, and ending with the rising of the crescent, stanza sixty-six. FitzGerald arranges them in succession: (A) What is the true nature of existence, and of man's relationship to God? (B) If God created man for a purpose, why does he stamp him back to earth again? Why does God create beautiful things, and then destroy them for no apparent reason? (C) If there is ugliness, why did God create it? (D) If God is all-merciful, would it not be against his nature to punish men? Stanza sixty-five offers no solution, but a way of escape from exhausting and insoluble paradoxes—the old familiar juice of the grape which at least ensures a jolly time while life lasts.

In later editions, FitzGerald removed the subtitle of "Kúza-Náma," or the episode of the pots; but he left the questions arranged consecutively and as parts of the episode. In the second edition, FitzGerald added a number of stanzas with a philosophical content, perhaps influenced by his reading of Nicolas' edition of the *Rubáiyát* from the manuscript he had found in Iran.

The sequence of stanzas fifty to fifty-five of the second edition are not in the first edition. Stanza thirty-six, which first appears in the second edition, draws upon an allusion in Attar's *Mantic uttair*, which FitzGerald also translated, for the image of the mourning sea:

> Earth could not answer; nor the Seas that mourn
> In flowing Purple, of their Lord forlorn;
>   Nor Heav'n, with those eternal Signs reveal'd
> And hidden by the sleeve of Night and Morn.

Since FitzGerald allowed himself great latitude in composing the English version of the *Rubáiyát*, allusions appear from his other readings, both Oriental and non-Oriental. He was fully aware of the common heritage of Eastern and Western thought, and he pointed out in a note to the *Rubáiyát* the occurrence of the metaphor of the Potter and the Pot in different literatures of the world. Thus he did not consider it improper to add a dash of Calvinism to Omar's Persian philosophy in stanza fifty-seven of the first edition:

> Oh, Thou, who didst with Pitfall and with Gin
> Beset the Road I was to wander in,
>   Thou wilt not with Predestination round
> Enmesh me, and impute my Fall to Sin?

Or even to contribute his own philosophy in the famous epigrammatic line of stanza fifty-eight:

> Oh, Thou, who Man of baser Earth didst make,
> And who with Eden didst devise the Snake;
>   For all the Sin wherewith the Face of Man
> Is blacken'd, man's Forgiveness give and take!

NOTES

1. Mary Eleanor FitzGerald Kerrich, "Memories of Edward FitzGerald," *East Anglian Magazine*, August, 1935, p. 84.

2. Edward FitzGerald and Bernard Barton, pp. 180–81.

3. Ibid., 182.

4. *Letters of Edward FitzGerald*, I, 328; dated April 22, 1857, to Mrs. Cowell.

5. Ibid., I, 336. Dated July 13, 1857.

6. Arthur J. Arberry, *The Romance of the Rubáiyát* (London, 1959), p. 81. Professor

Arberry includes a number of FitzGerald's unpublished letters to Cowell, written while FitzGerald was translating the *Rubáiyát*.

7. Thomas Wright, *The Life of Edward FitzGerald* (New York, 1904), II, 202.

8. *Letters of Edward FitzGerald*, I, 345–46; dated September 3, 1858.

9. C. Quaritch Wrentmore, ed., *Letters from Edward FitzGerald to Bernard Quaritch: 1853–1883* (London, 1926), p. 6.

10. Alfred McKinley Terhune, *The Life of Edward FitzGerald* (New Haven, 1947), p. 210. This is the best documented biography of FitzGerald, and includes a number of unpublished letters.

11. *Letters of Charles Eliot Norton*, I, 426.

12. Ibid., 1, 471.

13. Terhune, p. 212.

14. *Letters to Bernard Quaritch*, p. 32.

15. Ibid., p. 60; dated January 16, 1879.

16. FitzGerald was not the only poet to take liberties with his original. Matthew Arnold's "Sohrab and Rustum," which is widely regarded as recounting the episode of Sohrab from Firdusi's *Shah Nameh*, and is so described in anthologies of literature, differs widely in reality from the original version. Matthew Arnold put together the details of his story, not from any translations in English or in French of the *Shah Nameh*, but from short accounts of the episode of Sohrab in Sainte-Beuve's review and in Malcolm's *History of Persia*. For details of Arnold's debt to the latter, see my "Matthew Arnold's Version of the Episode of Sohrab," *Orientalia Suecana*, 16 (1967).

DANIEL SCHENKER

Fugitive Articulation:
An Introduction to The Rubáiyát of Omar Khayyám

Over a half century ago Ezra Pound remarked that FitzGerald's re-creation of Omar Khayyám was one of the finest works bequeathed by a generation of Victorian poets.[1] Today, the *Rubáiyát* receives little attention from critics, although the poem is frequently reprinted in sumptuously designed and illustrated trade editions. Probably few poems are so widely circulated (whether read I do not know) and yet so rarely talked about. The situation, of course, was very different in 1861, when Dante Gabriel Rossetti purchased his first copy from London publisher and bookseller Bernard Quaritch. The changing critical fortune of the *Rubáiyát* is one of its more interesting features, and in the first part of this essay I want to make a few brief remarks on the history of the poem. I begin with a hypothetical comparison that will outline some of the difficulties we have reading the *Rubáiyát*.

Let us imagine two hours of classroom discussion, one for the *Rubáiyát* and one for an unimpeachable contemporary masterpiece, T. S. Eliot's "The Love Song of J. Alfred Prufrock." One can easily guess which poem will yield the more fruitful hour of instruction. Even naive readers in our day have some idea where to begin with an Eliot poem: his work signals its own incomprehensibility and quickly shifts the reader into the interrogative mood. Consider, for example, "In the room the women come and go /

From *Victorian Poetry* 19, no. 1. © 1981 by West Virginia University.

Talking of Michelangelo." Someone will notice that the doggerel meter and foolishly simple vocabulary are inappropriate for such an oracularly composed line—oracular because the words appear out of the unexplained gap that twice punctuates the verse. Nor is this empty space without significance. The hiatus gives an audience time ("There will be time, there will be time") to cast about: how can this peculiar intrusion follow from the preceding monologue? Is this still Prufrock's voice (if it ever was)? Does "Michelangelo" fit the sense, or is it just a seductively fitting rhyme? And *what* room? The novice's initiation into the mysteries of the poem is well under way.

Our class members will be baffled—disconcertingly baffled into silence—by the seeming clichés and trivialities that are the substance of the *Rubáiyát*. Time is also a central motif in this poem, but it slips away at a leisurely pace, without the hint of life or death imperative in Prufrock's "'Do I dare?' and 'do I dare?'" The measured repetitions of quatrain and white space in the *Rubáiyát* are the soothing music of a complacent universe. As we linger through these lines near the end of the poem,

> Would but the Desert of the Fountain yield
> One glimpse—if dimly, yet indeed, reveal'd,
>   To which the fainting Traveller might spring,
> As springs the trampled herbage of the field![2] (XCVII)

fainting Travellers that we are after ninety-six quatrains of enervation, the verse does not impress us as unusual in meter or expression nor otherwise deserving of scrutiny. Nothing in its tone alerts us to a conundrum here, the cryptic "Desert of the Fountain." No unorthodox gesture interrupts the accretion of verses, nor does the harmonious assemblage of words in the quatrain encourage an investigation of this anomaly. *Some* meaning is easily enough reconstructed: fainting travellers *do* have mirages in the desert, so why not a verbal mirage? And the key word "spring" not only evokes all the life sustaining fountains that bubble up through the parched earth, but recalls the desideratum for rebirth that underlies the sentiment and sentimentality of the *Rubáiyát*. If all else fails, the inversion can be blamed on a conjectural peculiarity in the original Persian. Nothing to be alarmed about.

I will pursue at a later time this question of why we fail to respond to the *Rubáiyát* as a work of serious literary art. For now we will satisfy ourselves with an empirical glance at the critical history of the poem. I think that we can identify three approximate stages in the public reception of the *Rubáiyát* that mark its progress from exotic Prophecy to Victorian gimcrack.

Anyone who has spent some time with the poem probably knows the story of how copies of FitzGerald's translation sat many months in Quaritch's pennybox, "having proved hopelessly unsaleable at the published price of a shilling,"[3] until they were brought to the attention of Rossetti and of others through him. The still youthful Pre-Raphaelites and their allies were searching for alternatives to the pieties of mid-century English cultural life, and a note of quiet desperation became progressively more evident in their work throughout this period. By the time of the discovery of the *Rubáiyát*, Rossetti had long abandoned the naturalistic first principles of the original Brotherhood for the sake of his fancy. In the early 1850s, he began painting a scene reminiscent of the brighter moments in a Keatsian ode (*The Bower Meadow*, 1850–72) when all that lay before him were the rotting leaves of a Kentish autumn. Explaining this phenomenon he wrote to a friend: "The fact is, between you and me, that the leaves on the trees I have to paint here appear red, yellow etc. to my eyes; and as of course I know them on that account to be really of a vivid green, it seems rather annoying that I cannot do them so: my subject shrieking aloud for Spring."[4] Algernon Swinburne, a later member of Rossetti's circle, had become by 1861 a disciple of the Marquis de Sade, seeking transcendence in the morally perverse. As he was primarily interested in the *Rubáiyát* as a work of frustrated iconoclasm, Swinburne chose to highlight the angrier (and somewhat unrepresentative) quatrains of the poem, such as number LXXXI, his personal favorite:

> O Thou, who Man of baser Earth didst make
> And ev'n with Paradise devise the Snake:
>   For all the Sin wherewith the Face of Man
> Is blacken'd—Man's forgiveness give—and take!

A mellower Swinburne still had transcendence in mind when he praised the *Rubáiyát* near the end of his career, speaking now in a more traditionally religious idiom: "Every quatrain, though it is something so much more than graceful or distinguished or elegant, is also, one may say, the sublimation of elegance, the apotheosis of distinction, the transfiguration of grace."[5] Perhaps more telling of the impression the poem made than any critical appreciation was Swinburne's borrowing of the verse form FitzGerald adapted from the Persian for his reworking of the bizarre and erotic Tannhäuser legend, his "Laus Veneris":

> There is a feverish famine in my veins;
> Below her bosom where a crushed grape stains
>   The white and blue, there my lips caught and clove
> An hour since, and what mark of me remains?

O dare not touch her, lest the kiss
Leave my lips charred. Yea, Lord, a little bliss,
   Brief bitter bliss, one hath for a great sin;
Nathless thou knowest how sweet a thing it is. (ll. 165–172)

The transition to social respectability is discernible in the first review of the poem written in America (appearing fully a decade after the initial publication of the *Rubáiyát,*) by Charles Eliot Norton. Ironically, the exoticism of the work impressed him with the homeliness of its sentiments: Omar's message had universal application regardless of its origin. Norton proclaimed that "in its English dress it reads like the latest and freshest expression of the perplexity and of the doubt of the generation to which we ourselves belong."[6] The meaning was so plain that the critic's own voice trailed off after a few initial remarks and the review concluded with a selection of quatrains from FitzGerald's text without further commentary or elucidation.

But neither perplexity nor perversity seems to have been responsible for the wide appeal of the *Rubáiyát* as it went through third and fourth editions. Such phenomena as the Omar Khayyám societies that sprang up in England and America during this period sought rather to institutionalize a cult of spiritual resignation. Their intuition was not unsound, for certainly withdrawal from the world was a dominant theme in FitzGerald's own life. In a letter to Edward Cowell, his close friend and Persian teacher, FitzGerald wrote that his translation of Omar's rubaiyat had been "most ingeniously tesselated into a sort of Epicurean Eclogue in a Persian Garden" (November 2, 1858; Richardson, p. 606). The garden, in fact, is the preferred locale in many of FitzGerald's literary productions, both originals and translations. In this setting, the man who seems to have felt the onset of old age by his middle twenties because he could not escape the banal awareness that all things must pass indulged his predilection for melancholy. In 1857, he wrote to Cowell: "*July 1st*—June over! A thing I think of with Omar-like sorrow. And the Roses here are blowing—and going—as abundantly as even in Persia" (Richardson, p. 600). The popular audience of the day must have responded to the domestic possibilities of these Epicurean sentiments. Although we never hear FitzGerald muse upon the simple pleasures of home life, his garden eclogue was nonetheless easily assimilated to the beleaguered institutions of home and family. Walter Houghton, examining Victorian attitudes on this subject, has written:

[The home] was much more than a house where one stopped at night for temporary rest and recreation—or procreation—in the midst of a busy career. It was a place apart, a walled garden, in which certain virtues too easily crushed by modern life could be preserved, and certain desires of the heart too much thwarted be fulfilled.[7]

Under this aegis, the poem that was ignored in the pennybox by all but the young Turks in the world of letters became fit for inclusion on the bookshelves of millions of burgher households. People longed for the repose and security of a "walled garden," and FitzGerald, who knew his gardens as only an English country gentleman could, almost by accident provided them with a mental close in faraway Persia that they might retreat to again and again. However, the poem never eliminates all temptation to the more subversive counter-readings, and this I think is another reason for its success: for when the stresses of the day are so great that the *Rubáiyát* cannot be accepted as an emblem of domestic stability, the besieged master or mistress of the house may guiltlessly indulge himself or herself in a momentary escape into its amoral world without husbands or wives or fathers or children or even Englishmen (and yet how English!). FitzGerald's achievement is noteworthy: neither Rossetti nor Swinburne nor Tennyson ever constructed a garden that all at once answered so many pressing needs.

The majority of FitzGerald's published works are translations. This reclusive squire had catholic interests, ranging through classical, Romance, and oriental literatures; now Islamic allegory, now the repartee of the Spanish gracioso might occupy his talents. Refined promiscuity of taste is perhaps endemic to the genius of any great translator. The man or woman who adopts the role of creative artist with regard to his or her peculiar art may take up a polemical stance to reform if necessary prevailing standards of judgment. A translator, however, is bound Odysseus-like to furnish suitable blood for the shades of the departed dead so that they may be readily comprehended by the living. While poets are free to seek after absolutes, translators must look to a golden mean: their work must be both original *and* typical:

> Translations—exactly because of the peculiar conditions of their manufacture—are of special interest to a critic of poetry; for they show him in the baldest form the assumptions about poetry shared by readers and poets. To paraphrase Collingwood, every poem is an unconscious answer to the question: "What is a poem?" But the question is never the same question, any more than the question "What is a man?" is the same question when asked in 1200 or 1600 or 1900.... The study of translations,

especially from a literature produced by a civilization very different from our own, [is] one of the simplest ways of showing what is expected at various times in answer to the question of "What is poetry?"[8]

In the last third of the nineteenth century, FitzGerald provided a nearly perfect response to the final query, demonstrating his uncanny knack in the *Rubáiyát* for drawing level with his age without exceeding it. An epitome of contemporary writing, the poem is also a convenient benchmark for surveying neighboring precincts of art and expression: the *Rubáiyát* appeared midway between the death of Byron and the advent of Modernism, and is correctly interpreted as a document both of retrospection and of some prophetic power.

FitzGerald could be as successful in maintaining a status quo in literature as he was in preserving an archaic policy of land management on his estates in Victorian Suffolk. Just whose status quo was often hard to discern, though it had a familiar ring whatever it was. The editor of the *Athenaeum* apparently believed that an early FitzGerald composition, "The Meadows in Spring," came from the hand of Charles Lamb. Writing to a correspondent sometime later, Lamb himself pointed to the mistake, but confessed that he envied the writer "because I feel I could have done something like [him]."[9] Many years after he had written "Bredfield Hall," another original lyric, FitzGerald cleared up a mystery for an old friend, who running across the poem had thought it to be Tennyson's. In a letter, he admitted its authorship

> only to prevent you wasting any more trouble looking through Tennyson for those verses.... No; I wrote them along with many others about my old home more than forty years ago and they recur to me also as I wander the Garden or the Lawn. Therefore, I suppose there is something native in them, though your referring to A. T. proves that I was echoing him. (Cited in Groome, p. 109).

These brief remarks on the status quo in literature point to a distinction between the translating methods of FitzGerald and his chief inheritor in the next century, Ezra Pound. Both did their best work with the aid of a second language, but in the end Pound strove to escape the voices of past and present. Though committed to tradition, he took risks and asked his audience to do the same: the reassuring Canto I lay at the edge of a familiar horizon beyond which the reader is expected to journey. FitzGerald, when he gave an English life to a play or poem, was more careful to speak in the recognizable cadences of an accustomed language. Thus was he drawn to little projects like the cataloguing of the seacoast dialect of his native Suffolk (which in reality was much derived from the speech of "Posh," a seafaring buddy of his). Yet he did foreshadow Pound in his understanding that the translator should not so much fulfill a role as occupy an office—that of an impromptu shaman before the ell-square pitkin. FitzGerald wrote to Cowell: "At all cost, a thing must *live*, with a transfusion of one's own worse life if one can't retain the originals better."[10] He did not want to produce imitations of the originals, and although he decided to remain conservative in his choice of idiom, his finished products are incontestably English. If his work suffered at the hands of some nineteenth-century reviewers it was because, ironically, his eye was on the living Englishman and not the dead foreigner. "As for Poetry," he commented in the "Prefatory Letter" to his *The Downfall and Death of King Oedipus*, "I pretend to very little more than representing the old Greek in sufficiently readable English verse: and whatever I have omitted, added, or altered, has been done with a view to the English reader of Today, without questioning what was fittest for an Athenian theatre more than two thousand years ago."[11] Of course, this statement of purpose was wholly out of step with a Victorian literary establishment that believed the translator should make the reader aware of the abyss separating his language and culture from that of his predecessors: thus Browning's jawbreaker of an *Agememnon*. FitzGerald's motto, "Better a live sparrow than a stuffed eagle," leaves us with the amusing paradox of a private man, publishing anonymously and indifferent to a vulgar audience, who became the most renowned popularizer of an exotic literature in nineteenth-century England.

Collections and "editions" rank second in importance among FitzGerald's works, although he usually performed the functions of redactor and translator simultaneously. He felt obliged to do whatever was necessary to keep something he valued alive. Sometimes just publishing a version of an overlooked work was sufficient, as when he brought out his translations of Calderon's more obscure plays. But even here there was tinkering of the kind best exemplified in his *King Oedipus*, for just as the Victorians had no qualms about making architectural "improvements" in old cathedrals to render them more medieval looking, so FitzGerald saw nothing wrong in tightening up the tragic economy of a Greek drama. He honed Sophocles' plays with a mind to leave "the terrible story to develope itself no further than needs it must to be intelligible, without being descanted, dwelt, and dilated on, after the fashion of Greek Tragedy" (Wright, III, 165). George Crabbe's *Tales of the Hall* was edited with the hope of achieving a similar reduction, and contains prose summaries of sections FitzGerald thought unduly prolix.

FitzGerald, rural aristocrat, was unwittingly laboring for the same cybernetic man his contemporary Herbert Spencer had in mind when he formulated the theory that "a reader or listener has at each moment but a limited amount of mental power available."[12] Condensation was as much the key to success in literature as in business in a culture founded upon the cardinal sin of impatience. A biographer tells us that in his later years FitzGerald took an especial delight in planning abbreviations "of big books like *Clarissa Harlowe* and *Wesley's Journal.*"[13]

"How truly language must be regarded as a hindrance to thought," said Spencer (p. 3). FitzGerald, too, had proceeded in his redactions as if each word meant a further enervation of psychic energy. Omar Khayyám, whose impeccable sense of decorum had struck a chord in FitzGerald's soul, was thus an attractive figure for a more pragmatic reason: noted Professor Cowell, "He [Omar] has left us fewer lines than Gray" (cited in Heron-Allen, p. viii).

Before turning to the text itself, a comment on the first and final editions of the *Rubáiyát*.

Meditating over the infant Hartley Coleridge, Wordsworth inadvertently charted the next hundred years of English poetry. Wordsworth's typical inheritor in the nineteenth century would proceed "As if his whole vocation / Were endless imitation" ("Ode: Intimations of Immortality," ll. 107–108). Romantic mellowed into Victorian art. In the process, Tennyson and Browning turned the ambition of the poet from gaining distinction in philosophy toward achieving excellence in "conning a part." By 1909, the appearance of a volume unabashedly entitled *Personae* was anticlimactic. Edward FitzGerald, translator, and as such barometer of mid-century poetic decorum, was not immune to the impulse. His first *Rubáiyát*, the one that sat in Quaritch's pennybox, was as much soliloquy as eclogue, and was not ashamed to say so. The speaker in the poem had a name: the directive "come with old Khayyám" occurs twice in the original version. But with recognition, FitzGerald seems to have consciously decided to remove all traces of intimacy. In the final text, the name Khayyám is mentioned nowhere except in the title. This pattern of revision is the key to all the changes FitzGerald made through five editions. The avant-garde admirers of the poem, Swinburne most notably among them, regretted these alterations which blurred the dramatic immediacy of the original for the sake of an impression of timeless utterance. As the nineteenth century wore on, the poem became more and more a reactionary document, insuring its place in popular literary imagination. I should add that with retrenchment, this work seems to have completed the project Wordsworth had left unfinished: the *Rubáiyát* became the long-awaited great philosophical poem for many like

Professor Norton, who, suffering the disorientations of their era, looked to this walled garden of soothing aphorism for reassurance, if not indeed vindication.

The aphoristic quality of the *Rubáiyát* is at the heart of our inability—or disinclination—to say anything about the poem. Speech here is robbed of its potential for innovation just as the New Word of the prophets is continually reduced to an old tale or proverb:

> The Revelations of Devout and Learn'd
> Who rose before us, and as Prophets burn'd
>   Are all but Stories, which, awoke from Sleep
> They told their comrades, and to Sleep return'd. (LXV)

"Waste not your Hour, nor in the vain pursuit / Of This and That endeavor and dispute," Omar has counselled in a preceding quatrain (LIV). But proverbial wisdom, even when not directly averse to speech, is by nature the enemy of articulation: the wise saw is an instance of discourse divorced from the face-to-face encounters during which people actually speak to one another. As FitzGerald himself noted in his Preface to *Polonius*, the proverb is nothing more than the ossified remains of a collapsed narrative or fable (Richardson, p. 102). Like the bowls and other empty signs throughout the *Rubáiyát*, proverbs are created sufficiently void of meaning to be recyclable in any number of contexts. While this has meant nearly universal acceptance for the poem, it is also worth our remembering that an earlier teacher of wisdom, Ecclesiastes, used the strategy of citing one reasonable proverb against another in his proof of the vanity of all things.

This approach to the *Rubáiyát* emphasizes an underlying nihilism which unfortunately further deflects us from attempting the more serious reading the poem deserves. The poem is not without its more starkly tragic elements. It introduces, for example, various tangible forms, bearing little resemblance to Christian or Platonic genii which reside beyond the world of the senses. The most perfect form in the *Rubáiyát* would be the human body. I say "would be" because the body is something hopelessly mutable, which like "The Flower that once has blown for ever dies" (LXIII). Since the attempt to assemble a complete human form in the poem can never succeed, the *Rubáiyát* remains a veritable butcher shop of dismembered flesh: eyes in the earth, runaway moving fingers, and organs of speech all over the place. Nor is there much impetus to complete any such project: dissolution would overtake the human form the moment it was reassembled because every moment in time is itself a kind of emptiness.

Clay pots and bowls are signs for the body in Omar's world, but like ciphers are always vacant and desiring to be filled with "the old familiar Juice." Naturally, the clay pot is no less subject to decomposition than the human body. Omar toys with the metaphor when, in a more speculative moment, he tries to conceive a world elsewhere:

> I must adjure the Balm of Life, I must,
> Scared by some After-reckoning ta'en on trust,
>   Or lured with Hope of some Diviner Drink,
> To fill the Cup—when crumbled into Dust! (LXII)

The reader may easily envision the wine mixing with the pulverized cup to make more clay for new vessels which will again crumble to dust and so on ad infinitum.

More frightening is the prospect that wherever one looks, he will see nothing but a repetition of these bowl-shaped forms:

> And that inverted Bowl they call the Sky,
> Whereunder crawling coop'd we live and die,
>   Lift not your hands to It for help—for It
> As impotently moves as you or I. (LXXII)

The Bowl, round-rimmed like the *sifr* (or cipher, keystone of Omar's Arabic mathematics),[14] and invoked here through the empty pronoun "It," turns up in natural forms which themselves are emblems of the human body:

> As then the Tulip for her morning sup
> Of Heav'nly Vintage for the soil looks up,
>   Do you devoutly do the like, till Heav'n
> To Earth invert you—like an empty Cup. (XL)

Here is the same "empty Glass" turned down by the wine-pourer Saki at the end of the poem as a placeholder for the departed Omar; and when the serving boy is making his rounds among them, "the Guests Star-scatter'd on the Grass" will mirror once again the bowl-shaped starry heavens up above.

FitzGerald had become acquainted with such devices in his previous studies of Persian literature. In Jami's *Salaman and Absal*, which he had also translated, a Shah searched for his dissolute son. FitzGerald's text reads:

> Then bade he bring a Mirror that he had,
> A Mirror, like the Bosom of the Wise,
> Reflecting all the World.[15]

Far more interesting than the text at this point is the footnote he appends, glossing the "Mirror":

> Mythically attributed by the East—and in some wild Western Avatar—to this Shah's Predecessor, Alexander the Great. Perhaps ... the Concave Mirror upon the Alexandrian Pharos, which by Night projected such a fiery Eye over the Deep as not only was fabled to exchange Glances with that on the Rhodian Colossus, and in Oriental Imagination and Language to penetrate "The WORLD," but by Day to Reflect it to him who looked therein with Eyes to see. The Cup of their own JAMSHID had, whether Full or Empty, the same Property. And that Silver Cup found in Benjamin's Sack—"Is not this it in which my Lord drinketh, and whereby indeed he *Divineth?*"—Gen. xliv. 5. Our Reflecting Telescope is going some way to realize the Alexandrian Fable. (pp. 81–82)

Perhaps; but the great concave mirrors are just as likely to expand the empire of cosmic solipsism as to overthrow it. For if the guests be "Star-scatter'd on the Grass," is it not probable that the stars will be guest-scatter'd in the sky? That the sky is nothing more than an "inverted Bowl," whose worldly reflections should make us tremble as we stare up into its hollowness, was not a theme confined to the *Rubáiyát*. Charles Baudelaire addressed the question of what is above us in "Le Couvercle," In this last poem of the *Nouvelles Fleurs du Mal* sequence, "heaven becomes (by an inversion more serious than blasphemy, an inversion which has contaminated even the limping versification) the lid of a pot or coffin—something which clamps a ceiling on man's aspirations and renders them actually vulgar."[16] In a contemporary English poem on a related artifact, Dante Rossetti's "Troy Town," an empty cup molded in the shape of Helen's breast and given by her as an offering to Venus reflects a future of meaningless destruction on the Plains of Ilion. Actually, definitive annihilation would be a welcome end in each poem, for what terrified these men was not death, but the never ending dying into never ending dying, and the attendant knowledge of everlasting loss. Such was the fear that reigned in FitzGerald's daily existence. In a letter to Frederick Tennyson describing the summer of his thirty-fifth year he wrote:

> A little Bedfordshire—a little Northamptonshire—a little more folding of the hands—the same faces—the same fields—the same thoughts occurring at the same turns of the road—this is all I have to tell of; nothing at all added—but the summer gone. (October 10, 1844; Richardson, p. 522)

FitzGerald's Omar laments that after he expires and turns to dust he will still somehow be aware of an unabated monotony of enervation:

> Ah, make the most of what we yet may spend,
> Before we too into the Dust descend;
>   Dust into Dust, and under Dust to lie,
> Sans Wine, sans Song, sans Singer, and—sans End! (XXIV)

The modern reader can hear an echo in Beckett's Unnamable's gasping, "I can't go on, I'll go on"; FitzGerald heard in Omar a voice "as savage against Destiny &c as Manfred," but one disillusioned of Romantic passions, and with dulled sentiments, "mostly of Epicurean Pathos."[17]

I mentioned that organs of speech appear in a number of places throughout the *Rubáiyát*, especially the lips, which also resemble the zero or the circular edge rimming a cup or bowl. The lips encompass Omar:

> And this reviving Herb whose tender Green
> Fledges the River-Lip on which we lean—
>   Ah, lean upon it lightly! for who knows
> From what once lovely Lip it springs unseen! (XX)

This is a fine example of the claustrophobic sensibility of the poem, which complements in space Omar's awareness of temporal circularity. The form of dismembered lips moves from the blade of grass through the riverbank, only to close in again on a human subject. "Revives" offers no more hope of release into something different than the "reviving" of the new year back in the fourth quatrain which had brought with it unwanted "old Desires." All these lips never say much of consequence: speech rarely has a direction in the poem, and occasionally is unwilling or unable to progress from a phonological square one. One can hear the verbal claustrophobia in this well-known rubai:

> Into this Universe, and *Why* not knowing
> Nor *Whence*, like Water willy-nilly flowing;
>   And out of it, as Wind along the Waste,
> I know not *Whither*, willy-nilly blowing. (XXIX)

Or the human lips are deprived of speech altogether. David, the archetypal Biblical potentate, stands with locked lips in the sixth quatrain while a nightingale pipes on about wine in the ancient literary language of Persia, a language that was dead even to the ears of Omar's contemporaries.

The "Pehlevi" of both Omar and FitzGerald poses as a distinctly apolitical speech which has no force between persons in everyday life. We cannot therefore hold either of them to account for failing to deal with social and ethical problems because it is precisely their claim that language has no power to do so. Politics are merely a "whirlwind Sword" wielded by a "mighty Mahmded" who stands in apposition to the great dissolver of force and form, "the Grape" (LIX–LX), or wine—which returns us to the nightingale's Pehlevi song and the speech of impotence.

Speech is the placeholder of the sign of desire for a more intimate kind of touch between dissoluble forms:

> Then to the Lip of the poor earthen Urn
> I lean'd, the Secret of my Life to learn:
>   And Lip to Lip it murmur'd—"While you live,
> "Drink!—for, once dead, you never shall return."
>
> I think the Vessel, that with fugitive
> Articulation answer'd, once did live,
>   And drink; and Ah! the passive Lip I kiss'd,
> How many Kisses might it take—and give!
>
> For I remember stopping by the way
> To watch a Potter thumping his wet Clay:
>   And with its all-obliterated Tongue
> It murmur'd—"Gently, Brother, gently, pray!"
>   (XXXV–XXXVII)

The human presence Omar longs for escapes from lip to lip and all through this lip-sprouting world. Only at times of metamorphosis do we hear speech, for only as one form dies into the next, leaving behind a memory of what is now irretrievably lost, do we learn the differences between forms. Difference and distinction are at the root of "articulation," and are the sine qua non of intelligibility, as Saussure has demonstrated. But articulation in the *Rubáiyát* is always fugitive because visible forms are emblems of mutability; and the meaning of articulation is fugitive from itself when we consider the possibility of making genuine distinctions among these ever-changing shapes. In the lines above, Omar hears a murmur, the word (already repeating its one syllable) that stands for a vocalization on the verge of a linguistic utterance. Several quatrains later, Omar will compress all shapes in the universe between "Máh" (the moon, natural symbol of metamorphosis) and "Máhi" (fish in the sea) (LI). Speech is barely able to distinguish between these two words (with the implication that there is little distinction among all they represent), words which closely resemble the first word from the mouth of every Indo-European infant, the one who is *infans*, literally "without speech." FitzGerald's Omar had a Wordsworthian longing for childhood, but his melancholy, historically and biographically speaking, takes us further back than this. Ecclesiastes' wisdom might be appropriate here:

> If a man beget an hundred children, and live many years, so that the days of his years be many, and his soul be not filled with good, and also that he have no burial; I say, that an untimely birth is better than he. For he cometh in with vanity, and departeth in darkness, and his name shall be covered with darkness. Moreover he hath not seen the sun, nor known any thing: this hath more rest than the other. (Ecclesiastes 6.3–5)

Both Omar and the Preacher would agree that the mouth is better used to drink in the obliterating wine, or to give that last parting kiss.

The charge has been made that the *Rubáiyát* is a "period piece,"[18] and thus the question arises: Is it worth anyone's trouble to teach, talk, or write about the poem as if it were as much a living document as "Prufrock"? Or is an occasional reference to the poem necessary only to remind us that it lies mercifully buried in the archive?

The *Rubáiyát* is obviously not the best poem of its age. The various works by Rossetti and Swinburne I have referred to in this essay are more artistically accomplished. But the *Rubáiyát* is perhaps the archetypal Victorian poem. Those 101 quatrains have a little bit of everything from the nineteenth century: dramatic speech, mysticism, Weltschmerz, sentimentality, Manfred, Epicureanism, the palette of Rossetti and Burne-Jones, the "melancholy, long, withdrawing roar" of the sea in "Dover Beach." We see also that FitzGerald, who began with a very modern-looking poem, proceeded as the years went forward to bring his work in line with a more conservative ideal, with a diffidence and an anxiety about the future we now think so characteristic of the period. Yet even the "exotic injections" into Victorian art from Greece and Italy, for which Pound lauded Rossetti and Swinburne, are implied and encompassed in this poem that was itself a paraphrase of an alien culture.

There remains a word or two to be said about the supposed value of the poem as a piece of wisdom literature. Actually, FitzGerald wanted his readers to take an elegantly simple-minded view of Omar's message:

> [Omar's] Worldly Pleasures are what they profess to be without any Pretense at Divine Allegory: his Wine is the veritable Juice of

the Grape: his Tavern, where it was to be had: his Saki, the Flesh and Blood that poured it out for him: all which, and where the Roses were in Bloom, was all he profess'd to Want of this World or to expect of Paradise.[19]

Only the most scandalized among his audience took him at his word. Everyone else went ahead and read it as an orthodox theological document. The appraisal by Groome around the turn of the century is representative: "It seems to me beyond question that his version of the '*Rubáiyát*' is an utterance of his soul's deepest doubts, and that hereafter it will come to be recognized as the highest expression of Agnosticism" (p. 37). This, however, says little either for the depth of FitzGerald's soul or for agnosticism. Why should we be taken in by these easy pieties tailor-made for a middle-class clientele that couldn't be bothered thinking up its own solutions to metaphysical and moral questions? FitzGerald, perpetrator of these philosophical offenses, was himself never quite satisfied with the fallback position set forth in his *Rubáiyát*, and in much of the work of his friend Tennyson. In *Euphranor*, a dialogue on youth (1851) and in his letters, although one would never guess it from reading the *Rubáiyát*, he was unequivocal in his conviction that the great thinker and artist is fundamentally a man of action—a Dante, a Shakespeare, even a Byron.[20] Once, after reading of blockade and battle in the Fourth Book of Thucydides, he exclaimed in a letter to Cowell:

> This was the way to write well; and this was the way to make literature respectable. Oh, Alfred Tennyson, could you but have the luck to be put to such employment! No man would do it better; a more heroic figure to head the defenders of his country could not be. (January 25, 1848; Richardson, p. 546)

The Victorian era saw the development of all kinds of self-help books for the benefit of the masses, and perhaps this is the genre to which the *Rubáiyát* ultimately belongs: "infinite resignation made simple." But FitzGerald's skepticism in other writings about the attitudes expressed in his own poem is surely essential to a complete understanding of his work.

With what, then, are we left? A Victorian attic cluttered with antiques? Yes; but we should not find that a deterrent. Some of the finest productions of our own century are nothing but tatters and bric-a-brac in their constituent parts. Perhaps our past inability to salvage the *Rubáiyát* stems from our having forgotten how to read a Victorian poem—or not having forgotten quite enough.

The Russian critic Victor Shklovsky wrote:

> The purpose of art is to impart the sensation of things as they are
> perceived and not as they are known. The technique of art is to
> make objects "unfamiliar," to make forms difficult, to increase the
> difficulty and length of perception because the process of
> perception is an aesthetic end in itself and must be prolonged. *Art
> is a way of experiencing the artfulness of an object; the object is not
> important.*[21]

Nature is important to us, but not to art, whose purpose it is to make us
forget what we "know" of nature, so that we may learn to see nature all over
again, just as a nerve cell, having transmitted a sense impression, has to turn
itself off for an instant before transmitting information anew. I am saying, in
part, that the universal acceptance gained by FitzGerald's poem as a kind of
timely wisdom has rendered the poem overly familiar, less than a true object
of art, and therefore an uninteresting subject of inquiry for most modern
readers. "Habitualization devours works, clothes, furniture, one's wife, and
the fear of war" (Shklovsky, p. 12). This was obviously not the case in 1861,
for the *Rubáiyát* captured the imaginations of Swinburne, Norton, and others
of their generation precisely on account of its unfamiliar exoticism. Omar's
Persian accent was the result of careful and premeditated contrivance. In flat
contradiction to some of his other remarks on translation, FitzGerald
maintained in a letter to Cowell that the oriental flavor of Eastern works
should be preserved in English: "I am more and more convinced of the
Necessity of keeping as much as possible of the oriental *Forms* and carefully
avoiding anything that brings back Europe and the nineteenth century. It is
better to be orientally obscure than Europeanly clear" (Arberry, p. 46). Or
again to Cowell: "I like the Hafiz Ode you send me translated, though *that*
should be weeded of some idioms not only European, *but Drawing room-
European*" (Arberry, p. 46). I suspect that the *Rubáiyát* contained more
"*Drawing room-European*" than its author realized: so the transposition of
FitzGerald's "Some little talk awhile of ME and THEE" (XXXII) into Eliot's
sardonic "Among the porcelain, among some talk of you and me" might well
suggest. One can easily visualize the bookshelves of Prufrock's drawing room
lined with richly bound editions of the *Rubáiyát*.

Another problem has been that the relative exoticism of the poem too
effectively established its status as merely a literary artifact. "Art exists that
one may recover the sensation of life; it exists to make one feel things, to
make the stone *stony*" (Shklovsky, p. 12). But the Philistine wanted his art soft
and fluffy, and the *Rubáiyát* came to look, sound, and act like a poem that

knew its place in the world. When, for example, it struck an oracular pose by invoking a tradition of wisdom literature going back to Ecclesiastes, the poem was also signalling that its meaning need not in any disturbing way impinge upon the business of ordinary discourse. Little more than Drawing room-Exotic, it was reckoned fundamentally irrelevant to life, as all art was meant to be. Eventually the language of the *Rubáiyát*, like that of much late Victorian work, became so conventionally ethereal that it had etherized itself for many ears (ours today still included) and required exactly that word in the third line of "Prufrock," along with a whole series of ironic reversals, to electrify us back into unfamiliarity. The opening gesture toward the drawing room in Eliot's poem unexpectedly restored for his contemporaries the "experience of the artfulness": the new awareness that comes through the discovery of what we are through confrontation with what we are not. Perhaps now, after more than half a century, Prufrock and his peers have worn thin enough to allow the strangeness of Omar Khayyám to peep through once again.

NOTES

1. "How to Read," in *Literary Essays*, ed. T. S. Eliot (New York, 1968), p. 34.

2. Edward FitzGerald, *The Rubáiyát of Omar Khayyám*, 4th ed., in *FitzGerald: Selected Works*, ed. Joanna Richardson (Harvard Univ. Press, 1963); hereafter cited as Richardson. Unless otherwise noted, all citations are from this text of the fourth edition, the last to appear in FitzGerald's lifetime. (A fifth posthumous edition is virtually identical.) In Richardson's selection, the text of the first edition has been conveniently printed on the facing page.

3. Algernon Charles Swinburne, letter to Clement King Shorter, in *The Swinburne Letters*, ed. Cecil Y. Lang (Yale Univ. Press, 1962), VI, 96.

4. John Nicoll, *Dante Gabriel Rossetti* (New York, 1975), p. 58.

5. "Social Verse," in *Works*, ed. Sir Edmund Gosse and Thomas James Wise (London, 1926), XV, 284–285.

6. "Nicholas' Quatrains de Kheyam," in *North American Review*, 109 (October, 1869), 576.

7. *The Victorian Frame of Mind 1830–1870* (Yale Univ. Press, 1957), p. 343.

8. Reuben Brower, *Mirror on Mirror: Translation, Imitation, Parody* (Harvard Univ. Press, 1974), p. 161.

9. Charles Lamb to Edward Moxon, August, 1831, cited in *Edward FitzGerald: An Aftermath by Francie Groome with Miscellanies in Verse and Prose* (1902; rpt. Freeport, New York, 1972), p. 95; hereafter cited as Groome.

10. April 27, 1859, in Edward Heron-Allen, *The Rubáiyát of Omar Khayyám* [manuscript facsimile with translation] (London, 1898), p. xxvi; hereafter cited as Heron-Allen.

11. *Letters and Literary Remains of Edward FitzGerald*, ed. William Aldis Wright (London, 1889), III, 165; hereafter cited as Wright.

12. *The Philosophy of Style*, ed. Fred N. Scott (Boston, 1892), p. 3.

13. A. C. Benson, *Edward FitzGerald* (London, 1905), p. 51.

14. The historical Omar Khayyám was also famous as a mathematician, and this aspect of his career is touched upon in FitzGerald's quatrains LVI–LVII. The word "sifr" is the Arabic root of our "cipher" and "zero." The Arabic innovation of an empty placeholder was, of course, a momentous occasion in the history of mathematics.

15. J. Arberry, *FitzGerald's Salaman and Absal: A Study* (Cambridge Univ. Press, 1956), p. 81.

16. Robert Martin Adams, *Nil* (Oxford Univ. Press, 1966), p. 121.

17. FitzGerald to Alfred Tennyson, July 26, 1856, cited in Iran B. Hassani Jewett, *Edward FitzGerald* (Boston, 1977), p. 73.

18. Walter E. Houghton and G. Robert Stange, "Edward FitzGerald," in *Victorian Poetry and Poetics*, 2nd ed. (Boston, 1968), p. 341.

19. [Edward FitzGerald], *Rubáiyát of Omar Khayyám* (London, 1859), p. ix.

20. FitzGerald to Fanny Kemble, October 24, 1876, in Richardson, p. 713.

21. "Art as Technique," in *Russian Formalist Criticism: Four Essays*, ed. Lee T. Lemon and Marion J. Reis (Univ. of Nebraska Press, 1965), p. 12.

ROBERT BERNARD MARTIN

The Discovery of the Rubáiyát

Browne's death was of a piece with his life: brave, generous, proceeding directly from his love of sport. Perhaps not uncharacteristic, too, in that a cleverer man might have avoided it. Returning from a day's hunting at the end of January 1859, he was riding a high-spirited mare on which that morning he had asked the groom to put a curb bridle 'that his Mare could ill endure' and a '*high-pommeled* Saddle scarce ever used'. Browne saw a fellow rider punishing his horse and rode up to remonstrate with him, taking his mare too near the other animal, which kicked out at Browne's mount; she reared, lost her footing on the wet turf of the roadside, and fell backwards on her rider, 'crushing all the middle of his Body' as he slipped from the unfamiliar saddle.

Browne lived on for 'two months with a Patience and Vitality that would have left most Men to die in a Week'. FitzGerald was apparently not told of the accident for some weeks, and certainly he was not notified of the seriousness of Browne's condition until only a few days before his death, when he hurried to Goldington to be with his friend. For two days after his arrival he was not allowed to see Browne, then he received a summons to the sick room, a scrawl like a small child's, the last words Browne ever wrote, 'I love *you* very—whenever—WKB.'

FitzGerald afterwards confessed that he had to take a glass of brandy to

From *With Friends Possessed: A Life of Edward FitzGerald*. © 1985 by Robert Bernard Martin.

get up his courage. As he entered the bedroom, the tears came to Browne's eyes and he painfully forced out the words, 'My dear Fitz—old Fel-low' before his visitor broke down. It was nearly impossible to have a conversation with him because he could neither speak nor hear well; ever since FitzGerald met him, he had been deaf in one ear, and the accident had cut off the hearing in the other. Everyone around him had recognized for weeks that he could not possibly live, but Browne had continued to believe in his eventual recovery until the last fortnight of his life, when the doctors told him what all those with him already knew. He was bathed in tears as he told Fitz, 'They broke my Heart—but it was necessary.' More often he grieved silently to spare others. 'Once he had his Bed wheeled to the Window to look out abroad: but he saw the Hawthorns *coming into Leaf*, and he bid them take him back.' Throughout his illness he had been sustained by his strong religious belief; FitzGerald could not wish him deprived of any comfort, but it must have been painful to recognize the deep chasm that lay between them in this matter.

Mrs Browne, who had never been strong, was '*inspired*, as Women are, to lose all her own Weakness in his: but the Doctors dread the Effect on her—especially since she is four or five months gone with Child!' FitzGerald admired her selfless nursing of her husband, but it was hard to accept that she was almost constantly at the bedside from which he was kept for fear of tiring the patient. He loitered around the house in case Browne should call for him, and he whiled away the lonely time by looking at the little Crome painting and the hawking picture that he had given to Browne, and at the other pictures they had bought together over twenty years. Among the books were a large number with 'EFG to WKB' written in them, one of them a copy of Digby's *Godefridus*, which had always seemed to him to encapsulate the chivalrous values by which Browne lived. To the inscription in his presentation copy of *Euphranor* he added the words, 'This little book would never have been written, had I not known my dear friend William Browne, who, unconsciously, supplied the moral. E.FG., Goldington, March 27, 1859.'

When it was clear, after two or three days, that Browne would never again call for him, FitzGerald slipped away from Goldington, 'wishing to be alone, or in other Company, when the Last came'. For all his pity for Mrs Browne, he also felt something akin to envy: 'She has her Children to attend to, and be her comfort in turn: and though having lost what most she loved yet has something to love still, and to be beloved by. There are worse Conditions than that.' Of his own condition he said only, 'I ... have now much less to care about.'

As he left Goldington FitzGerald took away with him the riding crop

Browne had been used to carry in London, and Mrs Browne later sent him the snuffbox and the little Stubbs painting he had given to her husband. The summer of the following year, at Mrs Browne's suggestion, he took her sons for a seaside holiday to Aldeburgh, where they 'boated, and rowed, and shot Gulls and Dotterels, and flung stones into the Sea: and swore an eternal Friendship' with a young sailor, 'who, strangely enough, reminded me something of their Father as I first knew him near thirty years ago! This was a strange Thing: and my Thoughts run after that poor Fisher Lad who is now gone off in a Smack to the North.' But he never again went to Goldington, which held too many memories of the 'comely spirited Boy I had known first twenty-seven years ago lying all shattered and Death in his Face and Voice'. [II, 327–47, 371–3] Yet he was homesick for Browne's old home and yearned for 'Bedfordshire, not yet forsaken by the spirit of poetry, where trees are trees (not timber), and tapering poplars—likely enough thirteen in a row—contemplate their doubles in the placid Ouse. But the "dear shepherd" of those fields is gone.'[1] Even London was haunted at every turn by his 'old Companion in its Streets and Taverns', so that he kept away from it as long as possible and never returned with the same pleasure. Gradually he was cutting himself off from other places such as Cambridge where once he had been happy, and he even shunned Oxford and the area around Ipswich because of their association with Cowell before he deserted England.

The published correspondence between FitzGerald and Mrs Browne shows with what amazing candour and unself-consciousness he wrote to her after Browne's death of his love of her husband, in terms that seemed perfectly natural to him although one can easily understand that a widow might dislike them. Naturally, he did not ask her to return the £6,500 that he had lent to Browne, but by 1871, when the debt had been outstanding for some thirteen years, he recalled it, since he understood that Mrs Browne was a rich woman. His tactful letter to her about the matter, written in hope that she would have 'no bitter taste', is the last of his letters to her in the edition of his collected correspondence, and other letters from family friends indicate that she was furious that he had even mentioned the matter. It was a sad end to their friendship. But he never forgot a single detail of his years with Browne. In the last year of his life he recalled his 'rare intuition into Men, Matters, and even into Matters of Art: though Thackeray would call him "Little Browne"—which I told him he was not justified in doing. They are equal now.' [IV, 550]

FitzGerald was less shattered by Browne's death than might be expected, probably because he had already suffered half the pain of loss when he realized that he was no longer at the centre of his friend's existence.

Apart from a few fleeting visits to Boulge, he had not been in Woodbridge since his marriage, nearly two and a half years before. Mrs Smith's illness had made it inconvenient to go to Farlingay, and it was easier simply to avoid the hostility of some of the inhabitants by not appearing in the town. Crabbe of Bredfield had died just at the time when FitzGerald and his wife finally admitted that their marriage was effectually over. With Cambridge, London, and Oxford full of disturbing memories, most of his usual haunts were now denied to him. Two months after Browne's death he went to stay at Geldestone with the Kerriches, and from there he made an excursion to the fishing ports that had provided him with brief periods of pleasure during his marriage, from their likeness to marine paintings with views of the ships and the sea and the sailors with 'their brown hands in their Breeches Pockets'. It seemed an ideal locality to recuperate from his losses, and after another visit or two to confirm his impressions, he went to Lowestoft in November 1859 for a stay of half a year. It was the beginning of the association with the sea for which FitzGerald is most often remembered in East Anglia.

By the time he settled down in 10 Marine Terrace, Lowestoft, 'The Season' was over, so that he was not bothered with its provincial society, and there was 'not a Soul here but the Sailors, who are a very fine Race of Men'. [II, 346–7] Their presence was enough to reconcile him to the cold winds and the dirty yellow water between the town and an offshore shoal. They lived a hard life with great physical courage, in constant danger of being wrecked, often making little money but keeping their sense of fun and good humour: 'When one is in London one seems to see a decayed Race; but here the old English Stuff.' [II, 351] He particularly liked the look of the herring fishermen, who 'really half starve here during Winter', but he admired all the 'beachmen', as they were known, for their 'half-starving Independence' and their 'wonderful Shoulders: won't take one out in one of their Yawls for a Sovereign though they will give one a Ride when they go out to get nothing at all'. [II, 355] It was their very simplicity and nearness to the primitive that made them so attractive to FitzGerald.

All during his stay in Lowestoft he still ached at knowing he would never see Browne again. Slowly the resolution formed to find a new friend there, and he began searching deliberately among the sailors. In his loneliest evenings in London he had acquired the habit of walking the streets looking for a friendly face or a casual passer-by to whom he could talk. During the solitary winter in Lowestoft, he said, he 'used to wander about the shore at night longing for some fellow to accost me who might give some promise of filling up a very vacant place in my heart but only some of the more idle and worthless sailors came across me'. [III, 40] (Curiously, his confidante on this occasion was Mrs Browne, which indicates his extraordinary unself-consciousness about his behaviour.) To ensure his welcome among the sailors he carried with him a bottle of rum and rolls of tobacco, according to Donne: 'So armed, he spends his evenings under the lee-side of fishing boats, hearing and telling yarns.'[2] At the back of his mind floated a picture of Browne, which he was hoping to match among this wild, often handsome lot of men.

It is no wonder that all the sailors knew him by sight, for even without such remarkable behaviour, he was a distinctive figure on the lonely Lowestoft beach, his obviously expensive but ill-tended clothes thrown on anyhow, his top hat anchored against the sea wind by a scarf tied under his chin, on his face such a curious combination of apprehensive *hauteur* and excessive vulnerability that many of them thought he was mad. No one could have mistaken him for anything but a gentleman, but it would have been hard for the sailors to assign a reputable motive for his walks along the pebbles until he found an upended boat sheltering one or more of their kind. Inevitably he became the butt of innuendoes and jokes for the sailors, who were far more knowing than he. Among them was a handsome, somewhat stolid looking, young man, then only twenty years old, who stood back, silently observing him. Some years later FitzGerald became acquainted with 'Posh' Fletcher, as he told Mrs Browne: 'I asked him why he had never come down to see me at the time I speak of. Well, he had often seen me, he said, among the boats, but never thought it becoming in him to accost me first, or even to come near me. Yet he was the very man I wanted, with, strangely enough, some resemblance in feature to a portrait of you may guess whom, and much in character also.' [III, 40–1] There is little in his succeeding dealings with FitzGerald to suggest that Fletcher suffered from excessive generosity or propriety, and it must have occurred to him that there could be considerable profit from the friendship of an eccentric gentleman more than twice his age, but we know from what happened five years later that he had to take coarse jibes from his friends, so it is not surprising that he stood aloof in 1859, fearing the interpretation the other sailors would put upon his behaviour if he approached FitzGerald.

The rum and tobacco were apparently wasted on the Lowestoft sailors that winter, for FitzGerald wrote of none who had become his friend, but the following summer he employed a 'poor careless Devil' of a sailor, Alfred Hurrell, who subsequently broke into a house and was sentenced to prison for fifteen months. 'But he had Fun in him,' FitzGerald said, 'and the more respectable Men are duller.' [II, 396]

He became so attached to one young sailor from Aldeburgh ('strong as a Horse, simple as a Child') that he invited him to stay. The young man was at 'his turning Point of Life: whether he is to stay with Father, Mother, and

Sweetheart, fishing at Aldbro:—or go out in a Square-rigg'd Vessel (humph!) for five or six years, and learn what will qualify him to come home and be a Pilot. This would be best for him: but "Father and Mother and Sue"—and even E.F.G.—don't want to lose Sight of him so long, perhaps for ever, some of us.' [II, 391] In order to see the young man FitzGerald was willing to make the trip to Aldeburgh for a 'Smoke with the Sailors', usually with grog in the kitchen of a tavern, but occasionally on Saturday nights they sat drinking and singing in a net-house. FitzGerald was proud of the applause for his own performance of 'Pretty Peg of Derby O!'. His young sailor friend said to him: 'Somehow you know Songs something like ours, only better', which pleased him, as did the 'Childishness and Sea language of these People'. [II, 395–6]

Whatever the townsfolk of Lowestoft, Aldeburgh, and Woodbridge, or the sailors and even his own friends thought about the spectacle of a lonely elderly man consorting chiefly with young sailors, there can be little doubt that FitzGerald was completely guileless and open in his behaviour. Loneliness is seldom attractive, and his was probably graceless and embarrassing to others, but it was never disgusting or sordid, and anything that looked like ugliness to others was surely in the eye of the beholder.

His letters after the publication of the *Rubáiyát* bear resigned witness to FitzGerald's disappointment over its apparent failure, but he was too reticent to express it openly. Probably his frankest statement was to Cowell: 'I hardly know why I print any of these things, which nobody buys; and I scarce now see the few I give them to. But when one has done one's best, and is sure that the best is better than so many will take pains to do, though far from the best that *might be done*, one likes to make an end of the matter by Print.' [II, 335]

It was two years before the poem was 'discovered', the first step to its becoming one of the most popular works of the century. But it was much longer than that before FitzGerald himself knew that his poem had not been still-born. The story has often been told of how the poem was found in a publisher's bin, was puffed by the Pre-Raphaelites and their friends, and at last became one of the standard poems of the language. Because the account involves half of the most important Victorian writers and had such a happy ending, it has been called alliteratively the 'romance of the *Rubáiyát*', but to make it even more romantic, some aspects have been distorted. In particular it has been tempting to exaggerate the time that passed before the poem was noticed. Actually, only two years before the leading writers of the time were ecstatic about it would seem a short enough time for most other poets waiting for recognition. Even if FitzGerald was unaware of the fact, by 1861 the *Rubáiyát* was well on its way.*

Since few, if any, had been sold, Quaritch put the remaining copies of the poem into the bargain box of his shop for quick sale. The original price had been one shilling, but now they were offered ignominiously for a penny. In the summer of 1861 a young Celtic scholar named Whitley Stokes fished out several copies from the box, kept one for himself, and gave the others to friends, including Richard Monckton Milnes, Richard Burton, and Dante Gabriel Rossetti.

In his turn Rossetti bought copies for both Swinburne and Browning. According to Swinburne's account, which may owe some embellishment to retrospection, he returned with Rossetti the following day to buy more copies and found that the little flurry of sales had caused Quaritch to raise the price to the 'sinfully extravagant sum of twopence'. He secured copies for Edward Burne-Jones and William Morris and took one with him on a visit to George Meredith, where he arrived, as Meredith said, 'waving the white sheet of what seemed to be a pamphlet.... we lay on a heathery knoll outside my cottage reading a stanza alternately, indifferent to the dinner-bell, until a prolonged summons reminded us of appetite. After dinner we took to the paper-covered treasure again.'

Eventually the pamphlet reached John Ruskin, the unofficial apologist and mentor of many of the Pre-Raphaelites. On 2 September 1863 he wrote a letter to the translator, whose identity was still secret, and gave it to Burne-Jones to deliver if ever he discovered the translator's name:

> I do not know in the least who you are, but I do with all my soul pray you to find and translate some more of Omar Khayyám for us: I never did—till this day—read anything so glorious, to my mind as this poem ... and that, & this, is all I can say about it— More—more—please more—& that I am ever gratefully & respectfully yours.

Burne-Jones put away the letter and forgot about it for some years. In 1868 there was a second and enlarged edition, necessitated in part because Quaritch had inadvertently sold most of his stock of the *Rubáiyát* as waste paper. FitzGerald's anonymity had preserved his privacy, but it also deprived him of the pleasure of hearing about the respect of other poets for his work. A third edition appeared in 1872.

Before the third edition was published, there was one shrewd guess at the translator's name, by Fanny Kemble's daughter, who lived in Philadelphia. She wrote directly to FitzGerald, asking about the matter, and he acknowledged his identity, which then became known to a small group of readers in the United States, although it was still a secret in England.

Among the poem's American admirers was Professor Charles Eliot Norton of Harvard, who had first read Burne-Jones's copy in 1868. He helped to spread its reputation in America, among others to J. R. Lowell and Emerson, who paid it a characteristically chilly compliment in saying that it was 'very lofty in its defiance, with rare depths of feeling and imagination'. Four years later Norton was again in England and heard the rumour that the translator of the *Rubáiyát* was 'a certain Reverend Edward FitzGerald, who lived somewhere in Norfolk and was fond of boating'.

Norton sent a copy of the poem to his friend Carlyle, who had said in surprise when told of the rumour about the amphibious parson, 'Why, he's no more Reverend than I am! He's a very old friend of mine—I'm surprised, if the book be as good as you tell me it is, that my old friend has never mentioned it to me.' When he had read it, Carlyle thought that FitzGerald had wasted his time in translating the 'verses of that old Mohammedan blackguard'. Slightly more tactfully, in a covering note sent with Ruskin's letter, he told FitzGerald that he found the 'Book itself a kind of jewel in its way'. Fourteen years had elapsed since he first published it, but at last FitzGerald was beginning to know the pleasures of literary success. No editions of the poem appeared during his lifetime with his name on the title page, but his identity was an open secret in literary circles for the last decade before his death. The poem became even more popular in America than in England. One critic has estimated that by 1929 there had been 310 editions published in the world, and that thirty years later there were 'hundreds and hundreds of editions—how many hundreds no one knows'. And since then, there have been uncounted further editions.[3]

Any work as popular as the *Rubáiyát* acquires a certain critical mystery, one that Ezra Pound hinted at in his *ABC of Reading* when he proposed the exercise: 'Try to find out why the FitzGerald *Rubaiyat* has gone into so many editions after having lain unnoticed until Rossetti found a pile of remaindered copies on a second-hand bookstall.'[4] Pound's factual errors do not obscure the problem, nor does the facile answer that it is always a miracle for a work of serious poetry to become a popular success.

There may be one clue to the answer in the date of the first appearance of the *Rubáiyát*, 1859, which also saw the publication of Samuel Smiles's *Self-Help*, Mill's *On Liberty*, George Eliot's *Adam Bede*, Meredith's *Ordeal of Richard Feverel*, above all Darwin's *Origin of Species*. FitzGerald's work was not recognized at first as such, but we can see in retrospect that it was none the less representative of the distinguishing characteristic of them all, a repudiation of traditional religious morality and the attempt to find an alternative to it.

But nothing could be further than the *Rubáiyát* from the doctrine of work in Smiles or the competition for survival outlined in Darwin. It may be helpful to look again at the names of FitzGerald's 'discoverers': Rossetti,

Monckton Milnes, Burton, Burne-Jones, Swinburne, Morris, all of them
offering alternatives, some not wholly respectable, both to received religion
and to the apparent hardness of the scientific approach offered by Darwin's
hypothesis. It would be a mistake to try to huddle them into a group under
one label, but it may be said collectively of them that the warm-blooded
worship of beauty, 'aestheticism', was offered as a counter-proposition both
to the despair that poets like Tennyson recognized as implicit in the survival
of the fittest, where the mindless physical world is all, and to the cold
spiritual world of the 'pale Galilaean' that Swinburne saw as Christianity,
where body is punished to profit soul. It was surely the possibility of a middle
way that appealed to FitzGerald's contemporaries in his *Rubáiyát*. But besides
the idea of hedonism that seems suggested, FitzGerald meant by 'Epicurean',
which he so often applied to the poem, a stricter interpretation of the term,
in which man recognises that sense perception is his only guide to
knowledge, that his mode of distinguishing choices is by the enlightened
pleasure of the senses, and that the best life is a retired one where marriage,
the begetting of children, and civic responsibility are no longer paramount,
or even desirable. It was a doctrine of withdrawal that became increasingly
attractive in the face of the inhumane society caused by the combination of
the Industrial Revolution, intolerant Calvinism, and the theory of evolution.

Not a little of the lure of the *Rubáiyát* was that it tapped the great
attraction of the Orient for the Victorians, whether of Persian poetry, Indian
philosophy, or Japanese pots, symbols of a world where middle-class
conventionality had neither meaning nor validity. In the lushness of the
imagery of the poem lay suggestions of sensuality, mystery, satiety, all only
hinted at as they are held within the rigid framework of the FitzGerald
stanza; it was not unlike the Victorian love of feminine voluptuousness made
more irresistible by constraint within stiff confining garments. One suspects
that many of his readers were drawn to FitzGerald's work by impulses with
which he would certainly have felt little conscious empathy. The very
popularity of his translation, however, seems to indicate that he was far more
in tune with his contemporaries than he would have guessed.

The long wait for the discovery of the *Rubáiyát* made FitzGerald weary
at heart, and he began to feel a 'sort of Terror at meddling with Pen and
Paper.... The old Go is gone—such as it was. One has got older: one has lived
alone: and, also, either one's Subjects, or one's way of dealing with them, have
little Interest to others.' [II, 465–6] If publication was not worth considering,
it hardly seemed worthwhile writing. He continued to translate Persian in a
desultory way, and briefly he considered translating more Calderón, but he
published nothing of consequence for six years after the *Rubáiyát*. During
1860 and 1861 he contributed several brief items, concerned with his reading

or with local subjects, to *Notes and Queries*; he signed them 'Parathina', of which the translation is 'Along the Shore', which accurately reflects the change in his life.

'Somehow all the Country round is become a Cemetery to me: so many I loved there dead,' he wrote, 'but none I have loved have been drown'd.' [II, 371] Nothing could change the sea, but the countryside was being despoiled progressively: paths were fenced over by the squirearchy and guards set to prevent their use after they had been free to all since history had been recorded, commons were enclosed, trees were chopped down, and the land was systematically bought up by enormously rich families like the Thellussons of Rendlesham Hall and the Tomlines, who were FitzGerald's *bêtes noires*. 'I always like Seafaring People,' he said in justifying his attraction to the uncomplicated, unmercenary beachmen. Even their speech was freer, untainted by the city, more original and poetic, and his literary interests were revived by a sniff of sea air, so that he began collecting examples of the diction of the sailors, which he thought was the backbone of the Suffolk dialect that he had loved ever since his boyhood walks with Major Moor. 'Their very fine old English' was only a manifestation of the superiority of sailing men: 'We have a pretty word here for these fluttering light winds— you will see how pleasantly compounded—"No steady Breeze; but only little *fannyin'* Winds, that died at Sunset," etc.' [II, 397]

His delight in men of the sea led him naturally into sailing on a larger scale than he had undertaken since days on the Channel with his father and his grandfather. In 1861 he replaced a small boat he had on the River Deben with a two-ton, sixteen-foot river boat, sailed by two men and named the *Waveney* after the river on which she was built. 'She'll do all but speak,' said one of the crew in pleasure at her performance.

FitzGerald loved being aboard the *Waveney*, setting out for a sail with a cuddy well stocked with bottled stout for himself and the crew, but he immediately began hankering for a larger craft, one in which he could make short trips to the Continent or to Scotland and which could sleep a few guests. In the spring of 1862 he bought, sight unseen, a yacht that the Woodbridge plumber had found on the Thames at Greenwich; almost immediately he discovered that he had 'one of the biggest owls in Woodbridge (and that is no small thing) to choose and act for me'. The yacht had cost £43, and he paid two men to bring her from London, then discovered that she was nearly derelict and had to be almost entirely refitted. Rather than do that, it was simpler to admit that he had lost his whole investment in the boat.

After a long search for a replacement for the worthless yacht, he finally ordered a forty-three-foot schooner, built in Wivenhoe, Essex, for about

£350, which was launched in the summer of 1863. During her building he
was afraid he had made another mistake, but FitzGerald loved the new boat
when he saw her. Almost immediately he changed her name from the
Shamrock to the *Scandal*, which he said with feeling went faster than anything
else in Woodbridge; her skiff was appropriately named the *Whisper*. She
proved awkward in the Deben, 'but then she was to be a good Sea-boat'. For
all his love of her, he had few plans for long cruises after all: 'I can't sleep so
well on board as I used to do thirty years ago: and not to get one's Sleep, you
know, indisposes one more or less for the Day.' Gradually, however, he began
thinking of Dover, Folkestone, the Isle of Wight, and the Channel ports of
the Continent, 'which will give one's sleeping Talents a *tuning*'. [II, 484]

FitzGerald was quite happy to let his crew sail the boat without his
assistance, for watching the white sails and the beacons bothered his eyes: 'as
in other Affairs of Life, I only sit by and look on.' [II, 454] He contented
himself with good-natured shouts of advice to the helmsman from his own
position by the mainmast, where he spent most of his time lying with a book
in his hand, perfectly happy at being soaked in a heavy sea. He won the
respect of all who sailed with him by knowing nothing of fear in rough
weather. Although he took so small a part in their sailing, he was on
democratic terms with his crews, calling them by their Christian names and
delightedly going aboard other vessels with them to drink rum. He was a
good master, asking little for himself and expecting nothing but cold food on
board, to save work in the galley. If he kept the crew out over the weekend,
he would put into harbour to get them a hot meal. He even made his own
bed to save them trouble.

He had always declined to dress grandly for particular occasions, and
afloat he maintained the same sartorial indifference, wearing his customary
clothing, not 'yachting' costume. Like any other gentleman of the period, he
wore his top hat when sailing, in this case tied on to keep it from being blown
overboard. Some modern writers have questioned the testimony on the
subject of those who sailed with him, saying that a top hat would be
manifestly too impractical for the purpose. Contemporary photographs
show, however, that men of his class wore it as customary sailing gear;
certainly, he would not have worn a common sailor's cap, although he
probably took off his hat when the weather was too rough. Around his
shoulders was a huge shawl; one of those he owned, a plaid affair, is still worn
by the presiding officer at meetings of the Omar Khayyám Club.

But no one could have called him conventional, even when he was
sailing. Going ashore in the *Whisper*, he would sometimes be irritated by the
slowness and leap into knee-deep water to wade to dry land. Occasionally he
was swept off the deck by the movement of the boom in rough weather,

which he would forget when he was deep in a book, and more than once he was fished out still clutching whatever he had been reading, quite at his ease once his hat had been retrieved, content to lie down again and let the sea wash over him, since, as he remarked philosophically, he could hardly get wetter.

In 1863 he set out at last for Holland, where he had wanted for years to see the pictures in the Hague. They landed in Rotterdam and put up the boat in a 'sluggish unsweet Canal'. George Manby, a Woodbridge merchant who was his guest on the trip, persuaded FitzGerald to see Rotterdam before going on: 'So we tore about in an open Cab: saw nothing: the Gallery not worth a Visit: and at night I was half dead with weariness.' The following day they went to Amsterdam, where they were in such a rush that they missed two of the pictures they most wanted to see. They arrived at last at the Hague museum, but it was just closing for two days. In 'Rage and Despair' over the Dutch, Manby, and himself, FitzGerald immediately had the boat put out to sea and went back to England without ever having been in the gallery that was the goal of the trip. [II, 489–90]

Each year he kept the yacht under sail for increasingly long periods, taking her along the eastern and southern coasts of England and to the French Channel ports. In Lowestoft he often used her as floating summer quarters. Besides the fun of actual sailing, she provided him with a perfect excuse not to settle down permanently on land.

Mrs Smith, the mistress of Farlingay Hall, whose illness had made FitzGerald leave the house, died at the end of 1859, and he moved back there for the second half of 1860, but it was obvious that her widower was so ill that he would have to vacate the house and that the lodger would have to move elsewhere. The position of Farlingay a short way outside Woodbridge had been convenient, since it meant that FitzGerald did not have to face the hostility of the townspeople, many of whom were still resentful over his behaviour to Lucy, which became ever more reprehensible as it was endlessly discussed until it was the general opinion that he was either insane or totally without principles.[5]

It was surely a conscious decision to face up at last to his detractors that made him take lodgings in the exact centre of Woodbridge, over the gunshop of Sharman Berry across from the Shire Hall, with his windows overlooking the market place. It would have been hard to find a more conspicuous place to live. He said that he intended to stay there only as he looked for a house in the town, but he remained on that temporary basis in Market Hill for thirteen years: 'I am afraid to leave this poor Lodging, where I do pretty well, though I can scarce store half the things I want away in it.' But he had become acutely aware of his mortality and was afraid that the 'shaking of the

Dart over one's Head' might find him in rented rooms: 'I think one should not burden Landlord and Landlady with that.' [II, 434]

The Berrys were 'very kind and attentive'; his two rooms were cramped, uncomfortable, and dirty, but at least the last of these did not worry him. Mrs Berry hired 'at 1s. a week such a Slut as even I cannot put up with', and understandably had trouble keeping servants. FitzGerald's vegetarian diet demanded little of her culinary skills; on one typical occasion his early dinner was pease pudding, potatoes, and a small bottle of Chablis, which he presumably furnished himself. His only complaint about his quarters was that he found the 'Privy quite public'.

Furnishing his lodgings was the excuse for a new orgy of picture buying and restoring: 'I have been playing wonderful Tricks with the Pictures I have: have cut the Magi in two—making two very good Pictures, I assure you; and cutting off the dark corners of other Pictures with Gold Ovals—a shape I like within a Square, and doing away with much Black background.' [II, 459] Irreverently he turpentined and rubbed down two paintings that were, at least temporarily, ascribed to Velasquez and Titian. He bought an 'Early Gainsboro' from Churchyard and quantities of 'large *picturesque* China' to fill any gaps in the already overcrowded rooms, putting them with the pictures, statues, and even a parti-coloured mop that was so agreeable to his 'colour-loving Eyes' that he kept it in his sitting room. By the time he was finished, his rooms were as comfortable—which is to say, disordered—as his undergraduate lodgings or the cottage at Boulge.

The intellectual life of Woodbridge was as sluggish as that of any small market town, and at first FitzGerald was so conscious of the monotonous chimes from the nearby parish church, playing every three hours, that he threatened to hang himself. It was 'Ye Banks and Braes' and 'Where and oh where is my Soldier Laddie gone?' for weekdays, with a dolefully slow version of the 'Sicilian Mariners' Hymn' for Sundays. He had already cut himself off from invitations from people of his own class in the town, but he was not worried about that, and he found his company instead with tradespeople such as the bookseller, John Loder, and a bright young merchant's clerk, Frederick Spalding, whose interests in art and artefacts so commended themselves to FitzGerald that he set him up in business.

Spalding kept a worshipful diary in which he recorded FitzGerald's conversation and his own gratitude to him: 'I am getting selfish about him, I expect. I like him to *myself* best. I feel so at home with him, could ask him anything, could tell him anything.' In return FitzGerald talked frankly of his own family, of his broken marriage, of his disappointed aspirations. When he saw that Spalding's business was not prospering, he burnt the bond for £500 that he had lent to the younger man. 'I feel towards him as I do to no other man,' wrote Spalding. 'But how can he treat me as he does—with his vast knowledge, taste, and abilities, and I half his age?'[6]

The answer to Spalding's question was that he provided some of the intellectual company that FitzGerald missed in the locality, now that Barton and Crabbe were dead. But he continued to have a sense of humour about himself, even in this matter, and after complaining of his boredom in Woodbridge, he added, 'I see, however, by a Handbill in the Grocer's Shop that a Man is going to lecture on the Gorilla in a few weeks. So there is something to look forward to.' [II, 411–12]

Living in Woodbridge meant the danger of running into Lucy FitzGerald. In 1864 she was there twice for long stays, according to FitzGerald, 'though I never came across her'. Two years later she visited the town four times: 'We have different ideas of Propriety, to be sure.' After not having seen her for seven years, he met her in the street: 'I did not look, nor should have noticed her, but she rushed over the way, and put her Claw in mine, and the terrible old *Caw* soon told me. I said, "Oh, how d'ye do, Ma'am; how long have you been here?" I made off. All this is very wrong; but the Woman has no Delicacy: and if one gives an Inch will take an Ell.' [II, 617]

Lodging with the Berrys on Market Hill had one major advantage over living at Farlingay: he was twice as far from Boulge Hall and the FitzGeralds. There was, however, the inconvenience of being within a hundred yards of the Bull Inn, where the coach from Ipswich stopped and let out anyone going to Boulge. FitzGerald's brother John called on him several times a week, often bringing his sons with him; Edward would sit apprehensively waiting for a pause in the cataract of words to bring the visit to an end. He felt an amused love of John, but he never went to Boulge himself, and when the family was congregated there, he knew there would be a 'Levée of People, who drop in here, etc.' [II, 478], so that he had to leave Woodbridge at such times.

John, who seldom found it easy to make up his mind, was trying to decide whether to sell Boulge altogether, but he was to dither over the matter until his death. On one occasion it was put up for auction and the bidding went to £30,000, but John had set the reserve price well above that, so that it would not go out of his hands. Another time he actually negotiated the sale, then worried so much about it overnight that he bought it back the following day. Occasionally he would arrive at the Bull on his return home, ignore the Boulge carriage waiting for him, order a fly instead, then get into neither but walk three miles to Boulge with both conveyances following him; when he arrived home he would complain at having to pay for a fly he had not used. At the Hall he would ring for a footman to tell him the time from the clock at his elbow. FitzGerald said that John broke engagements from the 'feeling of being *bound*' to them, and that all he meant when he said 'D.V.' in accepting them was, 'If I happen to be in the Humour'. [II, 612] As his brother observed, John was a 'man one could really love two and three-quarter miles off'.[7]

In 1863 FitzGerald lost the one member of his family whom he loved without serious qualification, his sister Mrs Kerrich, who died at Geldestone. The day of her death he had the only extrasensory experience recorded in his life. He believed that he had seen from outside the house a clear picture of Mrs Kerrich having tea with her children in the dining room. As he watched, his sister withdrew quietly from the room, to keep from disturbing the children, and at the moment he saw this, Mrs Kerrich died in Norfolk. That he believed in the 'vision' even momentarily indicates how profoundly her death upset him.

He had been assiduous in visiting her in her long illness, but he refused to attend the funeral: 'There will be many Mourners, and I should, I am sure, do more harm than good.' He blamed his brother-in-law for 'having shortened the Life of this admirable Woman' and called him a 'self-Complacent Booby', but he then added with his usual contrition, 'yet he is five hundred times a better Man than myself'. [II, 480] Thereafter, he refused to go to Geldestone, even to see his beloved nieces, adding it to the growing list of places he could not visit because of previous happiness there. He had always hated funerals, and after this he refused to attend even those of his immediate family.

At the end of 1863 came yet another death, to make him feel that his whole past was being cut from beneath him. On the evening of Christmas Day he was walking alone in the dark gardens of the Seckford Almshouses in Woodbridge when he met George Manby, who gave him the news of the death of Thackeray.

> I have thought little else than of W.M.T. ever since ... as I sit alone by my Fire these long Nights. I had seen very little of him for these last ten years; *nothing* for the last five; he did not care to write; and people told me he was become a little spoiled: by London praise, and some consequent Egotism. But he was a very fine Fellow. His Books are wonderful.... [II, 509]

At any moment, it seemed to FitzGerald, 'he might be coming up my Stairs, and about to come (singing) into my Room, as in old Charlotte Street, etc., thirty years ago.' [II, 505] For all his sorrow, he refused to subscribe to the Thackeray monument in the Abbey, since he believed that no one should be commemorated there until a full century had proved the permanence of his reputation. [II, 537]

One by one the old friendships were vanishing. That with Tennyson had always been tricky, but it seemed to be disintegrating further. He so disliked the *Idylls of the King* that he said 'they might almost [have] been written by Matthew Arnold.' [II, 340] Although he continued to say how much he gloried in Tennyson's success and how he longed to visit the poet at home, he could somehow never find the time. He was tired of receiving answers from Mrs Tennyson to letters he had written to her husband: 'She is a graceful lady, but I think that she and other aesthetic and hysterical Ladies have hurt AT, who, *quoad* Artist, would have done better to remain single in Lincolnshire, or married a jolly Woman who would have laughed and cried without any reason why.' [II, 538]

When all his oldest friends were slipping out of his life, it hardly seemed worth keeping up newer acquaintances. In the eight years that the Cowells had been in India, he had continued his correspondence with them, and if something of the warmth of close friendship had gone, there was still their shared interest in scholarship to hold them together. But in 1864, when the Cowells came back to England, it was almost as if FitzGerald felt stifled by the renewal of an old intimacy. 'I am afraid you will find me a torpid and incurious Man compared to what you left me,' he wrote, and he began searching for reasons why they could not meet. He told them of his new boat and said they 'must come one day' to see her, but he did not specify when. After they had been in Ipswich for two months without seeing him, FitzGerald wrote that they were 'to have come over here one day, but somehow did not.... we shall meet before long, I doubt not.' When finally Cowell got to Woodbridge, FitzGerald told him the visit was a 'sad sort of Pleasure'. The letters still passed back and forth, but more infrequently and more coolly. His invitations to see the new boat were repeated without a specific date: 'I can't well make sure what day: sometimes I ask one man to go, sometimes another, and so all is cut up.' [II, 560] At last the Cowells had been only five miles away for a year and a half without FitzGerald's having laid eyes on Mrs Cowell.

Once he had been the most enthusiastic of friends, but after the deaths of Mrs Kerrich and Thackeray, a heavy lethargy had settled on him. Even in his correspondence much of the gaiety and spontaneity had disappeared, and for the first time the reader becomes aware of how often he repeated phrases from one letter to another, as if he scarcely had the energy to respond afresh to each new person.

His oddness had become far more than a matter of appearance, although that was eccentric enough. He had always dressed negligently, but now he was slovenly; his plaid shawl sometimes hung off his shoulders and trailed on the ground, with his old top hat wagging on the back of his head. He wore a carelessly tied black silk scarf around his neck, and no ornaments besides his gold watch chain. In the summer he was even seen to take off his shoes and walk barefoot. His whole demeanour was like a deliberate affront to public opinion, as if he were so weary of being distrusted that he was determined to be even more outrageous than the sober inhabitants of Woodbridge thought him. If he was spoken to in the course of one of his solitary walks by a neighbour who had not been introduced to him, he would say brusquely, 'I don't know you!'

For a long time his attendance at church had been little more than a polite observance of social custom, but now he ceased going almost completely. The rector of Woodbridge, the Revd Thomas Mellor, called on him and said, 'I am sorry, Mr. FitzGerald that I never see you at church.' FitzGerald replied curtly, 'Sir, you might have conceived that a man has not come to my years without thinking much on these things. I believe I may say that I have reflected on them fully. You need not repeat this visit.'[8] On another occasion Robert Groome, rector of Monk Soham, near Woodbridge, whom FitzGerald had known since their days together in the Camus Society at Cambridge, preached at the parish church across the street from FitzGerald's rooms and spent the following morning with him. 'I did not venture inside the sacred Edifice,' FitzGerald told a friend, 'but I looked through a Glass Door in the Porch and saw R.G. and heard his Voice (not the Words) ascending and descending in a rather dramatic way.' [II, 470]

The stories of FitzGerald's curious behaviour were no doubt exaggerated in the first place by Woodbridge residents who thought he was nearly insane, and they probably lost little in subsequent transmission, but there is enough objective evidence to suggest that most of them rested on a firm basis of fact, even if they had been given additional trimmings. It was no accident that his nickname among the beachmen of Lowestoft and the disrespectful schoolboys around Woodbridge was 'Dotty'. Sir Sidney Colvin remembered that as a boy he knew well the tall figure of the sad-faced elderly man drifting abstractedly along the roads, a sight so familiar that he was almost disregarded by passers-by.

FitzGerald was in his mid-fifties, but he was already an old man, and the thought of illness and death, like those of his family and friends, was so omnipresent that he determined to get a house of his own to anticipate becoming incapacitated. His eyes, which had never been strong, were failing badly, he had a constant ringing in his ears, and he had to go to London to see a dentist. In 1862, after the death of Mr Smith at Farlingay, he had been offered a chance to buy that house, and he hesitated long over it; it was the 'very most delightful Place' he knew, with 'Gardens *and* Furniture, *and* orderly Servants, all ready to my disposal', but he dared not risk its solitary situation: 'To be alone in the Country—even but a short mile of a Town—is now become sad to me: dull as this Town is, yet people pass, Children scream, and a Man calls "Hot Rolls" which is all less sad than the waving and mourning of Trees, and the sight of a dead Garden before the Window.' [II, 433–4] The days were long past when his cottage at the gates of Boulge had seemed too near to other people.

Unwillingly, he began looking seriously for alternatives to Farlingay. He got as far as having plans made for alterations to the house of the former parson at the end of Seckford Place, and then discovered to his relief that it was too small. He looked at other houses, even made enquiries about servants for them, but decided that 'all the better houses are occupied by Dowagers like Myself.' [II, 426]

It was 1864 when he finally bought a place of his own. An estate at the northern end of Woodbridge, Melton Grange, was parcelled off when it changed hands, and he bought its former farmhouse, a 'rotten Affair' with six acres, for £730. He was not sure what to do with his purchase, but he said he had talked so long of buying that he had to get something, even if he resold it at once. At least, he wrote, 'two or three People have asked to hire, or buy, Bits' of the property, 'so I have risen in public Respect'. [II, 525–6] Within a few months the builders were working on the first of his additions to the old farmhouse, but it was another ten years before he moved in completely and at last called it home.

Grange Farm, as the house was called, had once been two tiny cottages, which still made a small house when thrown together, with three cramped bedrooms above a kitchen, scullery, and sitting-dining room. To this FitzGerald immediately added one large and airy room on each floor and a lavatory. Outside the ground-floor windows he built the handsome garden terrace that still stands. He admitted that he often changed his mind after the builders had begun work on one section and asked them to tear out what they had done, but he was incensed to be given a bill of £1,150 when the addition was completed, half again as much as he had paid for the original house and six acres. He contested the bill as a matter of principle, calling in surveyors, lawyers, and adjusters, and after two years succeeded in having it reduced by £120, which surely did little more than pay his professional fees, but his honour was satisfied because the builder 'will have lost £200 at least by Law expenses, and being out of his money two years—and—*Serve him right*'. [III, 92] It was a brief glimpse of the hardness beneath the surface that sometimes showed when he was angry.

He planted the garden with trees and the bright flowers he loved, had a duck pond put in, bought more land to preserve his view of the river, and furnished the house completely, although he was careful not to hang many portraits on the walls, because he intended that his unmarried Kerrich nieces should use the house for their summer holidays; one of them was epileptic, and he did not want to frighten her with his 'dark Italian Faces', so that she 'would dream of them'.

When the house was complete, he should have taken that as a mark of its transformation into his own property, but he could not summon up courage to move into it: 'I believe I never shall do unless in a Lodging, as I have lived these forty years. It is too late, I doubt, to reform in a House of one's own.' [II, 579] It was more than five years after he bought it that he spent a night in it. He protested that he had no time for the responsibility of running a house, but he actually had that without living there, for he installed a resident couple to care for his nieces and other guests. When all other excuses failed him for not making it his home, he put on another extension of two more rooms in 1871, making it impossible to do more than 'dawdle about my Garden, play with the Cat, and look at the Builders'. What had been a pair of small cottages had now become a handsome and commodious house set in a large garden, far from the bustle of Woodbridge, with only the muffled sounds of Pytches Road to make him feel part of the life of the other townspeople. With great ingenuity and the expenditure of a good deal of money, he had succeeded in recreating all the disadvantages and loneliness that had frightened him out of buying Farlingay. The truth was that he had originally bought the house as a place to die, and it had now become an emblem of his mortality. 'My Chateau', as he liked to call it mockingly, 'is reserved for my last Retirement from the Stage.' [III, 7].

NOTE

* In the past, dispute over exact details has so often led to acrimonious explosions about the inaccuracy of other writers that recounting the discovery of the poem gives one the sense of going on tiptoe through a minefield that has often blown up before; it may be quiescent, but it is not safe to assume so.

1. Wright, II, 35–6.
2. Donne, p. 238.
3. For the 'romance of the *Rubáiyát*' see Terhune, pp. 207–13; Weber, pp. 19–31; FitzGerald: *Letters*, II, 417–18, III, 414–19. There are many other accounts, most of them less accurate.
4. Quoted, Kermode, p. 56.
5. Glyde, p. 249.
6. Spalding, 31.3.68.
7. Wright, I, 314.
8. Wright, II, 89.

FREDERICK A. DE ARMAS

The Apocalyptic Vision of La Vida es Sueño: Calderón and Edward FitzGerald

I

On April 27, 1859, Edward FitzGerald expressed his views on translation in a letter to Edward Byles Cowell, the orientalist who had inspired him to learn Persian: "I suppose very few People have ever taken such Pains in Translation as I have: though certainly not to be literal. But at all Cost, a Thing must *live*: with a transfusion of one's worse Life if one can't retain the Original's better. Better a live sparrow than a stuffed Eagle" (*Letters*, vol. 2, p. 335).[1] The *Rubáiyát of Omar Khayyám* certainly did live, bringing to the attention of FitzGerald's contemporaries not only the richness of Persian literature, but also the Victorian translator's own poetic abilities. Joanna Richardson comments: "Edward FitzGerald translated the *Rubáiyát of Omar Khayyám*. That, in one brief sentence, is all that most people know of him."[2] And yet, FitzGerald's interest in Spanish language and literature was as intense as his concern with Persian. Edward Byles Cowell, who was instrumental in inspiring and instructing FitzGerald in Persian, first led him to Spanish. They would often meet and read from the seventeenth-century playwright Pedro Calderón de la Barca. Before working on the *Rubáiyát*, FitzGerald turned to this dramatist, translating six dramas (1853). After

From *Comparative Literature Studies* 23, no. 2 (Summer 1986). © 1986 Board of Trustees of the University of Illinois.

completing his version of the Persian poem, he again turned to Calderón, this time rendering into English *El mágico prodigioso* and *La vida es sueño*. Both were printed in 1865. Although little attention has been paid to this endeavor by critics of FitzGerald's works,[3] he has found a modest place in the history of Hispanism in English-speaking countries. Edwin Honig asserts: "For the past century the most respectable versions of Calderón in English were Edward FitzGerald's prose and blank-verse translations of *Eight Dramas*. FitzGerald used a stock but modified Elizabethan diction, cutting long speeches, altering and adding lines as he saw fit, and generally polishing crude surfaces with his own debonair intelligence.[4] Beginning with the reviews of FitzGerald's first volume on Calderón of 1853 and continuing up to the present, critics have tended to deplore the many alterations found in these texts. In one of the most recent (1980) translations of Calderón into English, this view still prevails. Kenneth Muir explains: "Not everyone has approved of Calderón's style." He then cites a passage from FitzGerald and links his approach to Calderón to outmoded Victorian attitudes: "Victorian critics complained of the same things in Shakespeare's early plays, or blamed the groundlings, as FitzGerald blamed Calderón's 'not very accurate audience.'"[5] Is FitzGerald careless with Calderón? This essay will focus on the Victorian writer's translation of *La vida es sueño* in order to suggest some new ways of looking at this old problem. This *comedia* has been chosen from the eight adapted by FitzGerald not only because it is considered Calderón's masterpiece, but also because together with *El mágico prodigioso*, it represents the culmination of FitzGerald's efforts to interpret the Spanish theater.

FitzGerald's pride in his Calderón is evinced in the fact that he reworked the image he had used to describe his translation of the *Rubáiyát* (the live sparrow vs. the stuffed eagle) to refer to his Spanish translation. In a letter to James Russell Lowell, he says of his Calderón: "I am persuaded that, to keep *Life* in the work (as Drama must) the Translator (however inferior to his original) must re-cast that original into his own Likeness: the less like his original, so much the worse: but still, the live Dog better than the dead Lion in Drama, I say" (*Letters*, vol. 4, pp. 167–68). To prove his point, FitzGerald then asks: "Whose Homer still holds its own? The elaborately exact, or the "teacup-time Parody?" (*Letters*, vol. 4, p. 168). His answer is that Alexander Pope's Homer is the one that still holds its own even though it is far from exact. Contemporary criticism tends to agree with FitzGerald's assessment. Reuben Brower asserts: "Alexander Pope's *Iliad* is a triumph.... Since its appearance in the early eighteenth century (1715–20), scholars have kept saying with Richard Bentley that it is 'not Homer,' but readers have happily gone on reading.... It has been the most readable and most read of all English translations of Homer."[6] Brower details how Pope was able, as a great poet, to impose his own interpretation of the *Iliad*, one that captured the reader's imagination, making available at least "one level of meaning in the total Homeric vision" (p. 75).

FitzGerald's "dangerous experiment" (*Letters*, vol. 2, p. 85), as he was fond of calling his Calderón, is in many ways similar to Pope's *Iliad*. In both cases the translators turn to a culture and an epoch that is particularly foreign to them and to their readers. Brower comments: "Part of the excitement in doing a translation is the feeling of foreignness even of the obscurity, of the haunting original" (p. 14). He adds that the greater the distance between poet and translator, the more the latter can rely on his own creativity: "It might be claimed that the more ghostly-mysterious the text seems, the nearer the translator's process approaches free poetic creation" (p. 14). At the same time, it might be added that the translator hopes to unravel the mystery, to interpret the work to his own satisfaction. In this, he resembles those literary critics who believe that interpretation is their main task.

Although the mystery of the original is a spur to free poetic creation and to perceptive interpretation, the translator's own critical bias, the literary tastes of his public, or both lead to other textual alterations that are more predictable and restrictive. The translator thus reads and misreads the original text for his readers[7] in at least two ways: first by reveling in and attempting to unravel the mystery of the original, and second by adding a certain familiarity in the form or in the content. In Edward FitzGerald's alteration of *La vida es sueño*, both the expansive and the constrictive manners are encountered. The first part of the discussion will center on the latter since it is the most easily documented.

II

In 1881, at the bicentennial of Calderón's death, FitzGerald was presented a medal from the Spanish Royal Academy in recognition of his Calderón translations (*Letters*, vol. 4, pp. 461–62). This was also the year in which Marcelino Menéndez Pelayo gave a series of lectures at the *Círulo de la Unión Católica*, which were collected into a book entitled *Calderón y su teatro*. Studying this youthful effort, Bruce W. Wardropper concludes that Menéndez Pelayo "is, *malgré lui*, a Neo-classic critic. However much he might dispute Luzán's claim to speak in absolute terms about literature, Menéndez Pelayo was attracted to the Neo-classic school of aesthetics because its dogmatism and its doctrines of order and unity appealed to his conservative and Catholic mind. He espoused the Neo-classic precepts in spite of the fact that they threatened much of Spanish Catholic Art."[8] Much of the negative criticism that has been applied to Calderón is based on this neoclassical bias, a situation that has led Henry W. Sullivan to proclaim Calderón as a "victim of neoclassicism."[9]

These notions can be traced back to seventeenth-century France, a period that saw continuous adaptations of Spanish *comedias*.[10] Although utilizing the varied plots found in these Spanish plays, the French authors found them to be rough works that needed polishing in order to become true works of art: "Comment enfin achever et polir les formes qu'elle n'avait su qu'ébaucher ... ?"[11] These *comedias* were the *prima materia* that had to be refashioned into gold by the alchemists or artists who were aware of dramatic precepts derived from the Italian Renaissance commentators of Aristotle.[12] With the eighteenth century, these attitudes became commonplace. In France, they are most clearly expressed by Voltaire.[13] Even Spain absorbed these French attitudes and produced treatises that were critical of Baroque literature. Ignacio Luzán's *Poética* (1737) was to become a model for Menéndez Pelayo's condemnation of Calderón, but the most severe objections to Golden Age drama during the eighteenth century came from Blas Nasarre who "branded Lope de Vega as the 'first corrupter' and Calderón as the 'second corrupter' of the Spanish stage."[14]

Edward FitzGerald's opinions regarding Calderón's dramaturgy are not merely a reflection of Victorian attitudes, as Muir has argued. In his theory and practice FitzGerald often reflects the tenets of the neoclassical or French school. In his reductive and constrictive manner, this Victorian translator attempts to tame much of what he sees as "wild" (*Letters*, vol. 2, p. 547; *Works*, vol. 5, p. 99)[15] in Calderón's drama. He revises the original text so as to bring it closer to neoclassical ideals such as clarity of style, accuracy in geographical and historical data, verisimilitude, decorum, and unity of action.

In his letters, FitzGerald often evinces the concern that his translation of *La vida es sueño* may reflect too accurately Calderón's style: "I was really fearful of its being bombastic" (vol. 2, p. 554). He does not wish his version to smack of the "false heroic" (vol. 2, p. 551). The Victorian translator had expressed similar fears when he published *Six Dramas of Calderón*, adding that many conceits as well as repetitive thoughts and images had to be eliminated (vol. 4, p. 5). This stated preference on the part of FitzGerald is typical of neoclassic criticism. When Ernest Martinenche discusses the difficulty French seventeenth-century playwrights have in adapting *comedias*, he asks: "Comment ramener la négligence passionée et metaphorique de sa poésie au ton d'une savante simplicité?"[16] To achieve clarity of style in *La vida es sueño* FitzGerald eliminates much that the neoclassics would have considered excessive adornment. Puns, especially when uttered by noble characters, are often deleted. Not only are they excessive, but they also cloud the "otherwise distinct outlines of character" (*Works*, vol. 5, p. 5). Furthermore, they infringe upon decorum since characters ought to speak a language suited to their station in life. Rosaura's exclamation, "y apenas llega, cuando llegas a penas" (v. 20),[17] which as served as a point of departure for Bruce Wardropper's penetrating analysis of the initial scenes of the *comedia*,[18] is absent from FitzGerald's version. At the same time, the Victorian poet wishes to convey a sense of the original. In order to preserve both decorum and the original texture, puns are often relegated to the *gracioso*. Indeed, some of the humor is FitzGerald's own, such as: "Like some scared water bird, / As we say in my country, dove below" (p. 105).

The Victorian translator also shows his propensity for simplifying the style through his elimination of image clusters. E. M. Wilson has pointed out that the four elements are central to Calderón's dramaturgy.[19] As the Spanish play opens, the hipogryph is described thusly:

> ... rayo sin llama,
> pájaro sin matiz, pez sin escama
> y bruto sin instinto (vv. 3–5).

That Rosaura's horse, described in terms of a mythical creature and related to the four elements, unseats Rosaura and literally drops her into Poland has given rise to several interpretations. Angel Cilveti summarizes: "La identificación de hipogrifo con los cuatro elementos, dando de lado a Rosaura, conduce a la caracterización del primero como pasión sexual de proporciones cósmicas, o al símbolo de Segismundo representante del oscuro mundo de los sentidos."[20] The reader would search in vain for this image cluster in FitzGerald's version. This is unfortunate since Calderón clearly links the description of this mythical monster with the lament of a second "monster," that is, Segismundo, who considers himself as a "monstruo humano" (v. 209). In his first soliloquy, the imprisoned prince constructs his lament around the four elements. Describing and desiring the freedom of the *pez*, *bruto*, and *ave*, inhabitants of the elements water, earth, and air, Segismundo rages against his incarceration, utilizing the element of fire to characterize his own response: "un volcán, un Etna hecho" (v. 164). The volcano, according to Javier Herrero, is an image that partakes in itself of two of the elements, earth and fire. It is a symbolic representation of the "caos cósmico"[21] and is thus central to Calderón's iconic system. That FitzGerald chooses to eliminate this important image cluster is not so much a sign of carelessness or debonaire intelligence, but an indication of his neoclassical perceptions and a desire to update the original so as to make it more acceptable to his audience. The Victorian poet expresses his creativity by replacing the four elements, an "outdated" concept and a reiterative pattern, with other examples from the natural world. Segismundo rages because freedom is granted not only to "guiltless life" but also to "that which lives on blood and rapine" (p. 190), giving as examples the lion, the wolf, the bear, and the panther. Whereas Calderón emphasizes the majesty of nature, a text presented by God to man, FitzGerald focuses on the violence and rapine in nature which Segismundo comes to learn. This substitution allows him not only to move away from outdated and reiterative imagery, but also allows him to establish Segismundo's violent nature as an attempt to emulate the environment in which he is raised.

Although FitzGerald eliminates or substitutes a number of images, he preserves those he believes are central to the understanding of the *comedia*. In a letter to Cowell dated April 3, 1865, the English poet records his pleasure in capturing one such image: "By the bye, I think I have hit off the *Vida*'s Almond-tree very well" (vol. 2, p. 547). Curiously the almond tree is an image that is condemned by one of FitzGerald's contemporaries. The usually positive critic Richard Chenevix Trench comments: "His almond-trees, his phoenixes, his 'flowers which are the stars of earth,' and 'stars which are the flowers of heaven,' recur somewhat too often. He squanders ... seeing that what he has once used, he will not therefore feel the slightest scruple in using a second time or a hundredth."[22] Although FitzGerald must have realized that the almond tree was a commonplace in the theater of the time, he preserves it as a key to Segismundo's transformation. When the rebellious soldiers come to rescue the prince from the tower to which he has been returned after the "dream" or palace experience,[23] Segismundo has second thoughts about embarking on this new adventure since it may turn out to be one more dream that leaves him with nothing. FitzGerald mirrors Calderón in emphasizing the lessons that can be learned from the book of nature. The prince in both the original and the translation no longer holds on to concepts in his obsessive manner of thinking. Instead, as Christopher Soufas affirms, he discovers that: "The more one reads within that world text, the more one grows in wisdom."[24] Up to now, Clotaldo has attempted to teach him through natural examples. At this point, the prince grasps the manner in which this dialogue ought to be unfolded and posits the example of the almond tree to refrain his obsessive nature. FitzGerald has captured and condensed this image in his version, utilizing *almander* for almond-tree, a term he takes from Chaucer:

> Dressing me up in visionary glories,
> Which the first air of waking consciousness
> Scatters as fast as from the almander—

That, waking one fine morning in full flower,
One rougher insurrection of the breeze
Of all her sudden honour disadornes
To the last blossom, and she stands again
The winter-naked scare-crow that she was! (p. 182)

The almond tree which loses its flowers during a winter storm is a symbol of the impermanency of any temporal state and of the rule of fortune.[25] By speaking of the "insurrection of the breeze," FitzGerald adds immediacy to Calderón's conceptual approach. This phrase points to Segismundo's awareness that the breeze that destroys the flowers can be linked to the insurrection that the soldiers want him to lead. The prince has not only learned the hermeneutics of similitude, which according to Michel Foucault typifies the classical way of thinking,[26] but he is also aware that his violent actions can halve a devastating effect in the harmony and beauty of the cosmos.

Segismundo's transformation is here grounded to a central image in Calderón's text. Thus, FitzGerald does not always eliminate images in an attempt to stop that "lluvia de metátforas" which according to Menéndez Pelayo serves to drown Calderón's audience.[27] In the case of the almond tree the image is expanded to show how the violence that the prince had perceived in the blood and rapine of his first soliloquy has now given way to a more sensitive vision of the tragic possibilities of rebellion. With these images from the natural world, FitzGerald attempts to preserve the essential Calderón. They also serve to buttress Segismundo's transformation against the criticism of neoclassic scholars such as Menéndez Pelayo, who deplores "la violencia que hay en el cambio de carácter de Segismundo."[28] In FitzGerald, the prince's initial violence stems from a misreading of the book of nature. His tutor, Clotaldo, tries to show him how to read the world as text. But, it is not until Segismundo actually lives through the metaphor that life is a dream in the false dream of the palace that he begins to emulate his teacher. Only then does he engage in a positive dialogue with natural forces and adopts the almond tree as an example.

The French school often criticizes the Spanish *comedia* for weak characterization. To resolve this problem, FitzGerald overemphasizes the pupil-teacher relationship between Segismundo and Clotaldo. The latter, a representative of the status quo in the kingdom, is ambiguously portrayed by Calderón, as C. A. Merrick has demonstrated.[29] He had, after all, abandoned Rosaura's mother. FitzGerald replaces this shameful episode with a heroic one, granting further authority to Clotaldo. Indeed, Segismundo's famous second soliloquy is spoken by Clotaldo in FitzGerald's version, once the prince has been returned to the tower in the third act. The Victorian poet refashions the *comedia* into a *speculum principum* where Clotaldo becomes an idealized figure and the mirror to the prince. Segismundo's transformation is partially achieved by listening to his tutor, who understands the meaning of life and expounds upon it through the typical baroque metaphors that life is a dream and a stage:

> And all this stage of earth on which we seem
> Such busy actors, and the parts we play'd,
> Substantial as the shadow of a shade,
> And Dreaming but a dream within a dream! (p. 170)

The tone of the soliloquy elevates Clotaldo from a weak character lacking moral courage in Calderón to a heroic status as guide and preceptor to a rebellious youth. FitzGerald interprets and defines the central conflict in the play, leaving little room for the ambiguity that makes of Calderón's masterpiece a most engaging text.

This emphasis on characterization as the presentation of clearly defined traits can be seen as part of the neoclassical desire for verisimilitude. Events in a drama must be probable and likely. Thus the motivation of a character ought to be clearly defined. On the question of verisimilitude FitzGerald wavers between the neoclassical approach and his desire to preserve the mystery and foreignness of the text. In his letters, FitzGerald wonders if he ought to leave *La vida es sueño* "wild" or if he should argue "more probability" into the drama (vol. 2, p. 547). In a note to his translation he warns that he had not eliminated all improbable events from the *comedia*: "The bad watch kept by the sentinels who guarded their state-prisoner, together with much else (not all!) that defies sober sense in this wild drama, I must leave Calderón to answer for" (p. 99).

One clear way to increase verisimilitude in a work is to pay attention to geographical and historical detail. Ignacio Luzán's *Poética*, the most important neoclassical Spanish treatise of the eighteenth century, had criticized Calderón's dramas as "un conunto de absurdos, de anacronismos, de faltas de historia y geografía."[30] FitzGerald's desire to preserve historical accuracy is evinced in his letters when he speaks of his translation of *Guárdate del agua mansa* (vol. 2, p. 91). Here, all he must do is to preserve Calderón's historical details. However, when it comes to *La vida es sueño*, the task of a neoclassic translator is more complex. Menéndez Pelayo considers that: "La geografia y la historia del drama es de todo punto fantástica."[31] FitzGerald does little to increase historical accuracy since the play is not set during a specific historical period, although according to Ervin Brody, it does reflect the turbulent Russian Time of Troubles.[32] What the Victorian writer sets out to do is to increase geographic accuracy and detail. The data provided in *La vida es sueño* are minimal. The reader or audience only knows that the *comedia* takes place in Poland, in a tower close to the border and at Court. There is one more geographical clue. When Segismundo throws a servant from the balcony, he states: "Cayó del balcón al mar" (v. 1430). Neoclassical artists and critics saw in this statement an error since neither Warsaw nor Cracow, the two possible locations for the Polish Court, is by the ocean.[33] FitzGerald first tries to achieve geographical precision. The stage directions read: "The Palace at Warsaw" (p. 119). Cracow may have been a more accurate setting. One recent critic, Ervin Brody, sees in Segismundo's astonishment on waking at the palace the awe of a foreigner on experiencing the splendor of the beautiful Castle of Wawel in Cracow. Indeed, the seventeenth-century French adaptation of Calderón's masterpiece by the Abbé de Boisrobert has Cracow as the setting.[34] Aware of the inland location of Warsaw, FitzGerald also deletes the scene where Segismundo tosses a servant from a balcony into the sea. In this he is not only avoiding what he thought to be a geographic inaccuracy, but is also eliminating what he may have considered as a "wild" or impossible element in the plot.

Part of the wildness of the plot in FitzGerald's view consists of the excessive importance accorded to the subplot. The Victorian writer expresses his concern over the length of the Rosaura episode in Calderón's *comedia* in a letter of September 1858, where he wishes to "subdue" the Rosaura story "so as to assist and not compete with the Main interest" (vol. 2, p. 319). This negative attitude toward the subplot parallels the neoclassic stance which views the Rosaura episode as "una intriga extraña, completamente pegadiza y exotica que se enreda a todo el drama como una planta parasita."[35] In order to "tame" this "wild" element, FitzGerald deletes most of Rosaura's lines in the second act.

III

FitzGerald's many alterations of the Spanish original do not substantially transform the essential nature of Calderón's play. The work moves from one surprising event to another: From a prince imprisoned by his own father in a tower, to a woman dressed as a man and seeking revenge in a foreign land; from the lament of a monstrous being to the rationalizations of an astrologer-king. One neoclassic critic comments: "Con la inmensa fantasia de que pródigamente le doto la naturaleza, amontonó tantos lances en sus comedias, que hay alguna que cada acto o jornada se pudiera componer otra muy buena; y el vulgo, embelesado en aquel laberinto de enredos, se esta con la boca abierta, hasta que al fin de la comedia salen absortos sin poder repetir la substancia de ellos."[36] This is part of the mystery and excitement of Calderón's plays which FitzGerald wishes to capture and yet hold in check.

One way to tame this 'wild'[37] drama is to render it more familiar to his readers or audience. FitzGerald points to Shakespeare in his translation of Calderón so as to make the situations more familiar to the English public. In a letter dated April 10, 1865, FitzGerald claims that his translation is in "Ercles vein" (vol. 2, pp. 548–49). In *A Midsummer Night's Dream*, Bottom, one of the characters who is involved in the play within the play, boasts that he "could play Ercles rarely." Bottom's attempt at playing Ercles or Hercules turns heroic grandeur into comedy. Indeed, these rustic actors' play within the play, *Pyramus and Thisbe*, can serve "to satirize ... the crude mingling of tragedy and comedy."[38] By referring to Ercles' vein, FitzGerald is not so much adopting the neoclassic critical stance opposed to Calderón's mixture of the serious and the comic in *La vida es sueño*, but is pointing to one of the techniques he uses in his translation to make the text more familiar to an English audience. Considering that it may be difficult for his reader to accept the wild nature of the play's commencement, FitzGerald renders tame the fantastic elements of the first scene through the heightened role of the *gracioso* Clarín, now called Fife. But the mystery, danger, and romance of Calderón's initial evening scene is not lost. In FitzGerald we encounter a touching and comical exchange where Fife and Rosaura pledge to stay together "In a strange country—among savages—" (p. 104) where "bears, lions, wolves" (p. 105)[39] may abide. In their playful conversation they reveal apprehension about what they may find in this foreign land. It is the same apprehension that FitzGerald expects his reader to feel in entering Calderón's fiction. Indeed, Fife and Rosaura heighten the "marvelous" nature of their situation by alluding to *A Midsummer Night's Dream*. Rosaura and her *gracioso* are like the "fairy elves" (p. 104) of Shakespeare, and Fife is another Puck, "following darkness like a dream" (*Works*, p. 104; Shakespeare V, p. 393).[40] What the play has gained in lightness and familiarity it has not lost in mystery. By following a dream Fife and the audience will be delving into the very mystery of life which Segismundo comes to see as a dream.

It is fitting that FitzGerald allude to *A Midsummer Night's Dream* in his translation of Calderón; this play was one of Shakespeare's least popular until the nineteenth century, being considered by some as insipid and ridiculous. Its fantastic elements were a barrier to its acceptance until the German translation by Ludwig Tieck was performed in Berlin in 1827. Tieck not only revived Shakespeare, but also played a crucial role in the restoration of Calderón's place in literature. Indeed, Tieck's enthusiasm for the Spanish playwright led A. W. Schlegel to turn away from his translations of Shakespeare to those of Calderón.[41] In FitzGerald as in the German Romantics, Calderón and Shakespeare are seen as parallel figures.

The parallel between Shakespeare and Calderón is particularly striking when comparing *La vida es sueño* with *The Tempest*. The link between Prospero and Basilio is an obvious one on the surface; both are "wise" men who spend much time in esoteric studies, neglecting or erring in their duties as rulers. While Calderón portrays Basilio as delving into the secrets of the natural world, particularly astrology, in FitzGerald's version Segismundo views his father more as a magician:

> And you
> With that white wand of yours—
> Why, now I think on't, I have read of such
> A silver-haired magician with a wand,
> Who in a moment, with a wave of it,
> Turn'd rags to jewels, clowns to emperors. (p. 140)

This is the magic of Prospero whose books and wand can transform the fate of kingdoms. Indeed, Segismundo considers the power that transports him from the tower to the palace and makes him a prince, "some benigner magic than the stars" (p. 140). While the stars, he believes, were the cause of his imprisonment, this magician-father, a figure akin to Prospero, has saved him. He soon discovers that astrologer and magician are one and the same figure. The link between *La vida es sueño* and *The Tempest* is shattered by Segismundo's realization. Whereas Basilio, himself is the cause of the injustice by having imprisoned his son, Prospero is the object of treachery by a brother who deposes him. Prospero wants to regain his rightful position; Basilio places obstacles in his son's rightful claim to the throne. And yet, both Basilio and Prospero, through their attempts at control, are in danger of "playing God." Studying certain plays of Shakespeare and Calderón from the perspective of romance, William R. Blue concludes: "The power of art, of magic, of manipulation is something that must be mistrusted and finally abjured by Prospero here and by Basilio in a play by Calderón."[42]

Both *The Tempest* and *La vida es sueño* focus on the play within the play created by the magician-artist, leading Lionel Abel to devote a number of pages in his elucidation of metatheater[43] to a comparison of the plays. Speaking of Shakespeare's work, he comments: "Some dreams are antithetical to thought; the particular dream actualized in *The Tempest* is not. For a perfect revolution is not theoretically impossible."[44] The threat of violence in both works subsides with the dream, the fantastic elements becoming a tool for the achievement of harmony and justice. Prospero's bloodless revolution to regain power as Duke of Milan takes place in the dream-like ambience of the magical island. Segismundo's rebellion, on the other hand, loses its destructiveness when he learns from the "magical" palace dream and ponders on the metaphor that life is a dream. In both works, the realization of the insubstantiality of this life goes hand in hand with the restoration of precisely those earthly glories to the dispossessed. Following the play within the play, which is performed by spirits summoned by the magician, Prospero utters those well-known lines in *The Tempest*:

> And, like the baseless fabric of this vision,
> The cloud-capp'd towers, the gorgeous palaces,
> The solemn temples, the great globe itself,
> Yea, all which it inherit, shall dissolve
> And, like this insubstantial pageant faded,
> Leave not a rack behind. We are such stuff
> As dreams are made on, and our little life
> Is rounded with a sleep. (IV, vv. 151–58)

Pointing to the kinship in ambience and vision in Calderón and Shakespeare, Edward FitzGerald transforms Calderón's title from *La vida es sueño* to *Such Stuff as Dreams Are Made of*.

IV

Mystery through contextual reinforcement is not dependent solely on Shakespeare. Edward FitzGerald adds among others a Christian mystery, the unfolding of the Last Days, derived in part from the apocalyptic concerns of the Victorian era. In a discussion of the fantastic in literature, Eric S. Rabkin focuses on the Victorian period in order to argue that the notion of history as proceeding "inexorably towards a civilizing goal"[45] is confining to authors such as William Morris, who create "a history in a fairy land so that we can escape into a history that is demonstrably not progressive because it is not connected with our own times."[46] The concept of progress has shattered for some the notion of idyllic or paradisiacal beginnings. Northrop Frye notes that Charles Darwin was the Copernicus of the Victorian age: "The doctrine of evolution made time as huge and frightening as space: The past, after Darwin, was no more emotionally reassuring than the skies had come to be."[47] In FitzGerald's version, when Segismundo is taken to the palace, he believes that he has awakened in "Fairyland" (p. 140). The weight of his primitive and bestial past seems momentarily suspended. But Segismundo's escape is only illusory and temporary. The palace does not lie outside of time, but is an essential part of the historical process. Northrop Frye comments that a possible response to the fear of history is the elaboration of apocalyptic symbolism.[48] It provides not only a comprehensible beginning and end, but also it goes beyond escape and toward a personal or historical revelation that restores meaning to an increasingly alien and mechanistic process.

A recent essay by Mary Wilson Carpenter and George P. Landow has shown that Victorian authors such as Carlyle, Ruskin, Tennyson, and particularly George Eliot, use heavy allusions to the Book of Revelation as imagistic, thematic, and structuring devices.[49] To these writers must be added the name of Edward FitzGerald. He probably perused a few of the numerous treatises on the subject of apocalypse, popular during the Victorian era. The *Westminster Review*, a periodical that had been most critical of his *Six Dramas of Calderón* in 1853, would write favorably of Sara Hennell's pamphlet dealing with New Testament prophecy in 1861. The periodical also published that same year an essay on the apocalypse as literature, written by M. W. Call.[50] Furthermore, E. B. Elliott, in his four-volume commentary on Revelation entitled *Horae Apocalypticae*, singled out the year 1866 as the beginning of the millennium.[51] Thus, the apocalyptic references included in FitzGerald's version of *La vida es sueño* are most timely since the book was printed in 1865, the year before the supposed arrival of the millennium.

FitzGerald refashions Calderón by stressing the notion of judgment in the second act of *La vida es sueño*. Segismundo realizes that he has not escaped to Fairyland. The palace is not Prospero's island governed by a benevolent magician. Instead it is ruled by a stern father who chose to incarcerate his own son and raise him as a savage. The prince rebels against "lying prophecies and prophet kings" (p. 163). The weight of a bestial past and of an ominous future is on his shoulders as he fashions apocalypse from his father's fears:

> After a revelation such as this,
> The Last Day shall have little left to show
> Of righted wrong and villany requited!
> Nay, Judgment now beginning upon earth,
> Myself, methinks, in right of all my wrongs,
> Appointed heav'n's avenging minister,
> Accuser, judge, and executioner,
> Sword in hand, cite the guilty.... (p. 162)

Revelation to Segismundo is not a vision granted to him by God, but a realization of the injustice to which he has been subjected. This personal revelation will precipitate events that echo those foretold in the Book of Revelation. Segismundo appears to usurp the role of Christ as final judge and uses apocalyptic language to seek personal retribution. By setting himself up as Christ, Segismundo becomes Antichrist, since many believed that he would be a figure that imitates and yet reverses the actions of Christ. Segismundo assumes the role of final judge, but his justice is certainly not divine. Instead of mercy, he is driven by a desire for revenge. Segismundo also sets himself up as king and becomes a tyrant. It was believed that "the last king to rule over the whole earth"[52] would be Antichrist. He would be a tyrant who would bring about a final age of "terror and dread."[53] Segismundo may embody this historical terror.

Although derived in part from the apocalyptic concerns of the Victorian era, the element of Christian mystery may not be of FitzGerald's own making. Instead, he may be assuming the role of interpreter of Calderón, pointing out to his readers an important yet hidden aspect of *La vida es sueño*. Edwin Honig, a recent translator of Calderón's masterpiece into English, has also written a monographic analysis of Calderón's *comedias*. In the preface to this study we read: "These chapters grew out of two books of my own translation. The practical problems of translating the plays touched off speculations about their meaning and intention...."[54] A translator often acts as critic, and FitzGerald's emphasis on the topic of Revelation may be viewed as a contribution to Calderónian criticism. Having pointed out the theme, it becomes easier to pinpoint its presence in the original.[55]

When Segismundo sets himself up as a final judge and thus as an Antichrist, he is mirroring his father's apocalyptic fears, which can be gleaned from both the Spanish text and FitzGerald's version. The omens describing Segismundo's birth as described by Basilio can be interpreted as signs of the end. Such signs are necessary since: "The Medieval tradition holds that a number of terrible events or 'signs' will precede Antichrist's rise to power."[56] The writer is free to choose among many such events because "the tradition never developed a standard sequence of specific signs."[57] In *La vida es sueño*, when Segismundo is born, the world is plunged into darkness. FitzGerald renders Calderón's passage as:

> He coming into light, if light it were
> That darken'd at his very horoscope,
> When heaven's two champions—sun and moon I mean—
> Suffused in blood upon each other fell
> In such a raging duel of eclipse
> As hath not terrified the universe
> Since that that wept in blood the death of Christ (p. 124)

If Antichrist must parallel and yet reverse the figure and actions of Christ, what clearer sign than a birth marked by an eclipse as ominous as the one that occurred at Christ's death? The magnitude of the eclipse sets up the parallel between the two figures. As Antichrist, Segismundo's birth reverses events in Christ's life, since the eclipse occurs at the prince's birth and not at his death. The celestial portent thus augurs the coming of a destructive force. Images of light and darkness also point to the coming conflict between good and evil. Many other portents that can be equated with the coming of Antichrist are evoked by Basilio in both Calderón's and FitzGerald's text. They are of such import that:

> Earth and her cities totter'd, and the world
> Seem'd shaken to its last paralysis. (p. 124)

FitzGerald is here echoing Calderón's "último parasismo" (v. 695). Both writers emphasize that the signs appear to foretell the end of the world. Furthermore, Segismundo's birth brings about the death of his mother Clorilene:

> The man-child breaking from that living womb
> That makes our birth the antitype of death,
> Man—grateful, for the life she gave him paid
> By killing her.... (p. 123)

Birth ought to be the antitype of death, but Segismundo kills his mother at birth. The word *antitype*, added by FitzGerald,[58] emphasizes the *anti* nature of Segismundo: He is anti-life and Antichrist. As the first, he later becomes an image of death itself. Basilio calls him the "pale horseman of the Apocalypse" (p. 189). As Antichrist he kills his own mother. In FitzGerald's version, Clorilene, before giving birth, dreams that: "A serpent tore her entrail" (p. 123). The serpent is her own son and as the dream foretells, she dies giving birth. The dream reinforces Segismundo's potentially evil nature, since the serpent is commonly associated with Satan and with Antichrist.[59] The notion that Antichrist will be the slayer of his mother is probably derived from the fusion of the deeds of Nero with those of Antichrist. Emerson explains: "Early in the tradition this typological identification of Nero and Antichrist fused with the *Nero redivivus* legend, the belief that Nero himself would return as a great tyrant."[60] The fears expressed that Segismundo will be a great tyrant can be seen as further evidence that he is Antichrist. Although there is no direct reference to Nero in Basilio's speech, Calderón does refer to Nero in act 3 (v. 3050). FitzGerald, on the other hand, leaves out that reference to Nero, but includes the following in Basilio's speech concerning the portents at Segismundo's birth:

> I swear, had his foretold atrocities
> Touch'd me alone, I had not saved myself
> At such a cost to him; but as a king,—
> A Christian king,—I say, advisedly,
> Who would devote his people to a tyrant
> Worse than Caligula fore-chronicled? (p. 125)

The shift from Nero to Caligula heightens apocalyptic allusiveness. Caligula was reputedly as great a tyrant as his predecessor. Northrop Frye reminds us that his wish to place his own statue for worship in the Temple of Jerusalem linked him to Antiochus Epiphanes, who was the first to desecrate it by dedicating it to Zeus.[61] Indeed Emmerson notes that "Antiochus Epiphanes is the most widely discussed type of Antichrist during the Middle Ages.[62] If Segismundo is to be a tyrant worse than Caligula, then he will be either a type of Antichrist as Epiphanes or Antichrist himself, whose rule will be characterized by desecration and persecution. As a "Christian King," and prophet who foresees and foretells these events, Basilio must not allow this to happen. This is his justification for his imprisonment of his son.

When the king tests Segismundo in act 2, he cannot see that the savage in front of him is of his own making. The "trumpet sounds" (p. 162) that are heard throughout this act are a reminder to Basilio that the Last Day (p. 161) is at hand if he fails to contain his son, a possible Antichrist. The civil war that ensues in act 3 does little to change Basilio's views. Father and son are each following his own revelation. Basilio sees history in terms of apocalyptic fear, whereas Segismundo, yearning to escape to a land beyond the weight of history, is confronted with a prophecy that labels him as a potential tyrant. His own personal revelation of the injustices of the world make him into a character out of the Book of Revelation since, by setting himself up as final judge, he usurps the role of Christ and becomes Antichrist.

The guidance of Clotaldo, who teaches Segismundo how to read the marvelous book of nature, is the key element in the prince's transformation in FitzGerald's verses. Segismundo ponders on the "visionary glories" of the world through the image of the almond tree that loses its flowers. The transformation from Antichrist to Christian ruler is caused by the reversal of the "most frequently depicted marvel"[63] performed by Antichrist. While the figure of the end of time could make trees flower, Segismundo sees how easily these flowers are lost.

As Segismundo pardons the father in FitzGerald's version, he points to

Clotaldo as his teacher, calling him "this ancient prophet" (p. 194). The fears of the false prophet Basilio and the vengefulness of a prince who has been caught in a nightmare of injustice vanish as a new vision pervades the work. The whole world has been transformed in Segismundo's eyes into a magical spectacle akin to the play presented by Prospero's spirits in *The Tempest*. The events that surround the prince are perceived as insubstantial a pageant as that presented in Shakespeare's marvelous island.

When Segismundo labels the place of this incarceration as an "enchanted tower" (p. 149) in act 3, we know that the weight of the past has been removed and that the prince no longer regards it as a constrictive edifice, but as one of the contrasting extremes in a life that is no more than a play of light and shadow. Indeed, as he dispenses justice he admits that he may be doing so to "shadows / Who make believe they listen" (p. 195). Holding to this Platonic vision,[64] the prince is ready to face apocalypse. In his final lines, Segismundo merges the magic of this shadow-life with a vision of the Last Days. If the individual can subdue the passions through meditation on the "dream-wise" quality of "human glories" (p. 196), Segismundo argues that then there will be nothing to fear:

> Whether To-morrow's dawn shall break the spell,
> Or the Last Trumpet of the eternal Day,
> When Dreaming with the Night shall pass away. (p. 196)

In Matthew (24:35) we read after a description of the tribulation of the Last Days the well-known prophecy: "Heaven and Earth shall pass away, but my words shall not pass away." Segismundo's anguish over a savage past, a present of nightmarish injustice, and a future veiled in dark prophecy, has given way to a compassion and equilibrium based on the power of the word of God, on transcendental authority. He forgives the earthly father because he believes in and does not fear the heavenly counterpart.

While Calderón's play emphasizes that the apocalyptic events have brought about a new golden age in human history,[65] FitzGerald prefers to question the possibility of a future in time in order to stress Segismundo's ultimate revelation. In the Victorian translation, Basilio's constrictive view of heavenly signs makes of him a false prophet whose fears shape a dark vision of the future. His son actually becomes a figure akin to Antichrist when the revelation of injustice perpetrated by his own father impels him to usurp the role of final judge. Both Basilio and Segismundo have attempted to impose a restrictive and personal vision on the world. In the end, nature's mysteries save Segismundo, who goes beyond the confines of a history with a savage beginning and a frightening end to a vision of wonderment at the magic play of light and darkness wherein each must discover and perform a prescribed role. Northrop Frye concludes: "Apocalypse is the way the world looks after the ego has disappeared."[66] By surrendering to the mystery of creation, Segismundo paradoxically gains the freedom to act within and beyond time.[67] FitzGerald's prince explains that it matters not if apocalypse is now, if the magic spell is broken, because he resides within the mystery of eternity.

Just as Basilio misreads the heavenly signs, so FitzGerald approaches his translation as a "dangerous experiment" (*Letters*, vol. 2, p. 85), as a deliberate misreading of Calderón's text. His constrictive neoclassicism has sought to tame Calderón's masterpiece just as Basilio, within the text, wishes to subdue Segismundo through incarceration. FitzGerald curtails Rosaura's role, adds poetic probability and verisimilitude, and seeks accuracy of detail. But it is the mystery of the work that has attracted him to it, its mythical qualities and not its historical or geographical accuracy. As the Victorian writer struggles to solve Segismundo's puzzle along with the hero, and as he attempts to fashion the mystery in a way so as to make it more familiar, he begins to move away from the neoclassical frame and searches for a voice in the context of equally compelling visions such as Shakespeare's *A Midsummer Night's Dream* and *The Tempest*. In these texts, the magical qualities of nature and art break the bonds of historicity and probability so as to expand human awareness. The fantastic qualities of the parallel texts lead FitzGerald and Segismundo one step beyond. They seek to comprehend and express the mystery of the text—be it a text about the illusoriness of life (*La vida es sueño*) or the text of life itself, that "sapphire volume of the skies ... / writ by God's own finger" (p. 191). In this final attempt to render Calderón, FitzGerald takes heed of Segismundo's warning against "misinterpretation" (p. 191). The English version leads us from the constrictive constructs of Basilio and the neoclassic critics to Segismundo's and FitzGerald's new-found awareness. Revelation of the poetic inspiration of the Platonists is now allowed free expression. Calderón and FitzGerald coalesce in the presentation of mystery through an apocalyptic vision.

NOTES

1. Alfred McKinley Terhune and Annabelle Burdick Terhune, eds., *The Letters of Edward FitzGerald* (Princeton: Princeton University Press, 1980), 4 vols. All textual references to the letters are from this edition.

2. Joanna Richardson, ed., *FitzGerald: Selected Works* (Cambridge, Mass.: Harvard University Press, 1963), p. 7.

3. Alfred McKinley Terhune, FitzGerald's foremost biographer, presents a detailed history of the Victorian writer's translations of Calderón. He notes, for example, that as early as 1849 FitzGerald and Cowell were already discussing the Spanish playwright. *The*

Life of Edward FitzGerald, Translator of the Rubáiyát of Omar Khayyám (New Haven: Yale University Press, 1947), p. 162. Terhune also briefly analyzes the alterations made by FitzGerald to the original. in *Edward FitzGerald* (Boston: Twayne Publishers, 1977), Iran Hassani Jewett includes these translations as part of FitzGerald's "minor works" and also gives a brief account of some of the changes effected by the Victorian writer.

4. Edwin Honig, ed., Pedro Calderón de la Barca, *Four Plays* (New York: Hill and Wang, 1961), p. xxiv.

5. Kenneth Muir, *Four Comedies by Pedro Calderón de la Barca* (Lexington: University of Kentucky Press, 1980), p. 5.

6. Reuben Brower, *Mirror on Mirror* (Cambridge, Mass.: Harvard University Press, 1974), p. 56.

7. Misreading has been defined by Harold Bloom as "an act of creative correction." This is indeed what FitzGerald is attempting to accomplish in his translations. However, it would be difficult to see in this Victorian writer a "strong poet" who is intent on "perverse, wilful revisionism." *The Anxiety of Influence: A Theory of Poetry* (Oxford: Oxford University Press, 1973), p. 30. Bloom establishes a relationship between poetry and criticism since both are "acts of reading." *Poetry and Repression: Revisionism from Blake to Stevens* (New Haven, Conn.: Yale University Press, 1976), p. 26. This essay will point to a similar relationship: both translator and critic are engaged in acts of reading. For other contemporary theories on the relationship between text and reader, see Jane P. Tompkins, ed., *Reader-Response Criticism from Formalism to Post-Structuralism* (Baltimore: Johns Hopkins University Press, 1980).

8. Bruce W. Wardropper, "Menéndez y Pelayo on Calderón," *Criticism* 7 (1965), 366.

9. Henry W. Sullivan, *Calderón in the German Lands and the Low Countries* (Cambridge: Cambridge University Press, 1983), pp. 101–25.

10. On seventeenth-century adaptations of the *comedia*, see Roger Guichemerre, *La Comédie avant Molière. 1640–1660* (Paris: Armand Colin, 1972); and Alexandre Cioranescu, *Le Masque et le visage* (Geneva: Droz, 1983).

11. Ernest Martinenche, *La Comedia espagnole en France de Hardy a Racine* (Geneva: Slatkine Reprints, 1970; reprint of 1900 edition), p. 137.

12. Debating whether Calderón's *En esta vida todo es verdad y todo mentira* influenced Corneille's *Heraclius*, or whether the reverse was the case, Voltaire concluded that the French dramatist is like the alchemist who can transmute the chaotic *materia prima* found in the Spanish original into artistic gold. For a discussion of this concept, see Frederick A. de Armas, "The Dragon's Gold: Calderón and Boisrobert *La vie n'est qu'un songe*," *Kentucky Romance Quarterly*, 30 (1983), 335–48.

13. On Voltaire's attitude toward the Spanish *comedia* see Alfonso de Salvio, "Voltaire and Spain," *Hispania*, 7 (1927), 69–110, 157–64; and Donald Schier, "Voltaire's Criticism of Calderón," *Comparative Literature*, 11 (1959), 340–46.

14. Henry W. Sullivan, *Calderón in the German Lands*, p. 114.

15. All page and volume references to Edward FitzGerald's works are to *The Variorum and Definitive Edition of the Poetical and Prose Writings of Edward FitzGerald*, ed., George Bentham (New York: Phaeton Press, 1967; reprint of 1902 ed.), vols. 4 and 5. Subsequent revisions of the text have also been taken into account as detailed by Gerald D. Brown, "Edward FitzGerald's Revision," *Papers of the Bibliographical Society of America*, 69 (1975), 94–112.

16. Ernest Martinenche, *La Comedia espagnole*, p. 137.

17. All verse references to *La vida es sueño* are from Pedro Calderón de la Barca, *La vida es sueño (comedia, auto y loa)*, ed., Enrique Rull (Madrid: Alhambra, 1980).

18. Bruce W. Wardropper, "Apenas llega cuando llega a penas," *Modern Philology*, 57 (1960), 24–44.

19. E. M. Wilson, "The Four Elements in the Imagery of Calderón," *Modern Language Review*, 31 (1936), 34–47.

20. Angel L. Cilveti, *El significado de "La vida es sueño"* (Valencia: Albatrós Ediciones, 1971), pp. 164–65.

21. Javier Herrero, "El volcán en el paraiso. El sistema icónico del teatro de Calderón," *Co-textes*, 3 (1982), 106.

22. Richard Chenevix Trench, *Calderón: His Life and Genius* (New York: Redfield, 1856), p. 54.

23. On the palace experience as dream, see Julian Palley, *The Ambiguous Mirror: Dreams in Spanish Literature* (Chapel Hill: Albatrós-Hispanófila, 1983), p. 127.

24. C. Christopher Soufas, "Thinking in *La vida es sueño*," *PMLA*, 100 (1985), 288.

25. On the significance of the almond tree in Golden Age Spanish drama, see Frederick A. de Armas, "The Flowering Almond Tree: Examples of Tragic Foreshadowing in Golden Age Drama," *Revista de Estudios Hispánicos*, 14 (1980), 117–34; and "Los 'naturales secretos' del almendro en el teatro de Calderón," *Actas del VIII Congreso Internacional de Hispanistas* (forthcoming).

26. Michel Foucault, *The Order of Things* (New York: Vintage Books, 1973).

27. Marcelino Menéndez Pelayo, *Calderón y su teatro* (Madrid: A. Pérez Dubrull, 1910), p. 18.

28. Ibid., p. 278.

29. C. A. Merrick, "Clotaldo's Role in *La vida es sueño*," *Bulletin of Hispanic Studies*, 50 (1973), 256–69.

30. Marcelino Menéndez Pelayo, *Calderón y su teatro*, p. 18.

31. Ibid., p. 272.

32. Ervin Brody, "Poland in Calderón's *Life is a Dream*," *Polish Review*, 14 (1969), 47.

33. For other possible interpretations of the word *mar* in *La vida es sueño*, see Enrique Rull's edition of the play cited above, pp. 186–88.

34. Frederick A. de Armas, "The Dragon's Gold," pp. 341–42.

35. Marcelino Menéndez Pelayo, *Calderón y su teatro*, p. 278.

36. This citation from the prologue to Nicolás Fernández de Moratin's *La Petimetra* (1762) is included in the discussion of neoclassic critics of Calderón by Manuel Durán and Roberto González Echevarría, *Calderón y la critica: historia y antologia* (Madrid: Gredos, 1976), vol. 1, p. 21. For another discussion of Calderón and the neoclassics, see Ralph Merritt Cox, "Calderón and the Spanish Neoclassicists," *Romance Notes*, 24 (1983), 43–48.

37. FitzGerald's view of Calderón's drama as "wild" may derive from his mentor, Edward Byles Cowell, who, in his article "Spanish Literature" in the *Westminster Review* 54 (1851), 281–323, repeatedly uses this adjective in his analysis of Calderón's *comedias*. Cowell discusses, for example, the "wild profusion of imagery" in these plays; he complains of "Calderón's wild mistakes"; and stresses that a "wild and grand tone of fiction pervades his poetry" (p. 292), For Cowell's views on Calderón see Frederick A. de Armas, "Rosaura Subdued: Victorian Readings of Calderón's *La vida es sueño*," *South Central Review* (in press).

38. Kenneth Muir, *The Sources of Shakespeare's Plays* (New Haven, Conn,: Yale University Press, 1978), p. 77.

39. Bears, lions, and wolves are again encountered in Segismundo's first soliloquy. Thus FitzGerald, like Calderón, seems fond of reiterative imagery, although the Victorian writer replaces the "outdated" concept of the four elements with images he believes are more pertinent to the situation.

40. All references to *A Midsummer Night's Dream* and *The Tempest* are from *The*

Complete Works of Shakespeare, eds., Hardin Craig and David Bevington (Glenview, Il.: Scott, Foresman, 1973).

41. Henry W. Sullivan, *Calderón in the German Lands*, pp. 170–74.

42. William R. Blue, "Calderón and Shakespeare: The Romances." in *Calderón de la Barca at the Tercentenary: Comparative Views*, eds., Wendell Aycock and Sydney P. Cravens (Lubbock: Texas Tech Press, 1982), p. 91.

43. "Una moda superficial y passagera fue creada por el libro de Lionel Abel ... el cual le dedica varias piginas a *La vida es sueño* considerándola como obra metateatral." Frank P. Casa, José M. Ruano, and Henry W. Sullivan, "Cincuenta años de investigación sobre el teatro español del Siglo le Oro en Norteamérica, 1933–1983," *Arbor* 116 (1983), 82.

44. Lionel Abel, *Metatheater: A New View of Dramatic Form* (New York: Hill and Wang, 1963), p. 68.

45. Eric S. Rabkin, *The Fantastic in Literature* (Princeton, N.J.: Princeton University Press, 1976), p. 82.

46. Ibid., p. 93.

47. Northrop Frye, *Spiritus Mundi* (Bloomington: Indiana University Press, 1976), p. 88.

48. Ibid.

49. Mary Wilson Carpenter and George Landow, "The Apocalypse in Victorian Literature." In *The Apocalypse in English Renaissance Thought and Literature*, eds., C. A. Patrides and Joseph Wittreich (Ithaca, N.Y.: Cornell University Press, 1984), pp. 299–322.

50. Ibid., p. 309.

51. Ibid., pp. 307–8.

52. Marjorie Reeves, "The Development of Apocalyptic Thought: Medieval Attitudes," in *The Apocalypse in English Renaissance Thought and Literature*, p. 44.

53. Bernard McGinn, *Visions of the End* (New York: Columbia University Press, 1979), p. 1.

54. Edwin Honig, *Calderón and the Seizures of Honor* (Cambridge, Mass.: Harvard University Press, 1972), p. vii.

55. Little criticism has been directed to apocalyptic images in *La vida es sueño*. See Frederick A. de Armas, "The Return of Astraea: An Astral-Imperial Myth in *La vida es sueño*." In *Calderón de la Barca at the Tercentenary: Comparative Views*, eds., Wendell Aycock and Sydney P. Cravens (Lubbock: Texas Tech Press, 1982), pp. 135–59; and "The Serpent Star: Dream and Horoscope in *La vida es sueño*," *Forum for Modern Language Studies*, 19 (1983), 208–23.

56. Richard Kenneth Emmerson, *Antichrist in the Middle Ages* (Seattle: University of Washington Press, 1981), p. 83.

57. Ibid., p. 84.

58. Calderón's passage has a different emphasis. In the Spanish masterpiece the child by his actions is saying: "Hombre soy, pues ya empiezo / a pagar mal beneficios" (vv. 276–77).

59. Emmerson, *Antichrist in the Middle Ages*, p. 80.

60. Ibid., p. 28.

61. Northrop Frye, *The Great Code* (New York: Harcourt, Brace, Jovanovich, 1982), p. 94.

62. Emmerson, *Antichrist in the Middle Ages*, p. 28.

63. Ibid., p. 134.

64. On *La vida es sueño*'s Platonic vision, see, for example, Michele Federico Sciacca, "Verdad y sueño en *La vida es sueño* de Calderón de la Barca," *Clavileño*, 1 (1950), 1–9; and Harlan G. Sturm, "From Plato's Cave to Segismundo's Prison," *MLN*, 89 (1974), 280–89.

65. On the motif of the Golden Age in *La vida es sueño*, see Frederick A. de Armas, "The Return of Astraea."

66. Northrop Frye, *The Great Code*, p. 138.

67. "Faith ... means absolute emancipation from any kind of natural 'law' and hence the highest freedom man can imagine: freedom to intervene in the ontological constitution of the universe." Mircea Eliade, *The Myth of the Eternal Return*, trans. Willard R. Trask (Princeton, N.J.: Princeton University Press, 1971), pp. 160–61.

VINNI MARIE D'AMBROSIO

Young Eliot's Rebellion

Growing up in an Emersonian-puritanic family, young Eliot would have experienced, like the child in "Animula," the joy of transcendence (in the "patterns" formed by sunbeams) and the horror of failing to be strong (in the awe at "stags" and "Kings"). Armed with metaphysical vision and admiration for action, the child would grow only as he overcame challenges to each. Like the infant in "Animula," sensing the end of dependence on a parent's "arm and knee" and confused by the "actual and the fanciful," Eliot at the age of nine or ten experienced a melancholy out of which his earliest impetus towards writing came. Valerie Eliot reports that her husband told her he wrote "a few little verses about the sadness of having to start school again every Monday morning," and that he gave them to his mother.[1]

At fourteen, sadness over these strictures vanished as, suddenly, the boy responded to Omar with a daring and strengthened version of his old infant boldness. Now, like a great explorer, he saw "a new world."[2] If (in the phrases of a late interview) he began at that time to write, in the style of the *Rubáiyát*, "a number of very gloomy and atheistical and despairing quatrains,"[3] later lost, their gloom and despair were symptomatic not of the exciting new world but of the old gray world of the nonexotic quotidian. That his quatrains were "atheistical"—in the face of a family whose male head had been a powerful Unitarian—shows his joyous and even brash courage.

From *Eliot Possessed: T. S. Eliot and FitzGerald's Rubaiyat.* ©1989 by New York University.

We may imagine what the fresh response of a sensitive American boy of fourteen might have been to Omar's opening quatrains. Because their subject is so far removed from common daily life, the quatrains are all the more involving. That is, their foreignness would give the boy easier access to his own fantasies. With the first word, a powerful single-syllable imperative, Omar calls the boy to leave the state of sleep, of dreams, of passive impotence. The call is, be like the sun, an energetic warrior victorious over a universe full of stars:

> Wake! For the Sun, who scatter'd into flight
> The Stars before him from the Field of Night,
>   Drives Night along with them from Heav'n, and strikes
> The Sultán's Turret with a Shaft of Light.

That sun is like a strong and fiery field general, and the stars tumble away—lost, weak, effeminate soldiers. Night had been the gate-guard to that field ("Whose Portals are alternate Night and Day": quatrain 18), but the gate now lost, heaven has been freed, opened. The sun strikes the sultan's turret with a golden light that is masculine, cutlass-like, and the turret, authoritative symbol of an entire city, is conquered. Immobility, darkness, and blindness go. Action and vision arrive. A boy might identify with so attractively imperious a stance.

Then, quatrain 2 introduces another side of Omar:

> Before the phantom of False morning died,
> Methought a Voice within the Tavern cried,
>   "When all the Temple is prepared within,
> Why nods the drowsy Worshipper outside?"

Having pointed out the sultan's tall turret, Omar shows he is also interested in the lowly and the low. His commanding voice becomes more thoughtful as he reports the humble tavern keeper's cry. That cry echoes Omar's, not as an imperative to "Wake," but as an impatient argument *for* waking. It adds blasphemy to Omar's call, and Omar, undisputing, seems to assent to it. Thus, the tavern is (heretically) named a "Temple" and the drinker, a "Worshipper." The metaphor used by the disembodied and priestly tavern keeper must shock the boy. Yet, identifying with the imperious Omar, the boy would also feel ambivalent and frustrated over the lagging response to Omar's own call to "Wake!" The time is the one moment before the lowly world receives its light. In this drowsy moment, a phantom, false morning, is about to die as true morning comes. The world's drowsiness, sleepiness, inattentiveness, dullness, then, are connected to dryness, thirst, lack of wine—an engaging reversal for a boy who has been taught, surely, that drinking dulls the senses.

In 1902, Eliot may have had more than a glimmer of the poem's popularity, but at his young age he surely did not, could not, experience it in the formalist and purist terms of the aesthetic movement, as Aldrich had, for he could have no knowledge of the recent literary past. Nor could he read it as an evil product of the then ripe decadence, as More had. The youth's natural and innocent response would be closer to the earlier one of Norton: they shared not only a genealogy but a religion that did not recognize the Devil. The youth's reaction, of course, was different from Norton's in that to be manly and independent at fourteen is to rebel.

Yet, notwithstanding the warnings of More and the countercult, the rage for the *Rubáiyát* was indeed on. A retired "East Indianian" had a few years earlier written in England that the centuries-old survival of the *Rubáiyát* had raised the quatrains "to a position of almost Scriptural dignity," and that they were "inspiring modern artists in the busiest centres of Western life."[4] Now, in America, in the Eliot family's Midwest (at Chicago's Caxton Club), FitzGerald's memory was honored with an exhibition of his books and publications;[5] in the Eliots' Northeast (Cambridge, Massachusetts), in 1901, a twelve-volume set of FitzGerald's work was issued priced at $12,060 a set— and of thirty printed, twenty-two sold.[6] (By 1929, a mammoth bibliography quite incompletely named 586 editions worldwide, 410 in English, more than a third of which had been published in the United States.)[7]

The *Rubáiyát* had become, by the turn of the century, an object of admiration or attack on many levels, notably for its theology, for the politics that rose out of the theology, and for the call to free life that rose out of the politics. One long poem of the time directly associated Omar and Shelley as two poets alike in their call to revolution. A few lines tell much:

> A rebel our Shelley, a rebel our Mage.
> That brotherly link shall suffice us;
> 'Tis in vain that the zealots, O Prophet and Sage,
> From his creed—and from thine—would entice us;
> We seek not to stray from the path that ye trod,
> We seek but to widen its border;
> If systems that be are the order of God,
> Revolt is a part of that order.[8]

Because they were interested in moral issues, Eliot's family must have played a part in the general controversy; because they were literate, they were directly exposed to news of the poem which saturated the daily press and popular periodicals. If they had ever taken familial pride in the discovery of the poem's translator in 1872, then they were aware that in the minds of many people Charles Eliot Norton's view of Omar no longer held. In 1895, for example, in the *Philistine*, an American periodical styled as a "Magazine of Protest" ("it began its career by choking the various serpents of Conceit and Decadentism"), one commentator wrote that Homer and Omar are "the poles of verse—one standing for the heroic and romantic, self-unconscious and buoyant, the other for vampire introspection and fatalism which mistakes interior darkness for an eclipse of the universe."[9]

Like other American families, the Eliots probably were interested in nativist literature,[10] and news of such local colorists as James Whitcomb Riley and John Hay would have caught their eye. Riley's *The Rubáiyát of Doc Sifers*[11] was so far Americanized, however, as to have no tonal or imagistic resemblance at all to Omar; the connection between the two was undoubtedly the rationalist view—Riley's idealization of the local country doctor, speaking a kind of agnostic humanitarianism in dialect quatrains. Not quite as well-known a writer, but a much more newsworthy subject of discussion, was John Hay. Hay, who had tapped the culture of the American Midwest with his *Pike County Ballads* (1871), some of whose poems had "become virtual folk possessions,"[12] gave a long talk at the Omar Khayyám Club in London in December 1897.[13] In it he added to the renown of the "characteristic" American's love for Omar. To begin, Hay compared his own first reading of the *Rubáiyát* with Keats's first reading of Chapman. Then he recalled, as an example of the poem's broad influence, the unlikely experience he had had in the Rocky Mountains of hearing an American miner casually recite a quatrain from the Persian poem. At the time of the address, Hay held the post of United States ambassador to the Court of St. James's, and, as a noted public figure (becoming secretary of state to President McKinley in the following year), he was fully reported in American and British newspapers, his name lending further prestige to the poem: "the exquisite beauty, the faultless form, the singular grace of those stanzas," he had said, "were no more wonderful than the depth and breadth of their profound philosophy, their knowledge of life, their dauntless courage, their serene facing of the ultimate problems of life and death."[14]

In another American publication, the British folklorist, critic, and poet Andrew Lang, like Hay, alluded to the plain American's propensity for quoting the quatrains, noting that "one must keep repeating that a passion for Omar does not suffice for literary salvation." Lang then went on to say that thirty years earlier, when Omar had been the "favorite of a very few," John Addington Symonds gave him a copy "which someone had given to him" and which he, Lang, "was to hand on to another," and he did. At the time, Lang recalled, Symonds told him of an incident on a ship on which an American commercial traveler was a fellow passenger. "He seemed indifferent to literature," Lang's story went, "but was heard murmuring a quatrain of FitzGerald's which at once established a kind of free-masonry between him and the English admirer."[15]

Moncure Conway, a disciple of Emerson, reported a similar story about an American, in the widely read *Nation*. A Thomas Hinchliff, a British journalist,

> was once at sea near Panama, in a formidable storm, when some on board were expressing doubts whether they could weather it. Hinchliff said: "He knows about it all—He knows—He knows!" Instantly his hand was seized by an American, named Clarke, who cried, "You have been reading Omar Khayyám." The two men fairly embraced, on account of the ancient Persian, and remained friends through life.[16]

But the poem aroused controversy in many ways in the life that Eliot and his family knew. The views held at the extreme ends demonstrate the arguments that the American cult and countercult were making—in the one, that the quatrains expressed the healthy sensuality of the *vita activa* of the ordinary American, and in the other, that they sucked the very life out of the mind and spirit.[17] In the neat summary of one *Rubáiyát* scholar, the *Rubáiyát* "lined up agnostics against believers, materialists against idealists, sybarites against saints, bibbers against teetotalers."[18]

Eliot's grandfather, William Greenleaf Eliot (1811–1887), after retiring from his Unitarian ministry, was active full-time for his last seventeen years as the chancellor of Washington University and as a civic leader and reformer. W. G. took an impassioned part in the current movements to keep America sound and must have responded ethically and theologically to the *Rubáiyát* in America's debate-filled atmosphere.[19]

For example, W. G.'s notion of the stage was stern and, overall, indicative of his aesthetics: the theater "stimulates the imagination too strongly; it awakens dormant powers; it overtasks the sensibilities."[20] In 1875, Fanny Kemble's impressions of Edward FitzGerald appeared in a prestigious publication—the *Atlantic Monthly*—whose editors understood the public's interest in the long-standing friendship between the actress and the English translator.[21] In spite of his moral view of the theater (which harked back to Cromwellian puritanism), W. G. would have been interested in Kemble's reminiscences of the translator of the *Rubáiyát*, if only because FitzGerald so recently had been identified by a cousin of the Eliots.

Another journal of personal interest to W. G., Boston's *Unitarian Review*, which published a lengthy apology for an inadvertent slur on him in 1879,[22] took notice of the *Rubáiyát* in the same year with Rev. S. J. Barrow's essay, "Omar Khayyám." In it, Rev. Barrow rather unhappily pointed out that "a ministerial friend of ours" had already read the *Rubáiyát* "sixty times."[23] Then, in 1884, Elihu Vedder's illustrations of the poem made an admired and widely discussed debut in Boston. Although (or because) Vedder's style could be associated with the Pre-Raphaelites' mode of painting, and with their sensuous interpretations of religious subjects, the editions multiplied rapidly.[24] However, W. G.'s Unitarian theology, its position far from the "hellfire and brimstone" enthusiasm of the Calvinists, would not have been much threatened by the Pre-Raphaelite interpretation of the *Rubáiyát*, or by the various literary views of the poem, or—certainly not at all—by its hermit-author's fascinating connection with a theatrical personality.

W. G.'s theology might even fall short of that of the rationalists who protested that religious critics of the poem were dwelling too angrily on its "unbridled sensuality," and protested that "unbelievers" needed other than theological grounds for the control of sensual appetites.[25] Rather, W. G. probably would have joined the American reviewer of the *Rubáiyát* who, while deploring the true heretic's response, called Omar's poem "simply the cry of utter skepticism," in which there is "plenty of belief in a fixed order of the universe, but it is not a moral order.... [If Omar] reaches the depths of blasphemy, he touches the heights of magnanimity."[26]

The rationalist strain in Eliot's grandfather's religion ultimately was too strong for Eliot, who in a few years would feel that "if one discards dogma, it should be for a more celestial garment, not for nakedness."[27] In 1937 he alluded to the effects of his grandfather's religion in a letter to Paul Elmer More in which he claimed More's "spiritual biography" was "oddly, even grotesquely more like my own," because, in both, "the office of the imagination and the aesthetic emotions had ... been so ruthlessly evicted."[28]

The liberal theology of Eliot's grandfather included, as a first law, the "Law of Public Service."[29] W. G. was active in educational reform and the movement for women's suffrage, and, in a style of characteristic "plainness and clarity," he had written a book about an escaped slave whom he helped.[30] Of this awesome person, whose Unitarianism seemed, to the child and to the man, so cold, Eliot said:

> I never knew my grandfather: he died a year before my birth. But I was brought up to be very much aware of him: so much so, that as a child I thought of him as still head of the family—a ruler for whom *in absentia* my grandmother stood as vicegerent [*sic*]. The standard of conduct was that which my grandfather had set; our

moral judgments, our decisions between duty and self-indulgence, were taken as if like Moses, he had brought down the tables of the Law, any deviation from which would be sinful.... I think it is a very good beginning for any child ... to be taught that personal and selfish aims should be subordinated to the general good which [these Laws] represent.[31]

Neither the theology nor the sensual immorality of the *Rubáiyát* would have been the main problem for the powerful head of the Eliot family, who "lent his strength wholly to ideal enthusiasms." The major basis for his disapproval would be ethical and would lie in the many quatrains urging the reader to drink, for W. G. Eliot actively battled for the forces of temperance.[32] He was friend and college mate of Henry Ware, Jr., whose father had helped to found the Harvard Divinity School and who, as a temperance preacher himself, was the author of *The Criminality of Intemperance* and *The Combination Against Intemperance Explained and Justified*.[33] Honoring his friend's father, W. G. named his own son after Henry Ware, Sr.

W. G. died the year before this grandson's birth, but, notwithstanding the attribution of his vice-regency to the widow, the real residue of power lay in the daughter-in-law, Charlotte Champe Stearns Eliot, Henry Ware Eliot's wife, and soon-to-be-mother of Tom Eliot. Undoubtedly, along with other reform issues to be carried on from her idolized father-in-law's brief, Temperance had to be a prominent one, for that issue had more sensational coverage in print than any other in Eliot's boyhood: it was the era of Carry Nation.

Charlotte's influence over her son must have been very strong. A poet, she expressed zealous humanitarianism and fidelity to W. G.'s Unitarianism in her choice of subject for the narrative poem she wrote on the Catholic Puritan Savonarola,[34] who inspired women to make a bonfire of vanities in the public square in fifteenth-century Florence. Her interests in the rights of her sex (she fought for female wardens in women's, prisons) and in children's rights (she fought for the separation of child criminals)[35] allied her with the interest of the Temperance movement, whose foundation—the rights of women and children against drinking fathers—was the same. Later in life, Eliot viewed these busy nineteenth-century reforms as "bustle, programmes, platforms, scientific progress, humanitarianism and revolutions which improved nothing."[36] In F. O. Matthiessen's paraphrase of Eliot, they did not deal with "the real problem of good and evil"; rather, they set "groundless optimistic hopefulness" against "chaotic pointless despair."[37] His family, optimistic, hopeful, saw itself as courageous and as standing on firm ground.

To the Temperance movement the *Rubáiyát* was an enemy tract, one that had spread everywhere. The movement itself, of course, was strong. W. G.'s third cousin and president of Harvard since 1869, Charles William Eliot, was summoned to lead a Committee of Fifty in the 1890s "to explore the actual facts of the Demon's case."[38] The Demon's association not only traditionally with rum but now with Omar was being established firmly in the public's mind. The list of publication with titles like *Rubáiyát of Omar Khayyám, Translated into the Christian* lengthened considerably in those years.[39] But C. W.'s committee, liberal and objective, "found out" the Temperance movement's propaganda and called it "half-baked."[40]

The identification of Omar as the drunkard's friend, however, came easily. Richard Le Gallienne called him "the thinker-drinker" in 1897, and, by 1908, in a turnabout book of quatrains entitled *Omar Repentant*, he wrote, "The Wine! The Grape! / Oh, call it Whiskey and be done with it!"[41] In a more casual reference by a book reviewer, Omar is called "the bibulous old Persian."[42] Even Eliot's later interpretation of the poets of the 1890s has the stamp of his memories of the Temperance movement: "They all died of drink or suicide or one thing or another."[43] In the two decades between 1882 and 1902, including Eliot's formative years, the Women's Christian Temperance Union had become so strong that it obtained legislation requiring every state to give instruction in temperance; it then influenced the content and selection of the states' textbooks. Thus the McGuffey Readers began to include a "Temperance ethic" in the section on character.[44]

If Eliot was being educated on the subject at home by his mother, and at school by the WCTU, his was not a really atypical case. One Chicago periodical, pointing an accusatory finger at educators, asserted that there were no "school girls lacking to recite, 'I sometimes think that never blows so red / The Rose as where some buried Caesar bled,' tears in their voices and holes in their handkerchiefs."[45] It was logical, therefore, that the WCTU would welcome, as "an antidote to the popular FitzGerald Rubáiyát," a revised version of it. The organization happily dispensed one such: "an Omar which may be read in young ladies' schools without any apprehension of inflaming the cheek of outraged modesty.[46]

Nonetheless, the protected young must have heard the words of a musical composition that was a great hit all over the world, "In a Persian Garden," from a song cycle entirely based on Omar's quatrains. They might not have seen, though some could have heard excited talk about, the notorious artistic and sexual revolutionary whose dance was reported in an article in the New York *Critic* in May 1899, "'Illustrations': Omar Done into Dance by Isadora Duncan."[47]

Clarence Darrow praised the *Rubáiyát* for its beauty, but even more for being "one of the wisest and most profound pieces of literature in the world." An attorney, a proponent of "The Right of Revolution," Darrow became a "folk hero" because of his positions on religion, divorce, unionism, race, and Temperance. His stand against Prohibition was both shocking and amusing, and more fame came to him with William Jennings Bryan's accusation that he, Darrow, was "the greatest atheist or agnostic in the United States."[48] In his courtroom appearances, Darrow quoted the *Rubáiyát* whenever he could. The Puritan concept of human responsibility raised his ire, and, for him, Omar had powerfully pricked those who were so cruel as to judge people for what environmental forces had done to them, as did another midwesterner, Theodore Dreiser.[49] Coming out of Eliot's Midwest as the "American Legend," Darrow was sure to have been known by the boy and his family, and certainly the fame of his first book, which opened with a grand appreciation of the *Rubáiyát*, had helped. Darrow's essay "A Persian Pearl" was then extracted from the collection and bound up with the *Rubáiyát* in an edition that went through four printings in 1899 alone, and five more between 1906 and 1926.[50] The Prohibition question inflamed the nation in these years, and Darrow was outspoken on it. If you were to remove from the world down through history all the men who have drunk, he said, "you would take away all the poetry and literature and practically all the works of genius that the world has produced."[51]

If the free-thinking Darrow was the most publicized exponent of drink, the most publicized antagonist of the Demon was Carry Nation, whose character Eliot seems to have used in the poetry both of his youth and maturity. The saloon raid that made her famous on June 6, 1900, was reported on the front pages of New York and Boston newspapers and others across the country. In a historian's summary of the reports, the customers of that ill-fated saloon "had time only to gape before Carry started heaving rocks that smashed the immense gilt frame and tore through the canvas [of a life-size painting of the naked Cleopatra] as she shouted 'Glory to God!'" The most historic raid of all occurred in 1901, a year in which she scored over twenty times. Out of that raid came the symbol by which she is remembered, the hatchet, and she became "incomparably the most notorious female character in the United States."[52] Eliot, at thirteen, must have read the details of that epic battle, waged by a great female antagonist, who was six feet fall and wore a long black alpaca dress and poke bonnet. The adventure, therefore, is worth retelling.

All the country knew that St. Louis was the center for America's breweries, and that the heart of its economic life was endangered by Carry

Nation. The hatchet attack occurred in Topeka, capital of Eliot's neighboring state, where she, with, two disciples, went "to free [it] from, the shame of its saloons":

> With her she brought four brand-new hatchets that cost 85 cents each.... At the entrance of [Russam's] place, even at this early hour, the three women ran head-on into a couple of surly guards and were defeated after a brisk contact during which Mrs. Nation sustained slight wounds from her own weapon on forehead and one hand.
>
> Pausing only long enough to stanch the flow of blood with handkerchiefs, the three raiders plodded through the deepening snow across Kansas Avenue, to note there were no guards on duty at the elegant entrance to the Senate Bar, Topeka's finest drinking establishment. [They] pushed open the door and entered without disturbing Benner Tucker ... who was busy polishing glasses. He became aware of his visitors when he heard pounding and the tinkle of breaking glass.[53]

The three women chopped away at the cigar case and at "the glossy-smooth bar, raising chips of a size and depth beyond the ability of most women." The bartender "knew instantly who his callers were [and] grabbed the house revolver" to frighten them. Thoroughly unfrightened, Mrs. Nation swung her hatchet at the bartender, who dodged, snatched the hatchet, and left the bar in a dead run, calling for the police. Bellowing in triumph, Carry Nation attacked the big mirror and the rows of glassware. She turned to the cash register, lifted it above her head, and threw it halfway across the saloon, its No Sale bell ringing. Next she took on the huge refrigerator, which she demolished by hatchet and by hand. Finally she went to the heart of the matter, cutting the rubber tube that carried beer from the tanks to the faucets, and then, "using, the tube as a hose, sprayed good St. Louis beer over the walls and ceilings, to cascade down and drench herself and co-workers in malted foam." The police entered and, after disarming the "crusaders," arrested them. "The whole gorgeous story," the historian continued,

> went over the wires, and Carry and Hatchet went into the folklore of the nation. Cartoonists got busy. Almost before one knew it, too, miniature hatchets labeled with her name were being hawked in cities from coast to coast and offered for sale by news butchers on trains.[54]

Other hatchet women appeared in Kansas, such as Mary Sheriff and her Flying Squadron of Jesus, and in Illinois, Indiana, and Ohio. Carry Nation's fame was increased by her imitators. She began publishing a weekly paper, *The Hatchet*, and soon was drawn into the lyceum circuit, on which she toured the country as The Home Defender, The Smasher, The Wrecker of Saloons, and The Woman with the Hatchet.

Carry Nation's dramatization of the Temperance novel *Ten Nights in a Barroom* was renamed *Hatchetation*. The play was performed in Chicago, Cincinnati, Atlantic City, Philadelphia, New York, and also in Eliot's home city, St. Louis.[55] Her type reappears in Eliot's writing: in "A Fable for Feasters" (1905) as the "ghost"; in "Gerontion" (1919) as "de Bailhache" (the hatchet dance); and, in *The Confidential Clerk* (1953) as Lady Mulhammer, who is, coincidentally, married to a would-be potter. In Eliot's youth, Carry Nation's symbol was brought extremely close to home. The class of 1903, at the University that William Greenleaf Eliot had founded, published the first issue of a yearbook bearing a new title: *The Hatchet*.[56]

Written in the *Rubáiyát* quatrain form, poems about the Temperance movement came early from those on either side of Omar's fence. In 1898, in *Current Literature*, a poem appeared entitled "On Reading Omar Khayyám during an Anti-Saloon Campaign." It was reprinted in 1905 in recognition of Carry Nation's sensational campaigns, in 1909 during the FitzGerald Centennial, and again, for good measure, in 1911. "The Tipplers' Vow" appeared in San Francisco and New York in 1902. Then, during a three-month period in 1904, the *New York Mail* published "The Rubáiyát of Carrie [*sic*] Nation" twice; "Omar on the Wagon" appeared in a Boston anthology the following year.[57]

The number of *Rubáiyát* parodies, on all subjects, was enormous. Many of the writers used the FitzGerald form, applying its rhythms not only to the quatrains but to the titles also. Some versifiers, merely imitating the style, left the parody to inference: everyone, after all, by then knew that "Rubáiyát" simply meant a string of epigrammatic quatrains about some kind of confessing or complaining. Thus were born "Rubáiyáts" for poker players, bridge players, tennis players, golfers, footballers, smokers, commuters, young housewives, huffy husbands, cat lovers, motor car buffs, college students, spinsters, sausage makers, the unemployed, the bowery bum, linotype proofreaders, lawyers, Aztecs, refugees, examination candidates, rubes, umpires, pikers, amateur farmers, chorus girls, Paulines (in the *Pauline*), the Irish, and booksellers (by E. V. Lucas).[58] *The Rubáiyát of the Tourist* (1905) was one hundred quatrains in length.[59]

The earliest parody, the first to point up the humor of FitzGerald's title (humor, at least, to the ears of a speaker of English), was Rudyard Kipling's, in 1885. Punning on *rupee*, and attacking the legislators of a new income tax for their Protestant detachment, Kipling's poem was entitled "Rupaiyat of Omar Kal'vin" and was included in *Departmental Ditties*.[60] After Kipling, writers continued to top each other in complicating rhythm and pun. "The Ruby Yacht of Henry Morgan" and "Whereamiat Away from Homer Khayyam" were seemingly unbeatable when twenty-one quatrains entitled "The Budgai'at of I'm A-Khrying" came out and harked back to Kipling's theme. In November 1902, the *St. Louis Mirror* published "The Rubáiyát of the Old Red Moving Van."[61] It is likely that the poem caught young Eliot's attention, for that was the year in which Omar became so interesting to him. The subject of moving vans associated humorously with Omar's "Caravan" (Q.48), but the parodic rhythm and sounds of the title are what probably remained with Eliot until the time he created his own title, "The Love Song of J. Alfred Prufrock."

Eliot's childhood was surfeited with popular reaction to the *Rubáiyát*.[62] The publications cited here were merely the tip of the iceberg. In addition, between Eliot's eighth and eighteenth birthdays, at least ten dramatic or musical compositions of some importance on the subject of Omar were presented in England and America.[63] As for people's day-to-day encounters with Omarism, the *Rubáiyát* was drafted widely into use in commerce and in its art forms. Even to begin a catalogue of specific examples would have been a hopeless task, but one bibliographer attempted a broadly generic list:

> Tobacco, Cigarettes and Cigars; Stationery and Printing Press; Fountain Pens and Pencils; Coffee, Chocolate and Candy; Perfume, Dentifrice, Toilet Soap, Cream and Powder; Wines, Wine Bars and Cafes; Pottery and Canoes (Oxford); Calendars, Music, Drama, Films, Dances; Tombstone Inscriptions; Poster Advt. for Tube Railways, Xmas Shopping, quoting Quatrain XXIV; Shop Window Displays of Editions of Rubáiyát; Picture Post Cards, Book Plates, Crossword Puzzles, Text Cards, etc.[64]

Those who read the New York *Critic* found that Andrew Lang complained about the excesses. Omar, he said, "is chattered about, written about, translated, illustrated, dined over, poeticized about, to an extent which would scarcely be excessive if Omar were Homer." Lang did not blame FitzGerald, "who never blew the trumpet over his own achievements," nor Omar, "if any Omar there was," but the admirers, "who run about cackling like a hen which has laid an egg." Lang concluded that Omar was being made a bore.[65]

In England, the editor of the *Academy* tried to shed some light on America's overenthusiasm:

> The way America busted into Omar, when it got its advices, was real smart. Mr. Mosher easily sold 20,000 cheap copies of the poem, and for the millionaire youth wondrous editions were hatched. One such was advertised quite recently as follows:
>
> Rubáiyát.—Limited edition of fifty copies printed on genuine parchment, every page of each copy illuminated by hand in gold and colours, bound in vellum, with metal clasps set with semiprecious stones, 100 dols.
>
> We shall always believe that these "semiprecious jewels" were the beginning of the end. They had hardly ceased to burn their coloured lights in the advertisement column of the American *Bookman* when Mr. Edgar Fawcett, a writer of some repute, arose and proclaimed through the New York *Journal* that the Omar cult has been a silly "fad" and has illustrated the "hypocrisy of English ethics." He talked of the "ruffian heterodoxy" of "this Persian *bon vivant*." "The most pitiable stuff." "Commonplace is the word for it, since it merely decorates the obvious in wine-drenched garlands and tawdry spangles." And the Omarian message was interpreted: "Get drunk as often as you can, for there's nothing in life half so profitable."[66]

The parodists usually did not attack the *Rubáiyát* directly. Some were cultists who took affectionate liberties with their favorite poem; most were exploiting what obviously was a popular vein in current publishing. The form of imagery that these versifiers used implied their acceptance of, and, probably more, their attraction towards, the poem, even when they treated themes that were alien to the original theme of the *Rubáiyát*. Whether the parodies attacked "huffy husbands," or drinking, or, with Omar's poem as a model, Temperance, their ubiquitousness, and their easily comprehended low- and middle-brow wit, would have served to strengthen the secret interest that an adolescent such as Eliot might feel for the poem and the affinity he could feel for Omar.

The angriest antagonists of the cult and of the poem usually were not satirists but sermonizers.[67] They hated the poem not because they thought it cheapened America's culture but because of the role it played in the breakdown of America's Protestant religion and of the Temperance ethic that the religion had subsumed. Eliot's earliest preserved poem, "A Fable for

Feasters," written in 1905, reveals his internal conflict in this matter. The protagonist is an "Abbot" who, in the course of the narrative, is punished for his intemperance. His antagonist is a "ghost" whose aggressive behavior is very much like Carry Nation's and whose morality stems from William Greenleaf Eliot. While Carry Nation was an obvious object of satire for the more sophisticated public, she undoubtedly also was an object of both alarm and admiration for the young poet fresh from his reading of the *Rubáiyát*. A fiery version of Eliot's dead grandfather, she was unsexed enough, or even masculine enough, to be his "ghost." Hiding behind satiric language, the boy could take on the mantle of Omar and bravely fight them both.

If the cultural milieu of Eliot as a youth were not to be taken into account, his few retrospective remarks about "A Fable for Feasters" would be puzzling. It was a poem, he said, whose verses were. written "in the manner of *Don Juan*, tinged with that disillusion and cynicism only possible at the age of sixteen." Understandably, the verses were composed in the flush of "the first boyhood enthusiasm"; however, the images that were returned to his mind now by the memory of that enthusiasm were "accompanied by a [tedious] gloom."[68] The poem, therefore, represents more of the feeling that Eliot had expressed in his first lost "gloomy and atheistical and despairing quatrains."

Why the memory of such low spirits? The narrative contains boisterous episodes, witty rhymes, and other verbal surprises. The division into twelve parts is mock-epic. The stanzaic form is "easy-going"—the same *ottava-rima*, "with its habitually feminine and occasionally triple endings," that Eliot said had worked so well to keep "the continual banter and mockery" going in Byron's satires.[69] The young poet knew how to relieve the decorum of his poem without breaking it, and the reliefs are high-spirited.

Eliot's general gloom in maturity has been attributed to a quality his characters share with Byron's, both bearing "a characteristic burden of blight and guilt, attributable, it may be, to a common Adam's curse of Calvinism."[70] But Eliot has explained more personally and instrumentally what his commonality was with the poets of his youth, Byron among them. A very young man who wants to write, he said, is for the most part not critical or appreciative. He is, instead, seeking "masters" who will help him to understand what he wants to say or the kind of poetry that is in him. The taste of an adolescent writer is intense but narrow: it is determined by personal needs."[71]

There indeed is a logic based on "personal needs" in Eliot's use of Byron as the "master" through whom he expressed the Omarian message in his first extant poem. FitzGerald himself found an association between Byron and Omar that may elucidate the basis for Eliot's choice. In a letter to Tennyson, written as work on the Persian translation was beginning, FitzGerald noted that he had read "some curious Infidel and Epicurean Tetrastichs by a Persian of the Eleventh Century—as Savage against Destiny etc. as [Byron's] Manfred."[72]

The theme of "A Fable for Feasters" uncovers the "disillusion" the young poet felt on seeing his family's laws topple under Omar's arguments. The poem opposes Eliot's moral education to the attractiveness of the *Rubáiyát*, an attractiveness that included not only its current assertions against an unappealing Temperance movement but also its relativist assertions against "unalterable" universal Law.[73] The satiric mode, taken from the more savage Byron, would serve both as the antidote to Eliot's gloom and as its mask.

In the poem's battle between, on the one side, a group of seemingly sinful but really innocent hedonists, led by an Abbot, and, on the other side, a puritan ghost, the puritan wins. The forgiving, even indulgent, tone of the poem, however, indicates that the youth did not want to, but had to, allow the puritan to win. The youthful confusion and compromise rising out of this conflict probably are symbolized in the depression Eliot recollected in maturity.

But the poem is funny. The opening exposition quickly sets the poem's irony by purporting to take the good puritan view. The time is the Middle Ages—the bad old Catholic days. As the poem begins, (the future) Henry VIII is dealt quick blows for polygamy, greed, and philistine destructiveness. The present local politician is as rapacious as Henry will be. The Church, in contrast, has a "band" who are appealingly "merry":

> In England, long before that royal Mormon
>   King Henry VIII found out that monks were quacks,
> And took their lands and money from the poor men,
>   And brought their abbeys tumbling at their backs,
> There was a village founded by some Norman
>   Who levied on all travelers his tax;
>   Nearby this hamlet was a monastery
>   Inhabited by a band of friars merry.

In the *Rubáiyát*, as young Eliot must have noted, a very unmerry "Band" were prudent, temperate, and undemonstrative; they of course represented precepts that Eliot knew were also important to American culture. Omar satirizes them as yearning for "the Prophet's Paradise":

Some for the Glories of This World; and some
Sigh for the Prophet's Paradise to come;
   Ah, take the Cash, and let the Credit go,
Nor heed the rumble of a distant Drum. (Q. 13)

If but the Vine and Love-abjuring Band
Are in the Prophet's Paradise to stand,
   Alack, I doubt the Prophet's Paradise
Were empty as the hollow of one's Hand. (Q. 65, 2d ed.)

Thus, Eliot's next stanza introduced their opposite, the possessors of a hedonist paradise that includes a "vineyard." By contrasting the stingy and hypocritical barons of the neighborhood with the expansively sensualist monks, the young poet makes his sentiments clear:[74]

They were possessors of rich lands and wide,
   An orchard, and a vineyard, and a dairy;
Whenever some old villainous baron died,
   He added to their hoards—a deed which ne'er he
Had done before—their fortune multiplied,
   As if they had been kept by a kind fairy,
   Alas! no fairy visited their host,
   Oh, no; much worse than that, they had a ghost.

Young Eliot's stand against parsimony finds support as well in Omar's quatrains 13–16 and 24. Then, the third stanza reveals the ghost as a wanderer, an unburied man: "Some wicked and heretical old sinner / Perhaps, who had been walled up for his crimes." With an allusion to medieval punishment, or, even, to Poe's "Cask of Amontillado," the youth establishes the credibility of both the antiquarian atmosphere and the ghost. The allusion also is thematically appropriate—wine must lead to death. The punitive ghost, therefore, deprives the monks of "the fatter cows." Having himself led a wrongful life, he has come to punish other sinners. A zealous reformer, he even once "sat the prior on the steeple / To the astonishment of all the people." The image of the prior as a living exemplum atop a steeple amusingly echoes Omar's image:

And those that after some TO-MORROW stare,
   A Muezzin from the Tower of Darkness cries,
"Fools! Your Reward is neither Here nor There." (Q. 25)

With the fourth stanza, the time for ritual feasting approaches. Just as those thirsty for wine, in Omar's poem, are unhappy with the presence of the "hunger-stricken Ramazán" (Lent) and just as the saloon patrons, in America's Kansas, did not want the presence of Carry Nation, Eliot's Abbot, with Christmas at hand, vowed that the monks would "eat their meal from ghosts and phantoms free, / The fiend must stay home—no ghosts allowed / At this exclusive feast." The Abbot's vow to be free from "phantoms" for the holiday feast recalls the impatience of the "Tavern ... worshipper" in quatrain 2 as he waits for "the phantom of False morning" to die in order to begin his drinking bout. Preparing for battle if the ghost should happen to come, the Abbot chooses weapons, like the Kansas bartenders, that unfortunately will not have much force against the ingenuity of his antagonist:

> ... From over sea
> He purchased at his own expense a crowd
>   Of relics from a Spanish saint—said he:
> 'If ghosts come uninvited, then, of course,
> I'll be compelled to keep them off by force.'

"Spanish saint" works for the poem in several ways. It not only seems to salute Eliot's poetic model, Byron's Spanish *Don Juan*, but strikes the right note of satiric terror in its association with the Spanish Inquisition. It brings into the poem a mock-epic convention, for now the scope of the setting suddenly becomes vast as it covers another part of the world. The purchase of the Spanish relic "at his own expense" humorously enhances the quality of generosity, and open-handedness in the Abbot as a real "hero." That the Abbot's weapon is a Saint's relic foreshadows his rise to unwelcome sainthood at the battle's end. Finally, as an attack on the superstitions regarding saints, it shows the youth's brand-new "atheistical" bent and, simultaneously, his sympathy with the monks who actually are religious retrogrades. In the Persian, Omar's attack on "Saints" was antimystic, but in FitzGerald's translation the attack turned into full-blown agnosticism:

> Myself when young did eagerly frequent
> Doctor and Saint, and heard great argument
>   About it and about: but evermore
> Came out by the same door where in I went. (Q. 27)

The Abbot's second weapon against the ghost, in the fifth stanza, is "holy water," to insure that the reformer will be bested by his own asceticism.

The proponent of fasting must be made powerless by fleshless bone relics and unalloyed water. So the Abbot "drencht the gown he wore," and the "turkeys, capons, boars," and "he even soakt the uncomplaining porter / Who stood outside the door from head to feet." Young Eliot's "porter" plays the same role as Omar, who in the "Allegory" stood outside the Potter's shop where the thirsty pots were waiting for Lent to end:

> So while the Vessels one by one were speaking,
> The little Moon look'd in that all were seeking:
>   And then they jogg'd each other, "Brother! Brother!
> Now for the Porter's shoulder-knot a-creaking." (Q. 90)

The Abbot's action, furthermore, resembles Carry Nation's as she "soakt" the saloons during her raids. But the final line of the stanza contains as well a strong echo from a final line in quatrain 56 of the *Rubáiyát*. Omar had said that he "Was never deep in anything but—Wine." Eliot ends his fifth stanza with the identical fillip: The Abbot "doused the room.... / And, watered everything except the, wine," evidence that for the monks, as for Omar, the "wine" has paramount importance.

In the next two stanzas, the young poet puts on his puritan mask when he pretends not to know much about the "menus of that time." But he assures his audience, that "... as well's I'm able / I'll go through the account: They made a raid / On every bird and beast in Aesop's fable." Duly warned of a raid on *them* to be made by the ghost of Temperance, the gluttonous monks ignore the warning. Their prideful challenge to the powers of puritanism brings about their fall—and results in another moral "fable," this one about "feasters." Thus the list of foods mounts. Last is the great "boar's head," ritual food of sacrifice, presaging the rebirth of the sinning community.

The monks go into excesses of intemperance in stanza eight. Sated with wassail, a fine, old drink, though now gone out of use," they fall into peaceful regrets: the Abbot "with proposing every toast / Had drank more than he ought t'have of grape juice." The young poet's irony covers a view that is actually Omar's, who repeatedly argues in favor of the "Grape" and the "Juice":

> Why, be this juice the growth of God, who dare
>   Blaspheme the twisted tendril as a Snare? (Q. 61)

> "But fill me with the old familiar juice,
> Methinks I might recover by-and-by." (Q. 89)

> Ah, with the Grape my fading Life provide (Q. 91)

Better be jocund with the fruitful Grape
Than sadden after none, or bitter, Fruit. (Q. 54)

The stanza ends when the "lights began to burn distinctly blue," a signal
typical of a ghost's impending entry. The blue lights also recall Carry Nation
bearing blue laws into saloons, and by that means, the ghost becomes even
more characteristically puritan.

Stanza nine begins with locked "doors," an image that appears
frequently in the *Rubáiyát*. Even though Omar finally found "the Tavern
Door agape" (Q. 58) at the moment when Lent ended, he continually found
other doors symbolically locked. For example, his metaphor for the true
salvation (which lies in the body, and not in the spirit) is a key and door: "Of
my Base metal may be filed a Key, / That shall unlock the Door [the Dervish]
howls without." (Q. 76.) Perhaps because of his kinship to the invincible
Carry Nation, Eliot's ascetic ghost has more ingenuity and more strength
than Omar's "Dervish." Like the saloon doors, locked and guarded, against
the raider who overcame them anyway, in Eliot's stanza:

The doors, though barred and bolted most securely,
    Gave way—my statement nobody can doubt,
Who knows the well known fact, as you do surely—
    That ghosts are fellows whom you *can't* keep out;
It is a thing to be lamented sorely
    Such slippery folk should be allowed about,
        For often they drop in at awkward moments,
        As everybody'll know who reads this romance.

Lines 3 and 8 of this stanza contain an important echo of the line from Omar
that was most widely quoted: "*He* knows about it all—HE knows—HE
knows." (Q. 70.) In several instances in his later work, Eliot echoes the same
line.[75] Here, in its earliest appearance, he delays the final repetition of three
variants of *know* until the stanza's climax: "Who knows the well-known fact.
As everybody'll know ..." Using Omar's verbal strategy, Eliot laments such
"slippery folk" as the ghost, and claims that their sensational publicity is
"well known." The raiding Carry Nation indeed had filled the press with
news of her exploits.

Finally, in stanza ten, the climactic battle occurs. The ghost is quite as
rough as any saloon smasher ever was. The poor Abbot, wearing the gown
that had been so uselessly "drencht," is finally collared, and together ghost
and Abbot vanish "swiftly up the chimney." In *Rubáiyát* fashion, the Abbot
might have said, "I came like Water, and like Wind I go." (Q. 28.)

The humorous search for the physical Abbot, in stanza eleven, ends with the monks' near-sighted rationalization—he'd been "snatcht to heaven" by St. Peter. However, the skeptical think "that the Abbot's course lay nearer underground / But the church straightway put to his name the handle / Of Saint, thereby rebuking all such scandal."

In the final stanza, with their spurious saint gone, the monks are reformed and no longer merry. There, a youthful pun, bearing at least three meanings, points to Eliot's own underlying "gloom":

> Spirits from that time forth they did without,
>   And lived the admiration of the shire.

That is, the monks were freed of their spirit-reformer, but at a cost; their urge for spirited behavior had to be eradicated; and, from then on, they did without the spirits called "wine," finally respectable.

Closing like a medievalist antiquarian (just as the romantic poets used to do), or like one who came upon an old Persian manuscript (just as the Victorian FitzGerald had), or like one who in the future will come upon old newspaper accounts of midwestern saloon-raids, the young poet claims: "...We / Got the veracious record of, these doings / From an old manuscript found in ruins."

"A Fable for Feasters" is only superficially unsympathetic towards the Abbot "Saint," an Omarian protagonist who clearly engaged Eliot's feeling of fraternity. The youth's "Fable" is "for Feasters," not against them. The ghost who is the Abbot's enemy is the poem's actual object of attack, and he is, of course, the saint of asceticism, of America's puritanism. In "[A Lyric]," the next poem Eliot wrote, his dispute with "Sages" is developed. Together, "Saints and Sages" are coincidentally subverted in one of Omar's more sacrilegious quatrains:

> Why, all the Saints and Sages who discuss'd
> Of the Two Worlds so learnedly—they are thrust
>   Like foolish Prophets forth; their Words to Scorn
> Are scatter'd, and their Mouths are stopt with Dust. (Q. 26)

"[A Lyric]," like "A Fable for Feasters," was written in 1905 at Smith Academy, but Eliot revised it as "Song" in 1907 at Harvard.[76] Of the 1905 version, Eliot remembered that his English teacher, a Mr. Hatch, "commended warmly my first poem, written as a class exercise, at the same time asking me suspiciously if I had had any help in writing it."[77] A slightly different version of this memory, one which stressed the privacy of the youth's feelings about the poem, has been reported by Valerie Eliot:

These stanzas in imitation of Ben Jonson were done as a school
exercise when he was sixteen. "My English Master, who had set
his class the task of producing some verse, was much impressed
and asked whether I had had any help from some elder person.
Surprised, I assured him that they were wholly unaided." They
were printed in the school paper, *Smith Academy Record*, but he
did not mention them to his family. "Some time later the issue
was shown to my Mother, and she remarked (we were walking
along Beaumont Street in St. Louis) that she thought them better
than anything in verse she had ever written. I knew what her
verse meant to her. We did not discuss the matter further."[78]

The "help" appropriated by the sophisticated and imitative student
came as much from Omar as from Ben Jonson. Moreover, while the youth's
interest in the *carpe diem* theme could be reinforced by the Elizabethan's
poetry, it had been awakened by Omar three years earlier.

In the opening of "[A Lyric]," Eliot joined Omar in his attack on
metaphysical "Sages"—the word capitalized as in the *Rubáiyát*. "If Time and
Space, as Sages say, / Are things which cannot be," wrote the youth, then the
philosophers are wrong. The destroyer "Time" does exist, as does the
physical "Space" which it destroys. To enjoy our lives, though brief, we must
ignore the message of "Sages" and love each other now. In his revision of
1907, Eliot added a specifically Omarian image, by changing words in the
penultimate line from "days of love" to "flowers of life":

> But let us haste to pluck anew
>   Nor mourn to see them pine,
> And though the flowers of life be few
>   Yet let them be divine.

With the change the stanza echoes the *Rubáiyát*: "the leaves of life keep
falling one by one." (Q. 8.) The 1907 revision, also, includes a new and
second reference to "Sages." The Harvard freshman, less mannered and by
then five years past his first impressions of Omar, removed the capitalization:
"For time is time, and runs away, / Though sages disagree."

"[A Lyric]" is a spare Jonsonian poem, of few words and stark
vocabulary, yet its thematic words strike an authentically Omarian note:
"time," "Sages," "flowers," "vine," "haste," "mourn," "divine."

The third poem that Eliot wrote in that year was for his graduation from
Smith Academy. As an occasional poem, "Graduation 1905"[79] shows, to a

greater degree than "A Fable for Feasters," the external pressures exerted by young Eliot's society. But under such intensity, the internal pressures exerted by Omar came out there even more clearly.

In the public's reception of the *Rubáiyát*, the Omarian message was externalized, and rather uniformly articulated by the Omar cult as powerful, novel, adversarial, and transcendent—that is, as generically romantic. The sense of cultist uniformity, however, was bound to endanger each member's romantic individualism, and, when it did, those turn-of-the-century enthusiasts of the *Rubáiyát* frequently reacted by creating a public memorial to their own individuality.[80] Thus, personal reminiscences about "first encounters" sounded a steady refrain even in the poem's public reception. However, as the young Eliot encountered cultural (anticult) attitudes at variance with the personal meaning he had found in the poem, he was powerless to seek out relief or actively to join with the cult. But he leaned towards the cultists in his retention of the private vision that the poem had engendered and even was able to set forth the vision later in the Norton lectures.

"Graduation 1905" seems to indicate that publicly Eliot joined the anticult, the culture closest to him. As an occasional poem, however, it shares a conventional insincerity with all such poems. It was expected, strongly, that the youth would conjoin his feeling with those of his ritualizing audience. That audience consisted of peers, parents, and teachers—all exerting moral as well as academic authority. Allying himself with them, he nonetheless produced a poem that was a connate symptom of his, by then, serious identification with his literary idol. Indeed, two stanzas of "Graduation 1905," stanzas III and XI, represent an "absorption" of the *Rubáiyát* as a model—absorption of its cadences, prosody, and structure, of its themes and imagery, and, most important, of its persona.

With this third poem, the youth seemed to be practicing a plain rhetorical style that, in general, was the perfect obverse of the *Rubáiyát*. About his understanding of how acceptable such a valedictory style would be, Eliot commented later, "I was informed afterwards, by one of my teachers, that the poem itself was excellent as such poems go."[81]

Structurally, the poem is a series of fourteen stanzas; prosodically, each has a six-line rhyme pattern, and is Roman-numbered as in the *Rubáiyát*. Again, as in the *Rubáiyát*, each stanza has only two sonic line-endings: FitzGerald's are *aaba*, Eliot's are *abbaba*. FitzGerald's cadences, especially the dying fall typical of the final line of his quatrains, are often reproduced by Eliot. A simple syntactical inversion, for example, at the end of Omar's quatrain 5, gives the effect of a stanzaic sigh: "And many a Garden by the Water blows." Eliot end-sighs too, but sometimes, as in stanza IV, the fourth line of the sestet contains the end-sigh, and produces the effect of an enclosed quatrain:

> Although the path be tortuous and slow,
> Although it bristle with a thousand fears,
> To hopeful eye of youth it still appears
> A lane by which the rose and hawthorn grow.

Except for the relative pronoun "which," a youthful metrical error, the cadent line resembles Omar's cadent line in word order and sense.

The poem begins with the poet's public manner, in an appeal to a shared tradition. The description of the forthcoming journey, in stanza I, accounts for the graduates' normal doubts and fears. There Eliot uses an image that seems automatic, coming perhaps from America's conditioned faith in success. The image lacks color:

> ... sail we
> Across the harbor bar—no chart to show,
> No light to warn of rocks which lie below,
> But let us put forth courageously.

Still public, stanza 11 urges rationality. The graduates must "fully understand" that, like the colonists who may revisit their former country, "They there shall be as citizens no more." The thought, however, is reminiscent of Omar's pessimistic "And, once departed, may return no more." (Q. 3.) With it, Eliot's set goal of public optimism seems to take a temporary turn.

Suddenly in stanza III—and, as will be seen, in stanza XI—the youth shows how he has been "possessed" by Omar. Here he uses the images and even the rhymes of Omar's quatrain 48:

> A Moment's Halt—a momentary taste
> Of BEING from the Well amid the Waste—
>   And Lo!—the phantom Caravan has reach'd
> The NOTHING it set out from—Oh, make haste!

Eliot wrote:

> We go; as lightning-winged clouds that fly
> After a summer tempest, when some haste
> North, South, and Eastward o'er the water's waste,

Some to the western limits of the sky
Which the sun stains with many a splendid dye,
Until their passing may no longer be traced.

In Eliot's lines, Omar's skepticism about everything except the transitoriness of life is patent. Although Omar's "Caravan," rushing through the universe, becomes Eliot's "lightning-winged clouds," the imagery is familial.[82] The youth's rhymes are only a minor variant of Omar's, and the stanza ends, like Omar's, in nothing.

In stanzas V–VII, the youth is again the cheerful public poet who recommends with bravado precisely what Omar condemned: attention to "great duties." But, the single faltering clause in stanza V is the only passage that seems sincere. In it, Eliot's language is Omarian: "who knows what time may hold in store."

Omar's imagined ghostly revisit to this world is to be commemorated with wine: "And in your joyous errand reach the spot / Where I made One— turn down an empty glass" (Q. 101); in stanza VIII, Eliot touches the same languidly sad string in his reference to the graduates' return visit: "Grey-haired and old, whatever be our lot, / We shall desire to see again the spot ...." However, the school's memory will be honored with a narcotic more acceptable to Eliot's public than wine would be: "For in the sanctuaries of the soul / Incense of altar-smoke shall rise to thee ..." (stanza IX).

Like stanza III, stanza XI begins with "We go," and contains major parallels from the *Rubáiyát*. With them, the poet again controverts his public optimism:

We go; like flitting faces in a dream;
Out of thy care and tutelage we pass
Into the unknown world—class after class,
O queen of schools—a momentary gleam,
A bubble on the surface of the stream,
A drop of dew upon the morning grass.

The language in both III and XI shows Eliot's obvious, if private, absorption of the following lines from Omar, as well as from quatrain 48, above:

The Eternal Saki from that Bowl has pour'd
Millions of Bubbles like us, and will pour. (Q. 46)

And when Yourself with silver Foot shall pass
Among the Guests Star-scatter'd on the Grass. (Q. 101)

With them the seed of Wisdom did I sow,
And with my own hand had wrought to make it grow;
    And this was all the Harvest that I reap'd—
"I came like Water, and like Wind I go." (Q. 28)

With respect to imagery, both Eliot and Omar will "go" in the wind, "NOTHING" remaining. Both refer to the "waste," FitzGerald's being terrestrial and Eliot's watery. Both, finished with formalized wisdom, are now merely "Bubbles" and "dew upon the grass." Both use the vocative "O." Omar's "momentary taste" is Eliot's "momentary gleam."

Finishing bravely, the young poet closes with the school's motto, "Progress!"—and a firm "Farewell."

In "Dante," Eliot commented on the power of the "first" experience of any significant poem. It is the experience, he said, "both of a moment and of a lifetime," one that may be likened to the more intense experiences we have of other human beings. He described it as a unique "early moment" of shock, surprise, and even terror, a moment that is never forgotten but also never repeated. "The majority of poems," however, "one outgrows and outlives, as one outgrows and outlives the majority of human passions."[83]

If he finally outgrew the *Rubáiyát*, "Graduation 1905" certainly indicates that his first identification with Omar was intense. The poem's two Omarian stanzas were clearly written with more passion than the rhetorically plain stanzas, and their message of Omarian skepticism strongly contradicts the rest of the poem. Eliot may have felt he was not an imitator of Omar but a manly, if secret, disciple of him. Later in his life, writing on the ramifications of imitation, he distinguished between the disciple and the imitator, saying that the disciple is first impressed by "what" the master says, and therefore will give deep attention to the "way" he said it; the imitator, or borrower, is interested first and chiefly in the "way" the thing was said by the master.[84] The "way" Omar spoke was important to the imitative young poet, but "what" he said was just as important to him as disciple. Their private alliance slipped out in the most public poem of Eliot's youth.

NOTES

    1. *PWEY*, p. v. In 1950, Eliot had supervised the printing of these juvenilia in a limited edition of twelve copies.

    2. *UPUC*, p. 33.

    3. Quoted in Donald Hall, "T.S. Eliot," *Writers at Work*, ed. George Plimpton (New York, 1965), p. 92. Eliot's remark, made in 1957, seems to be a sign of the long complete liberation he felt, as an Anglo-Catholic, from FitzGerald's influence. Valerie Eliot's later report of her husband's memory of these quatrains emphasizes not so much Eliot's adult

repentance as his youthful possessedness: "At about fourteen he wrote 'some very gloomy quatrains in the form of the *Rubáiyát*' which had 'captured my imagination.' These he showed to no one and presumed he destroyed." *PWEY*, p. v.

4. H. G. Keene, "Omar Khayyám," in Nathan Haskell Dole, *Rubáiyát of Omar Khayyám* (Boston, 1891), 2:423.

5. Irving Way, "Omar Khayyám at the Caxton Club, Chicago," *Bookman* 8 (1899): 446–48.

6. Ambrose George Potter, *A Bibliography of the Rubáiyát of Omar Khayyám* (London, 1929), #249. This was the St. Dunstan edition.

7. Potter, *Bibliography*. Carl Weber observes, "It may well be believed that no bibliographer can claim knowledge of *all* editions," and that the Centennial Edition was "merely the last of hundreds and hundreds of editions—how many hundreds no one knows." He quotes one scholar's comment on the worldwide interest in the poem: "Publishing the *Rubáiyát* became the rage. It spread from London to Birmingham and Leicester and Worcester, to Edinburgh and Glasgow, to Leipzig and Venice and Singapore; to Bombay and Calcutta and Madras in India, and to Melbourne and Sydney in Australia." *FitzGerald's Rubáiyát*, Centennial Edition (Waterville, Maine, 1959), p. 31. Although Potter's fascinating and most helpful catalogue contains the 586 editions and some 700 additional articles, critical works, poems on the subject, theatrical productions, and so forth, I found that numerous articles published around 1900–1910 had been omitted.

8. Grant Allen, "Omar at Marlow." Allen was a philosopher and novelist, and an early member of the Omar Khayyám Club in London. The poem was reprinted in Edward Clodd's *Memories* (London, 1916) after its appearance in newspapers and periodicals, e.g., the *Sketch* in 1896. Clodd, pp. 32–34

9. Dole, *Rubáiyát*, 2:567.

10. They were interested enough to proscribe Mark Twain's *Huckleberry Finn* for their son. Horace Gregory, *The House on Jefferson Street* (New York, 1971), p. 54.

11. James Whitcomb Riley, *The Rubáiyát of Doc Sifers* (New York, 1897).

12. Wallace Stegner, "Western Record and Romance," in *Literary History of the United States*, ed. Robert Spiller et al. (New York, 1963), pp. 870–71.

13. John Hay, *In Praise of Omar Khayyám* (Portland, Maine, 1889). The address appeared in many editions of the *Rubáiyát*.

14. Cited as having been printed in the *Daily Chronicle*, on 9 December 1897, n.p., in Edward Heron-Allen, *Some Side-lights upon Edward FitzGerald's Poem, 'The Rubáiyát of Omar Khayyám'* (London, 1898), p. i.

15. Andrew Lang, "Omar Khayyám as a Bore," *Critic* 37 (1900): 219. Lang had written several poems on the subject of Omar Khayyám, the earliest, "Omar de Profundis," *Saturday Review of Literature*, 31 January 1885. His frequent articles and poems on the subject prompted H. L. Wale's "Lang and Omar," *Book-Lover* 2 (1901): 146.

16. Moncure Conway, "The Omar Khayyám Cult in England," *Nation* 57 (1893): 304. After completing his study of theology at Harvard, Conway became a Unitarian preacher, in 1854. In 1863, he went to England to lecture on the Civil War. From there he frequently sent his writing to the American press. In London he became head of the South Place Institute (for advanced religious thought). He was the author of *Demonology and Devil Lore* (1879), lives of Thomas Carlyle and Thomas Paine (1881 and 1892), and many other books including an autobiography.

17. The British seemed to be somewhat less concerned about the *Rubáiyát* in the latter respect. Arthur Waugh reported in 1897 that the guest of honor at the most recent of the quarterly Omar Khayyám Club dinners was Lord Wolseley. He was "a man of war," the "Commander-in-Chief" of all the armed forces of the British Empire. Yet he was able in

his address to speak with a "graceful and almost melancholy ... feeling" about the "indolent sweetness of Persian poetry in a land of fountains and garden-closes." Named among the "excellent company" at that occasion were James Barrie, Kenneth Grahame, Arthur Conan Doyle, Arthur Hacker, President Edmund Gosse, and two Americans—Moncure Conway and publisher Frank Dodd. Andrew Lang, Henry Newbolt, Austin Dobson, Thomas Hardy, and George Meredith, all members, were absent that evening.

As an interesting coincidence, Waugh noted that "on that very evening, as Mr. Gosse mentioned, the authors of New York were assembled to do honor to the veteran poet and critic, Mr. R. H. Stoddard, and they would have been pleased to see how the Americans present at the Omar Khayyám dinner shared in the British enthusiasm for the cause of letters." R. H. Stoddard, it will be recalled, was one of the "literary band of five" that included Thomas Bailey Aldrich, Arthur Waugh, "London Letter," *Critic* 30 (1897): 257.

Both British and American fears were mocked by another British cultist, Richard La Gallienne, who at the same time praised the unsettling power of Omar's poem: "It might be proved that this small handful of strangely scented rose-leaves have been dynamic as a disintegrating spiritual force in England and America, as no other written words have been during the last twenty-five years. Mr. George Moore has been nothing like so dangerous! One of Omar's forcible epigrams has proved mightier than a volume by Mr. Herbert Spencer." In *Book of Omar and Rubáiyát* (New York, 1900), p. 16.

18. John D. Yohannan, "One Hundred Years of FitzGerald's Rubáiyát of Omar Khayyám," *Epiterea, University of Athens Philosophical Journal*, n.v. (1959): 259.

19. Howarth, pp. 2–11.

20. Howarth, p. 348. In fact, for the Eliot family, it would seem, the Devil was to be found most often in the areas of sex and drink. W. G.'s second son, Eliot's father, viewed sex as "nastiness." Henry Ware Eliot "considered public instruction tantamount to giving children a letter of introduction Devil. Syphilis was God's punishment and he hoped a cure would never be found. Otherwise, he said, it might be necessary 'to emasculate our children to keep them clean.'" Gordon, p. 27.

21. Fanny Kemble, "An Old, Woman's Gossip," *Atlantic Monthly* 36 (1875): 725–26.

22. The editor agreed that Rev. Eliot's antislavery sermons most probably had kept Missouri from joining the Confederacy. "William, G. Eliot, D.D.," *Unitarian Review and Religious Magazine* 11 (1879): 544–46.

23. Barrow then quoted Jessie Cadell's review warning readers of the poem's many dangers. "Editor's Note Book," *Unitarian Review and Religious Magazine* 11 (1879): 384–86. See also n. 46 below.

24. *The Rubáiyát of Omar Khayyám* ... with an accompaniment of drawings by E. Vedder (Boston, 1884). This edition was widely reviewed: see *Nation* 39 (1884): 423; and *Atlantic Monthly* 55 (1885): 111–16. I own an edition published in 1894: Vedder's vision is both erotic and Dantesque. One can see how the youth might have been gripped by it, and then the man gripped by Dante.

25. A. W. Benn, *History of English Rationalism in the Nineteenth Century*, 2 vols. (New York, 1906) 2:292–94.

26. John W. Chadwick, "The Poems of Omar Khayyám," *Old and New* 5 (1872): 611.

27. Cited in John D. Margolis, *T. S. Eliot's Intellectual Development, 1922–1939* (Chicago, 1972), p. 62.

28. Ibid., p. 145. The "spiritual biography" to which Eliot felt so close was "Marginalia," in which More (p. 144) "described his rejection of the Calvinism in which he had been reared, his subsequent 'craving, a kind of necessity laid upon the intellect, to find some formula whether of creed or of worship which should respond to those elusive intimations and, as it were, build a new house for the evicted spirit'; his turning to the

Brahmanic theosophy of the Upanishads and the Bhagavad-Gita; and the influences on him of John Henry Newman and Joseph Shorthouse." "Marginalia" was published in *American Review* 8 (1936): 1–30.

29. Eliot, "American Literature and the American Language," *Sewanee Review* 14 (Winter 1966): 2.

30. William Greenleaf Eliot, *The Story of Alexander Archer* (Boston, 1885).

31. Eliot, "American Literature," p. 2.

32. Howarth, p. 10; T. S. Matthews, *Great Tom* (New York, 1974), p. 5.

33. Boston, 1823; Cambridge, 1832. "In 1811 [Henry Wade] began the University's first course of formal graduate instruction in divinity; from this grew the Harvard Divinity School." Daniel Walker Howe, *The Unitarian Conscience* (Cambridge, 1970), p. 14. Howe's study includes Ware's role in the formation of American intellectual and moral thought.

34. Charlotte Eliot, *Savonarola: A Dramatic Poem* (London, 1926).

35. Howard, pp. 24–17.

36. *SE*, p. 427. Even with this jibe at the kind of reforms his mother engaged in, at Faber and Faber Eliot had a brass plate on his door, inscribed STEARNS, "the relic of a Boston lawyer-forbear." John Betjeman, "The Usher of Highgate Junior School," in *T. S. Eliot, A Symposium*, ed. Richard March and Tambimuttu (Chicago, 1949), p. 91.

37. F. O. Matthiessen, *The Achievement of T. S. Eliot* (New York, 1935), p. 20.

38. J. C. Furnas, *The Life and Times of the Late Demon Rum* (New York, 1965), p. 330.

39. Potter, *Bibliography*, #1066. Some few of the many others cited in Potter: #726, "*A Dialogue in Hades*" (1902); #644, *A Holiday in Hades* (1907); #942, *Quatrains of Christ*, intro. Julian Hawthorne (1908); #668, *Omar or Christ* (1914). As early as December 1886, *Harper's* printed "The Cup of Death," a sonnet with illustrations after Vedder, Potter, #1064.

40. Furnas, *Late Demon Rum*, p. 330.

41. Richard Le Gallienne, *Rubáiyát of Omar Khayyám: A Paraphrase from Several Literal Translations* (New York, 1897), p. 17; idem, *Omar Repentant* (New York, 1908), n.p.

42. "The Book-Buyer's Guide," *Critic* 37 (1900): 277.

43. Hall, "T. S. Eliot," in Plimpton, *Writers at Work*, p. 92.

44. Joseph R. Gusfield, *Symbolic Crusade* (Urbana, 1963), p. 86.

45. Warren Barton Blake, "Poetry, Time, and Edward FitzGerald," *Dial* 46 (1909): 179. See also Potter, *Bibliography*, #247, for the edition of the *Rubáiyát* "printed by boys under 12 years of age."

46. Jessie E. Cadell, "The True Omar Khayyám," *Fraser's* 19 (1879): 650–59. Quoted in Yohannan, "One Hundred Years," p. 264.

47. Potter, *Bibliography*, #685, #700.

48. Clarence Darrow, *Verdicts Out of Court*, ed. Arthur and Lila Weinberg (Chicago, 1963), pp. 201, 57–64, 106–23, 21. On the WCTU, in the manner of Mark Twain, Darrow wrote (p. 115): "Now, if we put this [temperance] question to the members of the Women's Christian Temperance Union, I know I would be out my beer. But I know that all of them would stick to coffee and tea—every last one of them—and it wouldn't change their minds a bit if we told them it was killing them by inches; they would keep it because they like it."

49. Yohannan points out the similarity of Darrow's and Dreiser's views, especially clear in Dreiser's play, *The Hand of the Potter*. "One Hundred Years," p. 277.

50. Clarence Darrow, *A Persian Pearl: and Other Essays* (New York, 1899). The essay climaxes (p. 19): "It has ever been the same,—the punishment of the creature for the creator's fault. There might be some excuse if man could turn from the frail, cracked vessels, and bring to trial the great potter for the imperfect work of his hand."

51. Darrow, *Verdicts*, p. 106.

52. Stewart H. Holbrook, "Bonnet, Book, and Hatchet," *American Heritage* 9 (1957):

55. On April 6, 1901, the *Saturday Evening Post* published an article on Carry Nation by one of the most influential newspaper editors in the Midwest, William Allen White.

53. Holbrook, "Bonnet," p. 55

54. Ibid., p. 120. In 1909, she "wrought fearful havoc" in Washington's Union Depot "with *three* hatchets she told the police were Faith, Hope and Charity." In 1910, she battled with a female saloon keeper and the "old champ went down." p. 121. She died in June 1911.

55. John Kohler, *Ardent Spirits* (New York, 1973), p. 137.

56. *The Hatchet: Being the First Year Book of Washington University Published by the Senior Class*, 1903.

57. Potter, *Bibliography*, #1045, #1187, #1266, #1002. Some other titles in Potter's bibliography that deal primarily with Temperance are "Day of Wine," #1071; "The Bishop and the Booze," #1218; "The Grape," #1251; "Quatrains of Omar, trans. by Richard LeGallon," #1273; "Wine and Soda," #1275; "The Boozaiyat of Owe More Kiyi," #1287.

58. Ibid., #1107–#1308

59. Ibid., #1122.

60. Rudyard Kipling, *Departmental Ditties* (London, 1886), pp. 45–46. Kipling's epigraph reads: "Allowing for the difference 'twixt prose and rhymed exaggeration, this ought to reproduce the sense of what Sir A told the nation some time ago, when the Government struck from our incomes two per cent." As an example of Kipling's tone, the fourth of the ten quatrains goes:

> Indeed; indeed, Retrenchment oft before
> I swore—but did I mean it when I swore?
> And then, and then, We wandered to the Hills,
> And so the Little Less became Much More.

Kipling's fame rivaled Omar's. One astute publisher issued an edition of the *Rubáiyát* bound together with *Barrack-Room Ballads*. Potter, *Bibliography*, #248.

61. Potter, *Bibliography*, #1262, #1263, #1195, #1281. In 1906, the *St. Louis Mirror*, also published "Omar in Heaven," twenty-nine verses by Walter Malone. Eliot was then a student at Milton Academy. Potter, *Bibliography*, #1096.

62. In the year before Eliot's birth, Michael Kerney indicated the importance of America to the success of the *Rubáiyát* by dedicating his "Memorial Edition" of the *Rubáiyát*

TO THE AMERICAN PEOPLE, WHOSE EARLY
APPRECIATION OF THE GENIUS OF EDWARD
FITZGERALD WAS THE CHIEF STIMULANT OF
THAT CURIOSITY BY WHICH HIS NAME WAS
DRAWN FROM ITS ANONYMOUS CONCEALMENT
AND ADVANCED TO THE POSITION OF HONOR
WHICH IT NOW HOLDS

(London, 1887). Nathan Haskell Dole, *Rubáiyát of Omar Khayyám* (Boston, 1896) 2:507.

63. Potter, *Bibliography*, #685–#717.

64. Ibid., #718.

65. Lang, "Omar Khayyám as a Bore," p. 216. Two months later, "Omar on the Omar Craze" appeared in *Munsey's*. Potter, *Bibliography*, #1079.

66. A. H. Millar, "The Omar Cult," *Academy* 59 (1900): 55.

67. John D. Yohannan analyzes "the excessively strong feelings the *Rubáiyát*

engendered in both proponents and opponents—feelings which lay at levels of psychological bent or philosophical bias considerably below the level of purely aesthetic need." "Fin de Siècle Cult of FitzGerald's *Rubáiyát of Omar Khayyám*," *Review of National Literatures*, 2 (1971): 74–75.

68. *OPP*, p. 223. The "diabolism" of Eliot's early verse seems to be like Byron's, bogus: "the *innocence* of Juan is merely a substitute for the *passivity* of Byron ... [which itself] has a curious resemblance to innocence," p. 236. "Animula" as well describes the protagonist's essential passivity in adolescence.

69. *OPP*, p. 234. The twelve-stanza length functioned as a sophisticated allusion to classical epic: the necessary exposition, 1–3; *in medias res*, the hero's imposing stature and the preparation for battle, 4–5; the illusory scene of peace, with catalogues, 6–7; the turn, 8–9; the supernatural in an epic battle, 10; the post-battle scene, 11; the moral, 12.

70. Smith, p. 3. Smith may have based his conclusion on Eliot's "Byron," in which Eliot said: "It is ... impossible to make out of his diabolism anything coherent or rational ... the element that seems to me most real and deep is that of a perversion of the Calvinist faith of his mother's ancestors." *OPP*, p. 226.

71. "Yeats" (1940), in *OPP*, p. 295. In this passage, Eliot was referring to the period of his life when he needed a French "voice."

72. Alfred McKinley Terhune, *Life of Edward FitzGerald* (New Haven, 1947), p. 204. In a letter of July 1856.

73. Cf. the anti-Temperance character of Eliot's "Cousin Nancy," who seemed to be violating "unalterable law" as she "smoked / And danced all the modern dances." *CP*, p. 22.

74. Cf. "What puts the last cantos of *Don Juan* at the head of Byron's works is, I think, that the subject matter gave him at last an adequate object for genuine emotion. The emotion is hatred of hypocrisy." *OPP*, pp. 237–38. Howarth suggests that the youth was deeply affected by Lincoln Steffens' *The Shame of Cities* (1904), the opening chapter of which had been published as an article in *McClure's Magazine*, October 1902. Reform was in the air; even in the year before, Eliot's father offered a reward "with other gentlemen for any information proving malpractise at elections." According to Howarth, in Eliot "the voice of indignation was first heard in 'Burbank ... Bleistein.'" But it is quite clear that Eliot at least whispered his indignation beneath that mockery of these two stanzas of 1905. Howarth, pp. 43, 50

75. See chapter 4 below.

76. *PWEY*, pp. 9, 10.

77. Eliot, "American Literature," p. 3

78. *PWEY*, pp. v–vi.

79. *PWEY*, pp. 11–17.

80. One of the more hyperbolic of these reminiscences is Justin McCarthy's: "To say that the Rubáiyát were a revelation to me and that I adored the revelation, would be but to convey a pitiful and meagre sense of my enthusiasm. I drank the red wine of Omar from the enchanted chalice of FitzGerald, and gloried as joyously as Omar himself in the intoxication. The book was not mine to keep, but I knew it almost by heart before I parted with it.... I made myself a kind of little religion out of Omar. ... my writings ... seemed ... to do little save echo the name of Omar." McCarthy, quoted in Dole, *Rubáiyát*, 2:523; and in A. J. Arberry, *The Romance of the Rubáiyát* (London, 1959), p. 31.

81. Eliot added: "but that my delivery was very bad indeed." "American Literature," p. 1. In a letter of 1943, he wrote to his friend John Hayward, "I hope you will be impressed by the pathos of the hopes which I expressed for the twentieth century and for the future of a day school which was dissolved through lack of pupils a few years later." *PWEY*, p. 34.

82. The quatrain in the first and second editions is perhaps closer to Eliot's stanza III:

One Moment in Annihilation's Waste,
One Moment, of the Well of Life to taste—
    The stars are setting, and the Caravan
Draws to the Dawn of Nothing—Oh, make haste!

83. *SE*, p. 250.

84. Eliot, "American Literature," 13.

Influences of a literary kind on a young poet are treated in Eliot's prose as the development of "taste." In his 1919 article in the *Athenaeum*, he called it "The Education of Taste," and, in the Norton lectures of 1932–1933, he called it "The Development of Taste in Poetry." But in "Animula," where he was most probing of all, he claimed that the book crucial to his literary development had *affected the soul* and probably was a catalyst in the soul's subsequent descent to the Abyss.

If "taste" and "soul" are nowhere equated directly in Eliot's writings, "taste" and "character" are. This aspect of Eliot's private meaning for "taste" as soul probably was derived from Babbitt's teachings. Babbitt believed that criticism is not mere "taste" but an "articulation of more central attitudes." In Walter Jackson Bate, *Criticism: The Major Texts* (New York, 1952), p. 547.

Howard explains Eliot's identification of critical taste with central attitudes as "Puritan": "Eliot, before he sits down to report on a writer, reconsiders his theoretical position on the kind of work his man writes, and places the man in relation to the theory. He is committed to the Whole. The authority of his page is due to this procedure.... Sometimes; he has appeared to be what Rivière called ... a *marchand de valeur*.... No example of uncharted voyaging ... could wholly change him so deeply rooted is his critical procedure in his Puritan temperament." Howarth, pp. 168–69.

NORMAN PAGE

Larger Hopes and the New Hedonism: Tennyson and FitzGerald

In defiance of both seniority and the alphabet, 'Tennyson and FitzGerald' is a formulation that shapes itself much more readily than 'FitzGerald and Tennyson'; and it is of course a very different kind of pairing from Pope and Swift, Wordsworth and Coleridge, Eliot and Pound. It is the disparities between Tennyson and his friend (and again one instinctively puts it that way round) that most quickly seize the mind: the whale and the minnow; the vastly prolific major poet dedicated to the bardic vocation, and the dilettante translator-cum-man-of-letters whose creative stream usually ran shallow and sometimes dried up altogether; the celebrity or national institution, cosseted by his family and besieged by admirers, and the lonely eccentric single gentleman living a life of obscurity and self-imposed monotony. Yet their lives touch at many points; and, unequal though their achievement is, if *In Memoriam* was the Victorian age's favourite poem, the *Rubáiyát of Omar Khayyám*, which appeared in the same decade, was surely a close runner-up. After glancing at the history and nature of the relationship between Tennyson and FitzGerald, and the surviving record on both sides, I would like to make some comparisons between these two poems, the most celebrated sets of quatrains of their period. And if I seem at times to dwell a little more on FitzGerald than on Tennyson, this will be because *In Memoriam* and its history have received the larger share of attention in the past and will probably be more familiar to readers.

From *Tennyson: Seven Essays*, edited by Philip Collins. © 1992 by The Macmillan Press Ltd.

First, then, let me recall the origins and progress of a friendship that, whatever else may be said of it, was one of the longest in the lives of the two men concerned. They were almost exactly the same age (within less than four months),—as Arthur Platt once said, everybody was born in 1809—had a similar dark complexion, and were of about the same above-average height and build. They also share the same modern biographer, Robert Bernard Martin. Unsurprisingly, Martin's life of FitzGerald is much shorter than his earlier life of Tennyson, but there are one or two striking parallel passages. For example, of Tennyson's siblings:

> One of [his] brothers was totally insane most of his life, another suffered from some form of mental illness nearly as incapacitating, a third was an opium addict, a fourth was severely alcoholic, and of the rest of the large family each had at least one bad mental breakdown in a long life.[1]

While of FitzGerald's seven siblings, Martin writes:

> All his family were mad, FitzGerald used to enjoy saying, but at least he had the advantage of knowing that he was insane. The wryness of the statement nearly blinds us to its essential truth. All his brothers and sisters were, in one way or another, peculiar. Some of them suffered from periodic mental breakdowns, and one was so odd that he became the subject of a chapter in a book on English eccentrics.[2]

In rank and wealth the two families had little in common: the FitzGeralds had 'an enormous fortune', and Edward enjoyed a private income and, after the death of his mother, was a rich man.

What they did have in common, though, was Cambridge, where their periods of residence overlapped by more than two years. FitzGerald knew Tennyson only slightly at Trinity but was greatly impressed by him and later remembered him as 'a sort of Hyperion'. He also remembered his readings and recitations, and his account furnishes fascinating evidence of Tennyson's vocal and elocutionary powers and of his oddities of pronunciation. Later they met in London, and in 1835 were together for a memorable holiday in the Lake District; FitzGerald's comment on this time sets the tone for their later relationship for, while he believed his friend to be a great man, he was quite prepared to make fun of him—'his little humours and grumpinesses were so droll that I was always laughing' (*Mem*, i, 152).

From 1837 they saw each other often in London, and there were boisterous bachelor dinners at The Cock near Temple Bar and at Bertolini's (which they nicknamed Dirtolini's) in Leicester Square. FitzGerald brought out a vein of humour in Tennyson that was not always evident and that did not survive his youth undiminished. He recalls, for instance, his gifts as a mimic, 'tak[ing] off the voices and expressions of well-known public characters', and in particular one remarkable party-piece:

> He used also to do the sun coming out from a cloud, and retiring into one again, with a gradual opening and shutting of the eyes, and with a great fluffing up of his hair into full wig and elevation of cravat and collar; George IV, in as comical and wonderful a way (*Mem*, i, 184).

In their more serious moments, Fitz, as Tennyson called him, was a willingly captive audience for Tennyson's readings of his poems. In March 1841 Fitz saw him in London 'with a little bit of dirty pipe in his mouth; and a particularly dirty vellum book of MSS on the sofa'[3]. This was what Fitz elsewhere called the 'butcher's book', and it was Fitz who 'carried him off with violence' to the publisher Moxon to arrange for publication of what became the 1842 volumes. His faith in his friend's poetic powers must have been gratifying and may have been crucial: Alfred, he declared, 'will publish such a volume as has not been published since the time of Keats; and which once published, will never be suffered to die'. This, at least, is the version loyally given in Sir Charles Tennyson's biography of his grandfather;[4] actually FitzGerald seems to have prefaced his tribute with the phrase with all his faults' (*Letters of EF*, i, 315)—and the point is worth making, since his admiration, though genuine, was not uncritical.

In the mid-forties Tennyson's poor health and his indulgence in tobacco and port caused concern to his friend. Already, though, they were drifting apart: FitzGerald was making new friends, and the epoch of the closest intimacy was over. After Tennyson's marriage they saw very little of each other: apart from one visit to Farringford in 1854 Fitz seems to have consistently declined invitations. He was clearly not keen on being just a member of a house-party; he was slightly jealous of Tennyson's other friends and impatient with his admirers; and he did not much care for Mrs Tennyson. What he longed for was a return to what he rather poignantly called the 'ante-laureate days' (*Mem*, i, 184), and in doing so he was of course not only yearning for a revival of their vanished intimacy but hankering after a return of his own vanished youth.

The relationship that I have so far, and so baldly, summarised can also be traced through the letters that passed, or failed to pass, between the two of them over a period of nearly fifty years. As one would expect, there are some evident gaps in the surviving record; but enough is available to tell its own story and convey its own suggestive implications. Of FitzGerald's letters to Tennyson, a total of 50 survive, of which all but one were written after Alfred's marriage. The solitary exception is a letter of 1835 in which, with exquisite tact, he offers to lend money to his friend; the offer seems to have been taken up, and the letter may have been carefully preserved for this reason. There were certainly others, but Tennyson presumably saw no reason to retain them. To the 49 letters from the period after covering the last 33 years of FitzGerald's life, must be added a further 31 written to Emily and usually intended also for Alfred's eyes or ears. With Tennyson the tally is much smaller and the balance the other way round, since 11 letters survive (some mere notes, and not all of them complete) from his bachelor years but only two from the years after 1850. There may have been others but they can hardly have been numerous, for in 1869 we find Fitz remarking that he has just received the first letter from Alfred for fifteen or twenty years. We know that Fitz told Thackeray in 1852 that he had just burned most of *his* letters, partly to avoid the risk of eventual publication 'according to the vile fashion of the day' (*Letters of EF*, ii, 51); and some of Tennyson's may have received similar treatment; but there are few references to letters that have failed to survive and many allusions, teasing or mildly reproachful, to Tennyson's lack of eagerness as a correspondent. 'Do let me have a line from one of you one day,' he writes in 1854; 'at least let me have a line to tell about yourselves' in 1856; 'Write as little as you please, only write' in 1867; and, forgivingly, in 1872, 'I think you would generally give £100 sooner than write a Letter' (*Letters of EF*, ii, 135, 211; iii, 57, 346).

Remembering that Tennyson's pen was far from idle in other respects, we may be inclined to forgive his shortcomings as a correspondent; and Fitz would have known that they were nothing new, for as early as 1842 Tennyson had asked pardon for his 'ungracious silence in return for so many kind letters', pleading 'I know you like writing which I hate mortally', and in 1847 he had declared 'Aint I a beast for not answering you before?' (*Letters*, i, 204, 281). What must have been harder to stomach was the way in which Emily Tennyson interposed herself between her husband and his old friend: it was she who answered Fitz's letters, and she to whom, as we have seen, many of his were addressed. His situation resembled that of one who, hoping to have a word with the great man, has to make do with his polite but firm secretary; and although Fitz is invariably courteous and good-humoured in writing to Emily (though not always in what he said about her to others), he may well have felt sadness and even humiliation at his treatment. Even Tennyson's enthusiasm for the *Rubáiyát* must have lost some of its power to delight by being communicated through Emily. (It is pleasant to know that in about 1860 Tennyson was not only praising Fitz's Cambridge idyll in prose, *Euphranor*, to F. T. Palgrave but also 'commended to me warmly FitzGerald's famous *Omar* paraphrase' (*Mem*, ii, 505)—but the private praise did not of course appear in print until after Fitz's death.) Tennyson's earliest surviving letter to him, dating from 1835, is a touching tribute to their friendship at that period, though characteristically occasioned by Fitz's reproach that an earlier letter has gone unanswered. Relaxed, affectionate and humorous, it implies a rewarding relationship and, perhaps giving away more than was intended, casts Fitz in the role of Horatio to Tennyson's Hamlet by applying to him the lines 'as just a man / As e'er my conversation coped withal' (*Letters*, i, 132). But while Tennyson, married and famous, continued to play Hamlet, Fitz had been demoted to an attendant lord; if he ever re-read the letter he might have murmured 'Oh Alfred, what a failing off was there!'

FitzGerald's later letters resort to some odd contortions in response to the curious epistolary situation wherein his letters addressed to his friend would normally be opened and answered by another. A letter of 1881 begins touchingly, 'My dear old Alfred, I suppose that scarce a day passes without my thinking of you', but then perforce continues, 'have told you why I do not write to you; because of Mrs Tennyson's having to reply, which I do not like troubling her to do' (*Letters of EF*, iv, 455–6). If Emily or Alfred had cared to read between the lines they would have found plenty of food for thought; and such moments are numerous—in 1870, for instance, a letter ends, 'Do not trouble the Mistress to write in reply' (ibid., iii, 220).

Tennyson's lament for 'the days that are no more' would have found a ready echo in Fitz's bosom, and indeed he quotes the line in a letter written (not to Tennyson) at one of the few emotional crises of his life. One result of his feeling that the best days of their friendship were over was an impatience with Tennyson's later poetry with nearly everything, in fact, later than the 1842 volumes in the birth of which he had had a hand, though he made a partial exception in the case of *Maud*. As early as 1851, he avows a fondness for 'Tennyson's *old* poems' (ibid., ii, 28), pointedly underlining the adjective and implicitly showing scant respect, for Tennyson's new poem, *In Memoriam*. When *Maud* appears he admits to liking its '*Drama*' but draws the line at what he calls 'the Lyrical Execution' though even that, he quickly adds, is better than 'Princess and Memoriam' (ibid., ii., 234). With a consistency that must have been less than gratifying to Tennyson, he praises what he calls 'the old 1842 Volumes'; and a phrase in another letter brings his barely hidden motives right to the surface, 'Oh the dear old 1842 Days and Editions!' (ibid., iii, 59, 106). Elsewhere he recalls 'having heard nearly all I care for ... from your own Lips' (ibid., ii, 413). In 1876 he tells Hallam that he 'gave up all hopes of [Tennyson] after "The Princess"'—and again we may note that this uncompromisingly dismisses *In Memoriam*—adding that 'none of the songs had "the old champagne flavour"' (*Mem, i*, 253). On the same page of the *Memoir* Hallam Tennyson records: that the only song in *The Princess* for which FitzGerald had a good word to say 'was "Blow, Bugle, Blow," commemorating the echoes at Killarney', and he claims plausibly that 'Nothing either by Thackeray or by my father met FitzGerald's approbation unless he had first seen it in manuscript'.

Tennyson went on sending him his new volumes as they appeared, and they were politely acknowledged but received without enthusiasm. To Frederick Tennyson he wrote at the beginning of 1881:

> Alfred sent me his last Volume [*Ballads and Other Poems*], which to say the most of it, did not in my opinion add anything to what he had done before, and so (as I think) might as well have remained unpublished. (*Letters of EF*, iv, 388).

It was understandable that FitzGerald should think poorly of poems that came to him in the cold formality of print compared with those he had seen in manuscript and heard from the poet's lips—and which moreover were inseparably associated with the days of their youth and their closest friendship. Tennyson's marriage, the laureateship, his growing fame and his grander lifestyle must have produced in his friend a sad and painful sense of being left behind, stranded on the margin when he had once been close to the centre. He made no secret of his dislike of those he called Tennyson's 'aesthetic Worshippers'; and the same disapproving epithet was applied to Emily: telling his friend Pollock in 1864, with an unusual touch of sharpness, that he had received 'a kind letter from Mrs AT—who answers my yearly letter to her husband', he permits himself to add:

> She is a graceful lady, but I think that she and other aesthetic and hysterical Ladies have hurt AT, who, *quoad* Artist, would have done better to remain single in Lincolnshire, or married a jolly Woman who would have laughed and cried without any reason why. (Ibid., ii, 538)

A letter of 1874 to Richard Monckton Milnes sums up his grievances:

> I used to tell Tennyson thirty years ago that he should be a Dragoon, or in some active Employment that would keep his Soul stirring, instead of revolving in itself in idleness and Tobacco

smoke. And now he has sunk into Coterie-worship, and (I tremble to say it) in the sympathy of his most Ladylike, gentle, Wife. An old Housekeeper like Molière's would have been far better for him, I think. (Ibid., iii, 487)

In the light of what has been said, it is difficult to endorse Sir Charles Tennyson's claim that 'the two friends had never known any weakening of the bond between them'.[5] As we shall see later, their friendship was to have an unpredictable and touching epilogue; but for the last two-thirds of the half-century they knew each other it is hard not to believe that the 'bond' meant much more to FitzGerald than to Tennyson. It is his life of FitzGerald, not his life of Tennyson, for which Martin uses as a title the Shakespearian phrase 'with friends possessed', but FitzGerald's kind of possessing was an anxious, emotional preoccupation or possessiveness rather than a tranquil and secure enjoyment; and one wonders whether Tennyson's perhaps slightly conscience-stricken remark on hearing of Fitz's death—'I had no truer friend' (*Letters of EF*, iv, 598)—could have been used by Fitz if *he* had been the survivor.

All of this might lead one to suggest that it ought to have been FitzGerald rather than Tennyson who produced an *In Memoriam*, a painfully wrought monument to a friendship, though of course Tennyson's poem, like 'Lycidas', is a good deal more than a lament for or a tribute to an individual. What I want to suggest now is that FitzGerald's own masterpiece is, less overtly, itself a commemoration of an intense friendship and the expression of a sense of loss, and that in some respects its origins curiously resemble the more familiar ones of Tennyson's poem. The genesis and the 17-year gestation of the latter need not be rehearsed; but the birth of the *Rubáiyát* is a less familiar story, and, though Martin's recent biography reports the relevant facts, he does not, it seems to me, fully bring out the underlying pattern or draw attention to the significant conclusions.

'FitzGerald's translation of Omar Khayyám': the idea is such a tritely familiar one to us that it is easy to forget its inherent strangeness—the phenomenon of such a man producing such a work needs to be accounted for. There is nothing in FitzGerald's literary track-record before or after to encourage the supposition that he might be capable of producing one of the most widely admired, most oft-quoted and most frequently reprinted poems of the Victorian age. Most of his undertakings were little more than the recreations of a bookish gentleman with too much time on his hands: a glossary of nautical expressions, a calendar of Charles Lamb's life, a dictionary of the characters referred to by Madame de Sévigné, a children's version of the story of Little Nell, translations from Greek and Spanish.

There is not a shred of evidence of that 'incessant activity of mind' that V. S. Pritchett has identified as the hallmark of genius; and FitzGerald, who was wont to refer to himself as 'poking out' or 'puddling away at' or 'trifling with' his literary and philological enterprises; seems to have accepted at an early stage that his talents were of a minor order. As he told Frederick Tennyson in 1850, 'I pretend to no Genius, but to Taste: which, according to my aphorism, is the feminine of Genius' (ibid., i, 664). And yet, against all probability, this rather lethargic man tackled the daunting task of learning Persian; translated a medieval Persian poet into verse that became so widely known that it fills three columns in the *Oxford Dictionary of Quotations* (nearly as much as *In Memoriam*); and went on revising his poem over a period of twenty years. What can it have been that uniquely jolted FitzGerald out of his indolence and dilettantism?

The answer lies in his personal life; for the most emotionally turbulent period of an existence otherwise placid to the point of tedium was the years from 1852 to 1857, and especially 1856–71, and this precisely corresponds to his study of Persian and his translation of Omar Khayyám. The story of these years is one of deep attachment followed by loss and deprivation; but to understand it we need to go back nearly a decade to 1844, when FitzGerald made the acquaintance of a brilliant 18-year-old called Edward Cowell.

Cowell was to become a Cambridge professor and one of the founding members of the British Academy, but his origins were humble, and his early career testifies both to the effectiveness of self-help and to the vitality of provincial culture in the early Victorian period. The son of an Ipswich maltster, he left the local grammar school at 16 on the death of his father and entered the family business; but, well before this time, he had discovered in a local library the work of the eighteenth-century orientalist Sir William Jones and, at the tender age of 14, had become fired with an enthusiasm for Persian and Sanskrit. He taught himself Persian—as he casually observed nearly sixty years later, 'I soon learned the character'[6]—and at sixteen was already contributing verse translations to the *Asiatic Journal* and elsewhere. By a stroke of good fortune, orientalists and linguists were surprisingly thick on the ground in East Anglia in the 1840s, and Cowell took lessons from Major Thomas Hockley, who had retired to Ipswich after service in India. Another scholarly Anglo-Indian, Edward Moor, author of the popular *Hindu Pantheon*, was not far away, and George Borrow after his wanderings had married and settled at Oulton Broad.

FitzGerald met Cowell through a local clergyman; a close friendship based on a common enthusiasm for languages and literature developed between them; and FitzGerald, always ready to idealise someone who possessed the intellectual powers or the physical prowess that he felt himself

to lack, looked up to the boy who was half his age as his natural superior. The friendship survived Cowell's early marriage, and did not flag when, at the age of 24, he went to Oxford as a specimen of a rather rare Victorian species, the married undergraduate. It was Cowell who in 1852 suggested to FitzGerald that he should take up the study of Persian. FitzGerald's father had died earlier in the year, and perhaps his friend sensed that he needed a new interest in life to cheer him up. FitzGerald's initial enthusiasm was not great, but he persisted in what amounted to a correspondence course conducted from Oxford. By the end of 1853 he was doing 'a little every day' (ibid., ii, 116) and sending his translations for correction.

After graduating, Cowell remained at Oxford as a part-time employee in the Bodleian, and there in 1856 he came across an uncatalogued manuscript of some quatrains by a poet named Omar Khayyám who had received very little attention from scholars and to most educated men at that date was not even a name. These he promptly transcribed and sent to FitzGerald. The timing of events at this turning point of FitzGerald's quiet life is significant. In January of 1856 he learned to his dismay that his energetic and ambitious young friend was applying for a post in India; he had written to him on the 12th of that month that 'Your talk of going to India makes my Heart hang really heavy at my side' (ibid., ii, 194) and had tried— in vain, and not altogether disinterestedly—to persuade him to change his mind. In February Cowell accepted the appointment to Calcutta. Meanwhile, he was continuing to provide long-distance supervision of FitzGerald's Persian studies, and letters were passing frequently between Suffolk and Oxford: of FitzGerald's to the Cowells nearly thirty survive from the first four months of the year. Early in April, Cowell told his friend about his transcription of the Omar manuscript. At the end of June, FitzGerald went to spend a fortnight with the Cowells: a farewell visit, for they sailed for India on 1 August; and it was during this visit that Cowell gave FitzGerald a complete transcript of the manuscript of the *Rubáiyát*. It was in fact, and poignantly, a parting gift; for though pressed to go to see them off, FitzGerald declined, feeling that it would be unbearably painful (as he told Cowell at the end of July) 'to say a Good-Bye that costs me so much' (ibid., ii, 236).

But the most revealing document from this period is a letter that FitzGerald wrote to Tennyson on the day after leaving the Cowells at the end of his farewell visit. FitzGerald's friendships were passions—and tragic passions, since even their sunniest moments were haunted by the thought of the inevitability of separation. At what must have seemed like the desolating termination of an intense friendship (for he was not to know that the Cowells would survive the hazards of life in Calcutta and eventually return), it was natural that he should have turned for consolation to one of his oldest friends. In that letter he tells Tennyson that while staying with the Cowells they read together 'some curious Infidel and Epicurean Tetrastichs by a Persian of the 11th Century—as savage against Destiny, etc., as Manfred—but mostly of Epicurean Pathos....' (It is, incidentally, in this same letter that he confesses his lack of enthusiasm for 'Princess and Memoriam' (ibid., ii, 233–4).)

Three months after the Cowells sailed, FitzGerald married Lucy Barton, daughter of the deceased Quaker poet and friend of FitzGerald, Bernard Barton. This disastrous and short-lived venture can perhaps be partly explained by his state of emotional confusion after their departure. What he did cleave to was Omar: his first letter to Cowell in India refers to his Persian studies, and his second and third discuss his reading of Omar in detail. 'It is very pleasant to think,' he writes early in 1857, 'that we can go on exchanging our notes—in which you will still be Teacher—almost as easily as if we were only London and Oxford apart' (ibid., ii, 252). By a stroke of luck Cowell discovered in a Calcutta library another manuscript of the *Rubáiyát*, and sent a transcription of it to England, enabling FitzGerald to commemorate the anniversary of his farewell to Cowell by completing his first perusal of this new source. At about the same time we find the first references to his attempts at translation.

To FitzGerald, it seems clear, Omar Khayyám provided a lifeline to keep afloat a friendship that might otherwise have sunk without trace. To Cowell he confessed that he was 'still harping on our old Studies' and that 'Omar breathes a sort of Consolation to me!', while to Tennyson he was more explicitly self-aware: 'I keep on reading foolish Persian ... chiefly because of its connecting me with the Cowells' (ibid., ii, 273, 291). Before the end of the year he is thinking of sending to *Fraser's Magazine* 'a few Quatrains in English Verse' (ibid., ii, 305), the first fruits of a highly uncharacteristic burst of creative energy. In the context of what Carlyle once called FitzGerald's 'innocent *far niente* life' it is truly startling to find him telling Cowell, once the version of the *Rubáiyát* is completed, 'I supposed very few People have ever taken such Pains in Translation as I have ...' (ibid., ii, 335).

This bare summary perhaps makes the essential points sufficiently clear. For FitzGerald the study of Persian in general and of Omar Khayyám in particular were closely woven into the texture of his friendship with Cowell: his *Rubáiyát* might later be taken as an expression of the *Zeitgeist*, but its origins were intimately personal. FitzGerald's friend had not died of a stroke in Vienna, but his departure must have seemed almost as final ('Shall we ever meet again? I think not ...', he writes gloomily in one letter (ibid., ii, 260)); and, though less shocking, it was more painfully prolonged. Nor is it absurd to compare Tennyson's attitude towards the brilliance and promise of Hallam with FitzGerald's hero-worship of one whom an obituarist was much later to describe as 'not only the greatest Oriental scholar that England has produced, but probably also the most widely learned man of our time' (*Athenaeum*, 14 February 1903, p. 209). It also seems undeniable that, just as the excessively long-drawn-out labours on *In Memoriam* were a means of sustaining a kind of relationship with a dead man, FitzGerald turned to Omar—given to him by Cowell, read together at their last meeting, and a continuing justification for frequent letter-writing—as a link with the friend from whom he was separated not indeed by the grave but by what Matthew Arnold had a few years earlier called the 'estranging sea'.

But the two poems have more in common than a shared impulse to commemorate an intimacy terminated in its prime. Both were published anonymously (though Tennyson's authorship was common knowledge); both continued to grow after the original publication (though FitzGerald's expanded more dramatically, from 75 to 110 quatrains in the second edition); both were found to provide to provide consolation (though, as we shall see, not for the same readers). The *Rubáiyát* is ostensibly a translation but takes such liberties with both the structure and the details of the original as to entitle us to regard it as substantially an original work: *In Memoriam*, it is true, is more obviously autobiographical; but as Susan Shatto and Marion Shaw have recently shown, Tennyson's successive revisions tended to make it appear less personal.

When all is said and done, however, the differences (which sometimes amount to antitheses) are more important than the resemblances. Tennyson, after all, was famous (as I have pointed out elsewhere, the epithet 'Tennysonian', was current at least as early as the mid-forties, while FitzGerald was unknown and seems not to have been named as the author of his poem until nearly 16 years after its original appearance. *In Memoriam* was an instant success, but the *Rubáiyát* had a long wait for recognition. That delay was surely not just the result of FitzGerald's obscurity and disinclination for self-advertisement: his poem had to create the taste by which it could be enjoyed, or at the very least had to bide its time until there occurred a change in the intellectual and spiritual weather favourable to its flourishing. With remarkable appropriateness, Tennyson's poem appeared in the first year of the new decade and 11 months before the opening of the Great Exhibition; FitzGerald's appeared in the last year of the decade, the year of *On the Origin of Species*. Even as he confronts the threats to faith posed by the new science Tennyson is conservative and reassuring with the strength of his convictions; the *Rubáiyát*, a *fin-de-siècle* poem born before its time, is uncompromisingly unorthodox and challenging with the power of its scepticism.

The steady increase in FitzGerald's popularity during the remaining decades of the century was partly at Tennyson's expense. 'Everybody admires Tennyson now,' Walter Bagehot had declared in the year in which the *Rubáiyát* appeared; but John Jump has pointed out that criticisms of Tennyson became common, especially among the younger generation of readers, from about 1860.[7] A writer in the *North British Review* in 1864 drew attention to Tennyson's 'empire over some, and the indifference to his poetry of other by no means less able judges';[8] and things went far enough for Gerard Manley Hopkins, writing in 1879, to express his grief 'to hear [Tennyson] depreciated, as of late years has often been done'. Grieved or not, Hopkins had not a few reservations of his own: while (with ecumenical generosity) he thought *In Memoriam* 'a divine poem', he suggested that the *Idylls* should be called *Charades from the Middle Ages* and dismissed *Maud, The Princess* and other poems as 'an ungentlemanly row'. Ten years earlier, Alfred Austin claimed that Tennyson's 'fame has steadily increased precisely as his genuine poetical power has steadily waned', and (unconsciously echoing FitzGerald) suggested that 1842 represented the climax of his real achievement. Soon afterwards Swinburne—a notable early admirer of the *Rubáiyát*—attacked the ethical pretensions of the *Idylls of the King*.[9]

These were, of course, precisely the years that saw the rise in popularity of FitzGerald's poem. Charles Eliot Norton contributed a long essay to the *North American Review* in 1869 in which, reviewing the second edition, he declared that 'The prevailing traits of Omar Khayyám are so coincident with certain characteristics of the spiritual temper of our own generation'[10]—a point that was to recur frequently in subsequent criticism, and a clue to the growing popularity of the poem as the end of the century hove in sight. In the next decade a contributor to *Fraser's Magazine* (identified as Jessie E. Cadell) observed somewhat disapprovingly: 'That we have heard a good deal of late about Omar Khayyám is not due, we fear, to any increase in the number of Persian scholars, but to the fact that the existing translation harmonizes with a special phase of modern thought'.[11] On a less magisterial level, copies of the *Rubáiyát* became familiar items in the middle-brow cultural scene. Writing after the turn of the century, FitzGerald's great-niece testified to the popularity of the poem in her own generation:

> Quotations from Omar are in the mouth of every cultured 'miss' in real life and in fiction. Half-crown and penny magazines alike drag in his name. No novelist of pretension is happy unless one chapter boasts a quotation as headline or some heroine goes through the psychological moment of her existence with the

Rubáiyát at hand on her dressing-table to point out to her the nothingness of all things. In every conceivable binding and at all variety of price it lies on bookshop counters and railway stalls.[12]

One more recent commentator speaks of 'the extraordinary rage [in the 1890s] for FitzGerald's *Omar*'; another refers to the widespread use of Omar Khayyám's name for 'cigarettes, cigars, pipes, tobacco, wines, soaps, pens, and dozens of other commercial items, both in England and in America'.[13] One offshoot of the Omar cult was the foundation in 1891 of the Omar Khayyám Club, the list of whose members includes some of the best-known authors and critics of the day—among them Hardy, Gissing, Newbolt, Conan Doyle, Gosse, Lang and Clodd. Hardy's autobiography records that he attended a meeting in 1895 in the company of Meredith, and made his first public speech (and one of the very few he ever delivered) on that occasion; later he visited FitzGerald's grave; and it was a favourite stanza from the *Rubáiyát* that he asked his wife to read to him on his deathbed.[14]

So that when Hardy, in his first great novel of the nineties, speaks of Angel Clare as one who 'persistently elevated Hellenic Paganism at the expense of Christianity' (*Tess of the d'Urbervilles*, ch. 49), we may well be justified in enlarging 'Hellenic' to embrace Omar's Persia as well as in seeing this as a declaration of personal faith on the part of the author. During, his last minutes of consciousness, Hardy seems to have felt no craving to hear a stanza from *In Memoriam*, and, there is a sense in which he and his contemporaries had to choose between FitzGerald and Tennyson as they had to choose between Disraeli and Gladstone or between Huxley and Wilberforce, since the two poets could be seen as standing for contrasting responses to the anxieties of the age. Whatever it may be for us, for Tennyson's contemporaries, as Humphry House has pointed out, *In Memoriam* was primarily 'a great poem of spiritual and emotional victory'.[15] Victoria herself had found 'comfort' in the poem after Albert's death, and A. C. Bradley was to imagine 'readers who never cared for a poem before' turning to it at; a time of grief and murmuring '"This is what I dumbly feel"'. But as the century wore on, an increasing number found their instinctive convictions expressed—strikingly, memorably, and eminently quotably—in the pagan *Rubáiyát* rather than in Tennyson's Christian poem. Leslie Stephen and Charles Eliot Norton, who both lost their wives in the seventies, opted for FitzGerald to provide solace; and Stephen's *An Agnostic's Apology*, published in the year after his wife's death, seems not only to reflect his bereavement but to echo the pessimism of Omar as transmitted by FitzGerald:

There is a deep sadness in the world. Turn and twist the thought as you may, there is no escape. Optimism would be soothing if it were possible; in fact, it is impossible, and therefore a constant mockery.[16]

A revealing case-study of changing taste is furnished by Meredith, whose early enthusiasm for Tennyson evaporated far enough for him to declare at the end of the sixties that Tennyson was 'twenty years behind his time' and to speak of his latest work as 'lines like yards of linen drapery for the delight of ladies who would be in the fashion'. Earlier in the decade he had been one of the first to respond enthusiastically to the *Rubáiyát*: as he recalled in a letter written only a few weeks before his death, the unknown poem had been brought to his attention in 1862 by Swinburne:

> It happened that he [Swinburne] was expected one day [14 June 1862] on a visit to me, and he being rather late I went along the road to meet him. At last he appeared waving the white sheet of what seemed to be a pamphlet. He greeted me with a triumphant shout of a stanza new to my ears. This was FitzGerald's *Omar Khayyám*, and we lay on a heathery knoll beside my cottage reading a stanza alternately, indifferent to the dinner-bell, until a prolonged summons reminded us of appetite. After the meal we took to the paper-covered treasure again. Suddenly Swinburne ran upstairs, and I had my anticipations. He returned with feather-pen, blue folio-sheet, and a dwarf bottle of red ink. In an hour he had finished thirteen stanzas of his 'Laus Veneris', and rarely can one poet have paid so high a compliment to another as FitzGerald received.[17]

Both Meredith and Swinburne, we may reflect, belonged to a younger generation than Tennyson, and Swinburne was barely in his teens when *In Memoriam* appeared. For them, and for many others of their generation, Tennyson's reassuring surveyor's report that in spite of surface-cracks the edifice of faith was structurally sound must have seemed to belong, like the traditionalism of the laureateship and the optimism of the Great Exhibition, among the outmoded notions of their elders, while the pessimism and hedonism of the *Rubáiyát* were much more in tune with their own worldview. It was in fact in the mid-fifties, between the appearances of the two poems I have been discussing, that the words 'hedonism' and 'hedonist' seem to have entered the language: the *OED* records their first use in 1856, the year in which FitzGerald encountered Omar.

But 'the new hedonism', as Grant Allen called it in an essay contributed to the *Fortnightly Review* in 1894, came into its own in the eighties and nineties. Writing in the same journal in 1889, Edmund Gosse was able to look back on the causes for the *Rubáiyát*'s rise to fame:

> Whether it accurately represents or not the sentiments of a Persian astronomer of the eleventh century is a question which fades into insignificance beside the fact that it stimulated and delighted a generation of young readers, to whom it appealed in the same manner, and along parallel lines with, the poetry of Morris, Swinburne, and the Rossettis.... The same reassertion of the sensuous elements of literature, the same obedience to the call for a richer music and a more exotic; and impassioned aspect of manners, the same determination to face the melancholy problems of life and find a solace for them in art....[18]

Gosse's unintentionally ironic claim is that FitzGerald, the most reactionary of men, had written a modern poem without knowing it and had anticipated the aestheticism that he never lived to see but would certainly have taken a dim view of.

In the closing decades of the century, then, FitzGerald's stock was steadily rising, and for a generation or two his poem must have been a serious contender for the title of the most popular longer poem in English, with perhaps only Gray's *Elegy* (of which FitzGerald was a passionate admirer) and Housman's *A Shropshire Lad* (not very dissimilar to the *Rubáiyát* in its broad appeal) as non-Tennysonian rivals. (Housman, incidentally, who must have found FitzGerald deeply congenial, once observed of *In Memoriam* that its argument could be summed up as 'things must come right in the end, because it would be so very unpleasant if they did not'.) 'All the English are crazy for Omar' says an Arab character in Muriel Spark's *The Mandelbaum Gate*, and although the claim hardly holds good in a novel set in 1961, it faithfully echoes the reality of an earlier age.

Modern criticism and scholarship has, of course, reversed the process I have been describing: it is Tennyson, not FitzGerald, who is the hero of theses and conferences—and not unreasonably so, since beside the massiveness of his achievement even the *Rubáiyát* seems puny and anorexic. FitzGerald remains a one-poem man; the *Rubáiyát* in its final version is less than half the length of *Enoch Arden*; and the story of its birth is largely contained in less than three years of FitzGerald's long life, between that painful and creatively fertile visit to the Cowells in the summer of 1856 and the publication of the first edition. Still, he may be more of a presence in the twentieth-century than has sometimes been supposed: it has been suggested, for example, that T. S. Eliot not only unblushingly plagiarises A. C. Benson's biography of FitzGerald in the opening lines of 'Gerontion' but is greatly influenced by FitzGerald's letters throughout his early poetry.[19] And it is worth remembering that Tennyson himself commemorates their long friendship in what has sometimes been regarded (in my view rightly) as one of his finest shorter poems. 'Ally has been finishing one of his old world poems begun about the Ulysses period and discarded', wrote Emily Tennyson to Edward Lear in 1883.[20] The 'old world poem' was 'Tiresias', and Tennyson may have been partly prompted by the reflection that exactly half a century had passed since he had begun it. In these circumstances it was natural to think of dedicating the finished poem to the surviving friend closely associated with that period of his life, 1883 being also the fiftieth anniversary of their meeting. The dedicatory poem 'To E. FitzGerald' commemorates both their long friendship and their last meeting seven years earlier. That FitzGerald, who by an uncanny coincidence died a few days after the poem was written, never read it was perhaps on the whole a good thing, since (as Christopher Ricks has pointed out) his oldest friend, born in the same year as himself, had contrived to get his age wrong. But this final piece of thoughtlessness, so characteristic of Tennyson's side of the relationship, hardly mars a magnificent memorial that has something of the quality of an act of atonement.

Charting the currents of nineteenth-century belief and feeling, David Daiches has drawn attention to the changes that took place from the 'moral dandyism' of Byron's 'pre-evangelical sensibility' to the 'activist stoicism' of Henley and Housman: by the end of the century, he argues, it was no longer possible 'for a sceptic such as Housman to use his scepticism as a passport to hedonism'.[21] FitzGerald, born in the year in which *Childe Harold* was begun, seems closer to Byron than to Henley or Housman in temperament as well as background—which perhaps makes it all the more paradoxical that his greatest popularity should have been in the *fin-de-siècle* years. In the last third of the century the *Rubáiyát* advertises the hedonistic alternative; but FitzGerald's own distaste for the Laureate's unrelenting seriousness was articulated long before his own poem was even begun—to be precise, on the last day of the Tennysonian *annus mirabilis* of 1850, in a letter to Frederick Tennyson—and since the passage also conveys in a few lines the essence of their relationship it will serve as a fitting conclusion to these comparative observations:

> But you know Alfred himself never writes, nor indeed cares a
> halfpenny about one, though he is very well satisfied to see one

when one falls in his way. You will think I have a spite against him for some neglect, when I say this, and say besides that I cannot care for his *In Memoriam*. Not so, if I know myself: I always thought the same of him, and was just as well satisfied with it as now. His poem I never did greatly affect: nor can I learn to do so: it is full of fine things, but it is monotonous, and has that air of being evolved by a Poetical Machine of the highest order. (*Letters of EF*, 696)

NOTES

1. Robert Bernard Martin, *Tennyson: the Unquiet Heart* (Oxford and London: Clarendon Press and Faber & Faber, 1980); p. 10.

2. Robert Bernard Martin, *With Friends Possessed: A Life of Edward FitzGerald* (London: Faber & Faber, 1985), p. 22.

3. *The Letters of Edward FitzGerald*, ed. A. M. and A. B. Terhune (Princeton, NJ: Princeton University Press, 1980), 1. 272; hereafter cited as *Letters of EF*.

4. Charles Tennyson, *Alfred Tennyson* (London: Macmillan, 1949), p. 191.

5. Ibid., pp. 467–8.

6. Quoted in Cowell's obituary (*Athenaeum*, 14 February 1903, p. 209) from 'a memorable address given to the Royal Asiatic Society in 1898'.

7. *Tennyson: the Critical Heritage*, ed. J. D. Jump (London: Routledge & Kegan Paul, 1967), pp. 12–13, 216.

8. Quoted by Humphry House in 'Tennyson and the Spirit of the Age', *All in Due Time* (London: Rupert Hart-Davis, 1955), p. 123.

9. *Tennyson: the Critical Heritage*, pp. 295, 319, 334–5.

10. *North American Review*, cix (October 1869), p. 565. Norton's review, published anonymously, is, according to A. M. Terhune (*The Life of Edward FitzGerald* [New Haven Conn.: Yale University Press, 1947], p. 209), the first review of FitzGerald's poem to appear. It was prompted by the second edition of the *Rubáiyát* (1868), which is discussed in tandem with J. B. Nicolas's *Les Quatrains de Khayyam, traduits du Persan* (Paris, 1867). The first review to appear in England seems to be that in *Fraser's Magazine*, n.s. i (June 1870); the anonymous reviewer was Thomas W. Hinchliff, who draws a comparison between some of FitzGerald's stanzas and the 'infant crying in the night' stanza of *In Memoriam*.

11. J. E. C[adell], 'The True Omar Khayam', *Fraser's Magazine*, n.s., xix (May 1879), p. 650. The reviewer notes of the translation that 'its inexactness has allowed for the Infusion of a modern element'. FitzGerald himself describes the review as 'a temperate and just Article' (to E. B. Cowell, June 1879: *Letters of EF*, iv, 225). It is perhaps not unfair to mention that Mrs Cadell was herself at work on a text and translation of Omar that remained unfinished at her death in 1884.

12. Mary Eleanor FitzGerald-Kerrich, 'Edward FitzGerald: a Personal Reminiscence by his Great-Niece', *Nineteenth Century*, lxv (1909), p. 468.

13. John A. Lester, Jr, *Journey through Despair 1880–1914: Transformations in British Literary Culture* (Princeton, NJ: Princeton University Press, 1968), p. 8; Sol Gittleman, 'John Hay as a Critic of the Rubáiyát', *Victorian Newsletter*, xxiv (1963), p. 26.

14. F. E. Hardy, *The Life of Thomas Hardy* (London: Macmillan, 1962), pp. 268, 446.

15. *All in Due Time*, p. 135.

16. *Fortnightly Review*, n.s., xix, 1 June 1876, p. 857.

17. *The Letters of George Meredith*, ed. C. L. Cline (Oxford: The Clarendon Press, 1970), i. 407, ii. 1692.

18. 'Edward FitzGerald', *Fortnightly Review*, xlvi (July 1889), pp. 65–6.

19. J. A. Clark, 'On First Looking into Benson's FitzGerald', in *Fifty Years of the South Atlantic Quarterly*, ed. W. B. Hamilton (North Carolina: Duke University Press, 1952). The facetious tone of this essay makes it difficult to know how seriously Clark means to be taken: some of the alleged echoes are unconvincing, but others are undeniably startling.

20. *The Letters of Emily Lady Tennyson*, ed. James O. Hoge (Pennsylvania State University Press, 1974), p. 327.

21. David Daiches, *Some Late Victorian Attitudes* (London: André Deutsch, 1969), pp. 15–16.

ARTHUR FREEMAN

Bernard Quaritch and 'My Omar':
The Struggle for FitzGerald's Rubáiyát

As a publisher, Bernard Quaritch's principal claim to memory lies in his association with Edward FitzGerald. Quaritch's imprint appears on the first four editions of *The Rubáiyát of Omar Khayyám* (1859, 1868, 1872, and 1879), as well as on the 1876 'public' *Agamemnon* and the deathbed *Readings in Crabbe* (1883), and his instrumentality in popularizing *The Rubáiyát* was well recognized in its time. 'I am delighted at the glory E.F.G. has gained by his translation', wrote FitzGerald's old friend W. B. Donne in 1876, 'and Bernard Quaritch deserves a piece of plate or a statue for the way he has thrust the Rubáiyát to the front';[1] for his own part Quaritch treasured the relationship, increasingly as time passed and, FitzGerald's reputation took wing, and far more for its reflected 'glory' than its cash value.

But profit and proprietorship were never matters of indifference to the great bookseller, as the ensuing narrative will indicate. The tale of the first printing of FitzGerald's slender classic, its initial obscurity, its 'discovery' by various readers—including Swinburne and D. G. Rossetti—in Quaritch's penny-box in 1861, and its subsequent career as an international 'craze' (FitzGerald's own term) is too well-known to repeat in detail,[2] but the beginnings were simple enough. In 1858 FitzGerald had offered thirty-five quatrains to J. W. Parker at *Fraser's Magazine*, but after some six months of silence he reclaimed his manuscript, added forty more quatrains 'which I

From *The Book Collector*. © 1997 by The Collector Limited.

kept out for fear of being too strong' (EFG to E. B. Cowell, 2 November 1858), and resolved to 'print fifty copies and give [them] away'. In the event he commissioned about 250 wrapped copies from G. Norman, a Covent Garden printer, chose anonymity, and arranged for Quaritch—with whom he had corresponded over book purchases since 1853, and whom 'no wickedness can hurt' (EFG to W. H. Thompson, 9 December 1861)—to put his firm's name and address to the booklet, advertise it, and stock it. FitzGerald himself paid for the printing, the few advertisements, 'and other incidental Expenses regarding Omar', as 'I wish to do you'—he wrote to Quaritch on 5 April 1859—'as little *harm* as possible'. The British Museum stamped their deposit copy on 30 March, a day before FitzGerald's fiftieth birthday, but only two of the review copies that Quaritch sent out bore fruit,[3] and FitzGerald's personal supply of forty copies (requested 5 April, 'by Eastern Rail') might well have lasted him out the decade, given his diffidence in presenting them.[4]

How many Quaritch actually sold at a shilling we do not know, although in 1899 he, or the shop's cataloguer, maintained that it fell 'absolutely dead at the published price', and by July 1861 a number were consigned to the penny-box outside Quaritch's old Castle Street premises— his new shop at 15 Piccadilly having just opened. There they attracted the attention of two literary passers-by, Whitley Stokes and John Ormsby, and through them reached Rossetti and Swinburne, and latterly (when the price had risen, as Swinburne whimsically complained, 'to the sinfully extravagant sum of twopence') a host of new readers, including William Morris, Edward Burne-Jones, George Meredith, and John Ruskin. Perhaps this flutter of activity returned the title to Quaritch's Piccadilly shelves, for an old friend of FitzGerald's found a copy there in December (*Letters*, ii:417), and while part of the press-run may have been 'sold as waste-paper' or 'as much lost as sold' in the bookseller's move, 'some ten copies' turned up in January 1866 (*Letters*, ii:417–18 and iii:81) and temporarily satisfied retail demand. By October 1867 Quaritch was asking 3s. 6d. apiece for these relics ('I blush to see it!' FitzGerald twitted him), which encouraged the prospect of a second edition, with 'some 20 or 30 more Stanzas' (EFG to BQ, 14 October 1867). There is no indication that Quaritch credited FitzGerald's bookbuying account with any part of these late sales, however, as he regarded the remaining stock as his own, and FitzGerald clearly agreed.[5] For the enlarged second edition of 1868 FitzGerald again paid the printer, and left it to Quaritch to 'fix the most saleable price he can; take his own proper profit out of it; and when 50 copies are sold give me mine'. 'It seems absurd to make terms about such a pamphlet, likely to be so slow of sale', he told Donne (14 February 1868), adding that 'I should be inclined to make the whole Edition over to him except such copies as I want to give away ... but one only looks more of a Fool by doing so'.

No contracts survive for the 1859 or 1868 editions of *The Rubáiyát*, nor any formal agreements between FitzGerald and Quaritch over future sales, accountability, or—what became significant only in the 1870s, with its blossoming popularity—the copyright of FitzGerald text. The rights and privileges of the poet and his nominal publisher, never clarified in the first decade of their association, were rendered murkier by the idiosyncrasies of both parties—FitzGerald's unbusiness-like attitude toward his own literary property, and his practice of forever tinkering with his text,[6] set against Quaritch's seigneurial attitude toward his own never-bestselling 'authors', and his personal disinclination to obey copyright deposit requirements, even copyright registry instructions. And the anarchic situation of international copyright law, which led even in FitzGerald's lifetime to dozens of American piracies of *The Rubáiyát* (and one printed at Madras, India, in 1862),[7] complicated the picture by its challenge to any practical control by a *bona fide* trustee. While Quaritch may genuinely have wished to serve his client-friend's best publishing interests, and (less certainly) those of his executors after 1883, the later history of Quaritch's struggle for proprietorship of 'my Omar' is not always edifying. Misunderstanding and misdirection cloud his forgiveable pride in having 'thrust the *Rubáiyát* to the top', while the attitude of his steely-eyed opponent W. A. Wright, bent on curtailing an amicable thirty-year franchise, inspires little more sympathy. But the episode rounds out a celebrated publishing 'romance', and a chronology of the extant letters and drafts of letters between Quaritch, FitzGerald, and FitzGerald's executors—many unpublished—may help to defictionalize it.

*   *   *

No attitude toward ongoing 'rights' is expressed in the extant letters from FitzGerald to Quaritch of 1859 (*Letters*, ii:331–2) and 1867 (*Letters*, iii:39–40: 'You must tell me, Busy and Great Man as you now are, whether you care to take charge of such a shrimp of a Book if I am silly enough to reprint it'; and iii:50). Regarding the third version 1 of 1872, FitzGerald wrote '"*In re*" The Profits of Omar the Second [*sic*] ... I write to you from a recollection of our agreeing to share them, as we shared in the publishing: you taking all the trouble etc., I the expense of Printing etc.' He suggests that Quaritch, who apparently had offered him £5, should pay whatever his share might be to the Persian Relief Fund, adding 'I should think your £5 more than covers [it]' (27 August 1872, endorsed by Quaritch indicating that £5 was sent on 3 September).

Now Quaritch was accustomed to 'owning' the rights to books he published, or even of which he held all the stock, and frequently made a fuss about it, as when a provincial newspaper unwittingly reproduced illustrations from Owen Jones's *Grammar of Ornament*, or when a British bookseller advertised for sale an American piracy of another text published in England by Quaritch. But in this instance he cannot have thought matters worth regularizing, and when in 1878 he approached FitzGerald again over a fourth edition, he may have been a little surprised at FitzGerald's rather more precise reaction.

'Do let me reprint the Rubáiyát!' he pleaded (18 November 1878). Many in 'a small but choice circle' of admirers want to buy it; 'insatiable' American pirates (the adjective, present in the letter book, is eliminated in the letter as sent) reprint and *misprint* it '*ad libitum*': 'Allow me to publish another edition, and pay you twenty five guineas as the honorarium.'[8] But FitzGerald had previously (19 August) indicated that he did not want the *Rubáiyát* to be printed separately any more, as Quaritch preferred (having shrewdly perceived that this was its most saleable form), and had diffidently suggested a combination of Omar and Jámi (*Salámán and Absál*), which Quaritch could after all divide up again and sell individually if he chose;[9] and now (23 November) FitzGerald stood by his and his friend E. B. Cowell's preference for the pairing. On 9 December he asked 'whether you wish to undertake the Book: for an Edition of how many Copies; and on what terms', a letter which Quaritch endorsed 'offered £25 for privilege to print 1,000'. FitzGerald objected to quarto format (11 December: 'I have a dislike to see my minor things swelled out into 4to margin as if they were precious'), and thought 1000 copies excessive; on 16 January 1879 he reiterated his preference for 500 copies, which 'will see *me* out', and made three uncharacteristically firm 'stipulations', viz.: (1) 'That Omar, who is to stand *first*, be never reprinted separate from Jámí'; (2) FitzGerald is to have proofs and revises and they are to be 'strictly' followed; and (3) FitzGerald's name is not to appear in the book or in advertisements, unless quoted 'from some independent Review'. But the key condition for permitting 1000 copies rather than 500, is 'some understanding as to the Copyright reverting to my Heirs, Executors or Assigns, in some stipulated time after my Decease ... if you do not care for all such Bother, you have but to drop the thing, and no harm done on either side.'

This is apparently the first mention, on FitzGerald's part, of legal title to his own literary work, and it may well have reflected the advice of his friend and future executor William Aldis Wright, of Trinity College, Cambridge, a formidable Shakespeare and biblical scholar. For to Wright he had reported, a month earlier, Quaritch's repeated applications to reprint *The*

Rubáiyát, culminating in 'a humbugging Letter of his about "his Customers"—"twenty years connection", etc.'. Only for Cowell's sake, who favoured a reprint of *Salámán and Absál*, and 'who has more faith in Quaritch than I', did FitzGerald capitulate (he explained), although he resisted Quaritch's plan for large-paper copies, and mocked 'what he calls an "honorarium" of £25' (EFG to Wright, 17 December 1878). No doubt Quaritch, whose brusqueness belied a painfully sentimental streak, especially concerning his more luminous acquaintances, would have been doubly mortified—had he known—at FitzGerald's condescension, and Wright's sharing it. To FitzGerald's demands, however, he responded unambiguously and at once, 'as I am very anxious not to sever the bond which has connected us for above 20 years'. 'I agree to all the stipulations of your letter of yesterday', he wrote, viz., (1) small format; (2) Omar 'to stand first' and never to be reprinted separate from Jámí; (3) proofs and revises to be supplied; (4) anonymity to be respected; (5) Quaritch to pay FitzGerald £25 on completion of printing (FitzGerald had not actually stipulated this); (6) 1000 copies to be printed (Quaritch explained that he would only 'recoup' on the second 500); and (7), later the nub of it all, 'The copyright to remain yours; of course no new edition to be brought out by you or your representatives whilst I have a stock of say fifty unsold copies' (17 January 1879, Letter Book I, p. 222; *Letters*, iv:175–6, from a transcript by Wright).

To this FitzGerald replied on 21 January, 'Well then—take Omar and Jámí on the terms proposed in your letter of Jan. 17. It is not worth more fuss on either side', and requested twenty free copies. The ensuing correspondence never returns to the matter of 'rights'. In May 1880 FitzGerald wrote 'I am glad that Omar has, as I suppose, pretty well cleared his Expenses. I was afraid that Jámí might hang about him: but Cowell wished for him [i.e., the united format]'—not quite the version of the matter he had vouchsafed to Wright.[10] In October 1882 FitzGerald again sought Quaritch's agency for his *Readings in Crabbe*, an edition of fifty copies, 'of which fifty copies you may perhaps sell about twenty-five if you will bestow on them the usual Publisher's care, at the usual Publisher's remuneration' (*Letters*, iv:533–4). As in early days FitzGerald would pay for the printing himself, and 'if you agree to undertake this very lucrative [*sic*] business' would place Quaritch's name on the title-page. This time there were no stipulations.

* * *

FitzGerald died in June 1883, with the Crabbe booklet still in uncirculated sheets. He left a box of corrected copies of most of his writings, with a letter to William Aldis Wright, whom he designated his literary executor. Wright took his duties seriously, and immediately set out to collect and reprint FitzGerald's far-strewn *opuscula*, according to his own firm editorial notions, together with a selection of letters and a biographical memoir of his own. How Quaritch would figure in his plans, if at all, was unclear at the outset, but two more temperamentally incompatible partners could hardly be imagined—Wright cool, precise, patient and donnish, intent on an academically respectable tribute, Quaritch demonstrative, impetuous, market-minded, and—yes—something of a vulgarian. Although common cause, in honouring FitzGerald, might once have united them, manners alone would have set them at odds; and once Quaritch backed down in a bluffing game over prior arrangements, Wright held all the cards. The traditional impression that Wright behaved coldly toward a vulnerably sentimental old man is not altogether unwarranted, but perhaps owes in part to the selectiveness exercised by Quaritch's daughter, in the appendix to her 1926 *Letters from FitzGerald to Quaritch*.

On 22 June 1883, a week after FitzGerald's death, Wright asked Quaritch to replace part of the preface to the Crabbe booklet with revised sheets, 'if there are any copies ... yet unbound', and hinted that he had embarked on his own edition of FitzGerald—for he mentioned 'the letter of instructions which [FitzGerald] has left for me', and corrected copies of various books by FitzGerald which he possessed, and those which he sought. The executors had found about thirty copies of FitzGerald's Calderón translations (1853), theoretically suppressed, and 'would no doubt be willing to negotiate with you for them' (*Letters to Quaritch*, p. 89).

Quaritch replied promptly (23 June 1883, TCC Add. MS a.283[79]), but rather at cross-purposes, offering to buy 'any books, whether written by Mr. Fitzgerald or owned by him',[11] and to publish a 'Memorial Volume' of FitzGerald's works 'at my expense, giving to you a number of copies in lieu of an honorarium. I do not think there would be sale enough to make the posthumous works a commercial success,—but I gladly risk a loss because I should look upon the last, work as a Monument to be erected to E. F.'s memory.' 'I am very proud', he added—as if Wright might forget—'of the fact, that I contributed to make the fame of Omar Khayam.' Wright evidently did not respond, and Quaritch returned to the matter on 19 November 1883, offering to reprint the 1853 Calderón 'uniformly with my last edition [of] Omar' and subsequently 'your volume of Biographical Memoirs the *same size*, so as to form a uniform series.' He offered the services of Michael Kerney, his polymath chief assistant, 'who used to assist Mr. Fitzgerald in bringing out his Omar' (TCC Add. MS a.283[80]).

Wright may well have regarded Quaritch's approach as presumptuous, and answered sharply on 25 November: 'my plan has grown and ... in the event of my being able to command sufficient material for carrying out this larger work I shall naturally place it in the hands of my own publishers Messrs Macmillan & Co. With this design on my part Mr. Crabbe one of the executors fully agrees, as do other of Mr. FitzGerald's friends.' He will not allow Quaritch to reprint Calderón, for the present (*Letters to Quaritch*, p. 90).

Quaritch was 'very much astonished and grieved' by this letter, protesting on 27 November that 'it was understood between you and me, that I was to be the publisher of your Memoir', reminding Wright again of his part in FitzGerald's fame ('I consider that it was due to my commercial agency, in distributing at a mere nominal price, the *first* edition of "Omar Khayam", that Fitzgerald obtained his subsequent celebrity'), adding smugly that 'the books Mr. Fitzgerald published elsewhere never had any circulation', and offering to pay for an engraved portrait (£25) as well as £25 more 'for the Manuscript [of "your Memoir"] ... A *mere* publisher would simply look upon the venture as a commercial one, and as such, I think, it will not be remunerative. I am anxious that my name should remain associated with that of Fitzgerald, regardless of profit. Please reflect again on the subject' (*Letters to Quaritch*, p. 91; original in TCC, Add. MS a-282[81]). To this letter Wright replied sharply again (2 December 1883, *Letters to Quaritch*, p. 92), pointing out that no understanding about publishing had ever been reached, nor even mentioned: 'You must allow me to be the best judge of what I shall ultimately do with my own work. I do not undertake it for profit and therefore should not in any case accept your offer.'

Here the published *Letters to Quaritch* leave Quaritch and Wright, but they continued to correspond and to bicker. On 19 March 1884 (TCC Add. MS a.283[82]) Quaritch pressed Wright 'about Mr. Fitzgerald's unpublished works, letters, etc.', concerning which 'I had some grounds for expecting to hear from you'. There were further exchanges in 1886, 1889, and 1897–9, as we shall see.

But in the meantime Quaritch had become involved in what he professed to abominate, the American *Rubáiyát* industry. Houghton Mifflin & Co., the Massachusetts publishers, distributed through Quaritch a fancy edition (pirated, as always), illustrated by Elihu Vedder: letters to Quaritch of 17 and 24 November 1884 discuss forwarded proofs, 'electros', and positive reviews. Frustrated by Wright in his ambition to publish, distribute, or attach his name to FitzGerald's works, Quaritch took the surprising step of commissioning his own 'Collected Edition', produced in America. He engaged Theodore De Vinne, the distinguished New York printer, to set and print it in large and small paper, a two-volume work including every text known to him, plus an unsigned introduction by Michael Kerney (Quaritch Letter Book I, pp. 321 (15 October 1886) and 329 (18 November 1886)). He offered Houghton Mifflin the opportunity to be 'the American publisher of Fitzgerald's Works, edited by Michael Kerney—if so, your name shall as such appear on the title pages'. His terms were enticing: 'I do not wish you to "speculate" on the book—you can have copies "on sale" on the same terms as I have your illustrated edition of Omar by Vedder.' Five hundred small-paper and fifty large-paper copies were planned, the cost yet unknown, but 'you could publish the work at whatever price you like'.

I do not think that Quaritch ever admitted responsibility for this project, nor acknowledged that Kerney oversaw it, but a proof of the engraved portrait and signature of FitzGerald (taken from a letter supplied by Quaritch) were sent to Quaritch by H. Costello, a commercial engraver, in March 1886; these appear as the frontispiece to the New York 1887 *Works*, published with the imprint 'New-York and Boston, Houghton, Mifflin & Co. / London, Bernard Quaritch'.[12] Quaritch sent a print of the finished engraving to E. B. Cowell, who thanked him on 3 April 1886, and to Wright, who apparently disliked it: for Quaritch was 'like you, much disappointed with Mr. Costello's etching of Mr. Fitzgerald's photographic portrait [for which] I paid £26/5/—. I hoped for a success and I have had an artistic failure' (5 April 1886, TCC Add. MS a.283[83]). Had Wright known at once of Quaritch's involvement with the unauthorized 1887 collection it is hard to imagine that he would not have protested directly—his own 'standard' collection being well on the way towards publication in 1889. Quaritch sent copies of the 'American' edition to William Simpson, Oliver Wendell Holmes, and E. B. Cowell; Cowell acknowledged Quaritch's 'long regard & esteem' for FitzGerald, but declined to write 'any notice of this Edition and Memoir' because of 'my friendship for Mr. Aldis Wright' (*Letters to Quaritch*, p. 101). Quaritch advertised the collection in his retail catalogues, but as if he were only its English distributor; he also offered Costello's etching separately, for 10s. 6d., with a no-doubt unsanctioned quotation from Cowell's letter of acknowledgement (Letters to Quaritch, p. 99).

But Wright was proceeding with his own authorized *Letters and Literary Remains*, and it may not be coincidental that a new correspondence began in November 1887. George Moor, a solicitor of Woodbridge, Suffolk (FitzGerald's home), wrote to Quaritch on behalf of the FitzGerald estate—disingenuously?—asking professional advice about 'the value of the published works and of those unpublished' (28 November 1887, original in Quaritch Letter Book II, p. 11; all the ensuing correspondence is in Letter Book II, between pp. 11 and 23). Quaritch sprang for the bait, and on 29 November declared that 'the copy-right value ... involves no large pecuniary interest for his estate; since it does not comprise his chief book, the Omar Khayyám, which has been my property since the issue of the first edition in 1858 [*sic*] ... as for the other books which he printed, I should consider their copy-right value as slender, to be measured, in fact, rather by sentimental than by commercial appreciation'. Quaritch followed this misleading letter with another one, offering £100 for the copyright of everything published and unpublished apart from Omar (which 'I already possess'), as a matter of convenience and sentiment, 'as the author was a dear personal friend of mine'. Or he would make it £150, if manuscript memoranda, etc., were thrown in.

Did Quaritch really imagine that the estate would regard him as the copyright holder for 'Omar' without further demonstration? Or had he simply forgotten the 1878 exchange with FitzGerald on the subject, as he was later to claim? The affair soon got out of hand, as far as Quaritch was concerned. Moor wrote civilly (1 December) that 'if we can get 100£, that sum ought to be acceptable', and Quaritch must have been mentally setting type, and composing his final rebuff to Wright. But on 5 December Moor requested, politely, 'sufficient evidence to satisfy the executors' that Quaritch 'had purchased the copyright of "the Omar Khayyám"'—the executors having been 'not aware' of that circumstance.

Quaritch continued to bluster, but more cautiously. On 6 December he was

> slightly surprised by your letter which is not quite an answer to mine [about selling the other rights]. You have evidently misunderstood [!] my statement with regard to the Omar Khayyám copyright. I am the owner of it not 'by purchase', but by the free gift of the late Mr Edward Fitzgerald, at the time when I <produced *deleted*> published the first edition of the book in 1858.
>
> He was not, as you must be aware, a man of business-like habits, from whom legal documents could have been expected—which indeed were hardly required under the circumstances. But he gave very valid confirmation of his gift, by a still further extension of his friendly liberality in conducting through the press, gratis, the successive editions which I produced, in 1868, and 1872, and 1879. All of them were sold entirely as my property and for my sole benefit [!].

To these extraordinary claims—considering that FitzGerald himself paid for the printing of the first three editions and that Quaritch divided the profits for the third and paid for the right to print a specified quantity of the fourth—Quaritch added the odd argument that although his largesse in offering £150 was mainly 'sentimental', it might also forestall American piracies. 'An edition of Mr. Fitzgerald's works in two octavo volumes has recently been produced at Boston', he solemnly informed Moor, so that 'interest and sentiment alike combine to make me more desirous of having Mr. Fitzgerald's remaining copyrights.' The draft of this devilish letter (Letter Book II, p. 13) is almost entirely in Michael Kerney's hand (see below).

Before Moor could reply, Quaritch had second thoughts, or, as he put it,

> made a discovery, which must modify the terms of that letter [of two days ago]. The late Mr. Fitzgerald was in the habit of writing and speaking to me continually for many years of the *Rubáiyát of Omar Khayyám* as 'your book' and 'Your Omar', and that created an impression in my mind that the entire copyright of that book was mine in absolute ownership.
>
> I made a search yesterday amongst my old papers and letters, and I find that he so far altered his intention, on the occasion of producing the <fourth edition *deleted*> first edition of the *Omar-Jámi* (a single book, usually styled the fourth edition of *Omar*) as to reserve for his representatives a right of royalty on any republication, after the exhaustion of my *Omar-Jámi*. He has thus left it questionable whether he <had revoked *deleted*> then cancelled his original <purpose *deleted*> presentation of the *Omar* to me, or whether he reserved to his estate merely the copyright of the *Omar-Jámi*.
>
> In either case, it matters but little at present, as I have still a stock of about 200 copies of the book, and no one has the right to reprint it in England, or to bring out a book which shall comprise it.

Owing to his 'altered view of my position, above stated', Quaritch now offered £250 for all FitzGerald's copyrights (8 December 1887).

On the same day Quaritch wrote to E. B. Cowell, under the impression that Cowell was 'one of the parties in whose name Mr. Moor is acting', sending a copy of the new letter to Moor, explaining the earlier contradictory claim, and asking for help in swaying Wright to let Quaritch publish 'his projected *Life & Letters of Mr FitzGerald*'. Cowell replied on 9 December that he had 'nothing to do' with Wright's project, though they had discussed it at length: the disposition of it 'rests entirely with Mr Wright and the executors'. Quaritch underlined 'and the Executors' in blue pencil, as if planning a flank campaign.

On 11 December Aldis Wright sent Moor a transcript of Quaritch's concessionary letter of 17 January 1879 (*Letters*, iv: 176n.), from the archives of the deceased. On 13 December Moor wrote to Quaritch, briefly as ever, 'I am sorry to say you cannot have the refusal of the Copyright of the late Mr Edward Fitz-Gerald's literary works'. Quaritch replied on 14 December, regretting this decision, finding it incomprehensible in terms of the interests of the estate, and wondering 'if there be any private influence which is <hostile *deleted*> against me', which would thereby 'be greatly <hostile *deleted*> adverse to the family which you represent, and to the due continuance of the growth of Mr. Fitzgerald's literary reputation'. Not surprisingly, Moor never answered, and his correspondence with Quaritch ceases here: all these painstakingly-worded letters from Quaritch are in the handwriting of Michael Kerney, the *éminence grise* of the firm, to whom Quaritch habitually deferred in matters of social or legal delicacy.

On the very same day, however (14 December), Kerney also prepared a letter from Quaritch to Theodore De Vinne in New York. No copyright, no scruples: this was publishing hardball. 'I desire to bring out a *cheap* duodecimo edition [of] Omar Khayyám's Rubáiyát as contained in the two-volume edition of Fitzgerald's Works which you have printed for me'. It was to contain Kerney's biographical preface and his editorial notes from the 1887 *Works*, and the text of both the first and fourth versions, i.e., 1859 and 1879. One thousand copies were desired, and 'the book is to be a very cheap one'. So much for Quaritch's 1879 undertaking to FitzGerald that 'Omar ... [was] never to be reprinted separate from Jámí,' and so much for his candour as publisher: the title-page Kerney designed for De Vinne (Letter Book II, p. 17) ends with the imprint 'New York/J. W. Bouton/1888'. De Vinne's staff acknowledged Quaritch's letter of 27 December (De Vinne was now in London, and would visit Quaritch personally). Specimen proofs of the 'very cheap' separate *Omar* were sent Quaritch on 3 January 1888 and passed by Quaritch shortly afterward (Letter Book II, pp. 23–4).

Returning to the copyright home front, Quaritch received a letter on 15 December from Colonel Kerrich, on behalf of FitzGerald's executors, requesting details of the publication of *The Rubáiyát* in 1859 and *Agamemnon* in 1876, for the purpose of registering their own copyright. Quaritch replied that

I never registered any of the books of Mr. Fitzgerald which I published, either at the time of their publication or afterwards, except the fourth edition of the Rubáiyát of Omar Khayyám, and even that was done a long time after the publication [in fact in 1884, after Quaritch's impasse with Wright], in deference to the suggestion of some friend. I have always regarded such registration as a mere useless formality. Indeed the whole of the copyright law is in an unsettled, or rather chaotic state, so that nearly every question arising under it seems capable of contradictory decisions by different judges.

Quaritch (or Kerney again) topped off this casual opinion with a reiteration of his offer to buy the copyrights for £250, but three further letters to and from Kerrich (17–19–21 December) made no headway whatever. For purposes of keeping his name 'linked' with FitzGerald's, Quaritch at last must come back to the cold shoulders of W. Aldis Wright.

Three days before Christmas Quaritch tried that unlikely correspondent again, brazenly offering Wright one hundred guineas for 'unpublished copies of four pieces by the late Mr. Fitzgerald—two translations, from Sophocles and one from Calderon'. Wright must by now have been fed up to the teeth, for his Christmas Eve answer is testy and final: no sale, and please note that

> Mr. FitzGerald ... never parted with the copyrights of his published works although you in 1884 after his death registered the fourth edition of Omar Khayyám as your own ... .
>
> I have now arranged with his Executors for the transfer to me of the copyright in all his work, published and unpublished, and I have therefore to call your attention to the unauthorized American reprint circulated by you which is an infringement of that copyright. if after this notice you continue to advertise and sell copies of this reprint in this country you will do so at your own risk.

Wright concluded by demanding 'a printer's certificate' of the number of copies of Omar-Jámí produced in 1879.

Quaritch's reply to this chilly dismissal is almost touching. On 27 December 1887 he pulled out all Stops ('25 years most friendly relations ... a question not of business, but of sentiment ... would gladly pay you double what you can obtain from any other publisher') along with the litany of tradition ('In 1859 Mr. F made me a present of the first edition ... it was through my exertions that the reputation of the book was established ... claimed no royalty'). He offered his one trump, however: as long as he possessed fifty copies—and he had now 'little more than a hundred'—no new edition might appear save his own. Therefore he pleaded for the right to print 1000 more copies of a fifth edition, 'for which I would pay any fair price you choose to fix'. He transmitted the printer's certificate, and took 'due notice of what you say about the American "Works"'. Finally, a conciliatory appeal, man-to-man: 'Will you allow me to call on you?'

Wright gave not an inch. On 1 January 1888 he pressed Quaritch for 'more explicit assurance' that he would cease distributing the American *Works*. He declined to allow Quaritch to reprint *Omar* alone, as

> it was Mr. FitzGerald's express wish that it should never again be published separately, and he made this a condition with you when he gave you permission to print it with Salámán and Absál. I cannot therefore violate his distinct orders. Nor can I now make any change in my arrangement for the publication of his Letters and Remains. As I told you when you tried to tempt me with the offer of £25 for my part of the work when ready for press, my object is not gain.

Wright concluded with a devastating thrust, '*and you must not claim a monopoly in the sentiment*'. As an afterthought he offered to buy out Quaritch's stock of the 1879 Omar-Jámí, which of course would remove the impediment to republishing.

What chance of the last? Quaritch had already written to Moor (14 December 1887) that 'under the circumstances, I shall naturally feel no eagerness to divest myself of such [a] possession', although he deleted from the letter as sent the veiled threat which followed, '*unless the public is desirous of buying up my copies at an advanced price*'. In other words, Quaritch knew that he could block a new edition of *The Rubáiyát* as long as he chose to hold more than fifty copies in stock unless, of course, the copyright holders or their agents systematically ordered them at the published price until they fell below the prescribed level. Quaritch decided not to play that game, however, and on 2 January he appeared to capitulate: the American *Works* would be 'withdrawn from sale by me, and the copies now in my <possession *deleted*> hands shall be sent out of the country'. The remaining copies of Omar-Jámí 'I prefer to keep', but—and this seems curiously magnanimous—'since you do not intend to reprint the Omar *separately* from the "Remains" ... I am willing to waive any objection to your collective edition, arising from the stipulation in my agreement with Mr. Fitzgerald that no reprint should be made while I held at least fifty copies'. Wright must have been startled into civility: he replied 'exceedingly obliged by your letter' on 3 January, adding that 'nothing could be more satisfactory, and I accept your assurances with full confidence'.

On the very same day (3 January 1888) De Vinne wrote to Quaritch with 'proof showing the type we propose to use in the new edition of Omar Khayyám'. Do we remember that small exercise in publishing spite? Its resolution borders on the comic: Houghton Mifflin again took up the slack. On 8 May (Quaritch Letter Book II, p. 31) they 'have received from Mr. De Vinne a dummy showing the style of binding ... for the new edition of the "Rubáiyát", and also a set of proofs ...'. They submitted details of costing and terms, asking Quaritch how to proceed. Quaritch, now at peace with Wright, washed his hands of the whole affair, but not without profit, for on 23 May he proposed 'that you pay De Vinne's bill (to be ascertained), and £50 to me, and that I transfer to you all the present stock and the stereos'. All that seems to have happened.

The last echoes of these copyright campaigns come in letters preserved in the Wright MSS at Trinity College Cambridge. Wright sent Quaritch the three-volume *Letters* and *Literary Remains of Edward FitzGerald* as a gift, and Quaritch acknowledged 'your extremely beautiful and excellent edition' on 29 June 1889, adding wistfully, 'I wish I had had the honor of being the publisher of these volumes'. On 12 August 1897 Quaritch warned Wright about American piracies circulating freely in England, from which the estate receives nothing, and asked

> Will you grant me the privilege of importing American editions of the book now? I am 78 years of age and cannot hope to be alive in 1901 when the copyright expires. You see I am still anxious to connect my name with the memory of Fitzgerald.... If you demanded it I should still be willing to pay a moderate premium for the right of importing American editions.

Wright refused yet again, but Quaritch persisted, 'extremely sorry that my letter ... has given you so much offence', and offering £50 for the permission to import. Nothing, expectably, came of his appeal, but he repeated it on 26 November, and again on 24 February 1898: his point was (as always) that the public favoured the first version text, not the 'authorized' fourth, and that was just what the piracies provided. 'In April I shall be 79 years of age, it is therefore not likely I shall remain alive much longer to trouble about Omar', he reflected, concluding with a rare bookseller's observation, appropriate from the firm which remaindered the book for a penny: 'You have no doubt heard I bought at Sotheby's the first edition of

Omar 2 weeks ago for £21.' Three months earlier he had offered just £5 to Cowell for a 'spare copy' of the book, if he had one (Arberry, p. 97), but this sale-room purchase made headlines. Lest anyone should doubt Quaritch's conviction, frowned on by FitzGerald himself, that the 1859 text would retain its ascendancy, 'the 2nd, 3rd & 4th editions [still] sell at low prices'. Once more Wright did not see fit to reply. '*The Worldly Hope men set their Hearts upon*', their unsentimental friend might have reminded the applicant, '*Turns Ashes—or it prospers: and anon, / Like Snow upon the Desert's dusty Face / Lightning a little Hour or two—is gone*' (first—and in this instance the final—version).

NOTES

1. *The Letters of Edward FitzGerald*, ed. A. M. Terhune and A. B. Terhune (Princeton, 1980), i:57; hereafter cited as *Letters*. The letters from FitzGerald to Quaritch are quoted by the Terhunes from C. Quaritch Wrentmore, ed., *Letters from Edward FitzGerald to Bernard Quaritch* (1926, hereafter cited as *Letters to Quaritch*), the originals apparently having not been consulted by them: see below, notes 9 and 10.

2. A summary appears in A. J. Arberry, *The Romance of the Rubáiyát* (1959), pp. 25–30, but the best account of the celebrated 'remaindering' is by Terhune and Terhune (*Letters*, ii:417–18).

3. Arberry (p. 24) and others are wrong in saying that no reviews appeared before Charles Eliot Norton's famous notice of 1869: see Terhune and Terhune, ii:336–7.

4. On 6 December 1861 EFG declared that he had given away only three copies: to E. B. Cowell, George Borrow, and 'old [W. B.] Donne' (*Letters*, ii:419).

5. Terhune and Terhune (ii:332) cast reasonable doubt on one of Quaritch's later anecdotes, describing a visit by FitzGerald to the shop with 'a heavy parcel' of 200 copies, of which he 'made me a present'; but FitzGerald himself told Cowell in December 1861 that 'I gave Quaritch what Copies I did not want for myself' (*Letters*, ii:416).

6. The four lifetime editions of *The Rubáiyát* (1859, 1868, 1872, and 1879) are substantially different, and even the 'final' text is subject to posthumously recorded variants, bequeathed by FitzGerald to his executors.

7. FitzGerald was rather proud of the unlicensed activity, at first: 'I have not lived in vain, if I have lived to be *Pirated*!', he told Quaritch (31 March 1872), with specific reference to the Indian reprint.

8. Quaritch Letter Book I, p. 219; original in the Wright papers at Trinity College Cambridge (Add. MS a.7⁶⁷).

9. *Letters to Quaritch*, p. 56; inexplicably omitted from *Letters*, ed. Terhune and Terhune. Quaritch endorsed the original 'Permission to reprint Omar Salámán'.

10. The passage quoted (a postscript) is printed in *Letters to Quaritch*, p. 79, but is omitted without explanation by Terhune and Terhune, *Letters*, iv:330.

11. On 10 August he sent one of the executors, the Rev. George Crabbe, £20 for 'Mr. FitzGerald's books', noting that '26 Euphranors in sheets'—i.e., copies of FitzGerald's *Euphranor*, 1851—were still outstanding (letter in private collection).

12. The copy itself was provided by Quaritch from London, which may explain the odd-looking 'New-York' in the imprint. See a description in the Bernard Quaritch list 'Seventy-five New Acquisitions, English Literature' (Autumn 1996), item 30.

JOHN HOLLANDER

Paradise Enow

In 1856 Edward Byles Cowell, a British scholar who would eventually become Professor of Sanskrit at Cambridge, turned up in the Bodleian Library a fifteenth-century Persian manuscript containing 158 epigrammatic quatrains by the mathematician and philosopher and perhaps sometime tentmaker Omar Khayyám (1048–1131 C.E.) of Nishapur in northeastern Persia. Khayyám was not known as a poet during his lifetime; indeed, the first quotation of one of these quatrains or *ruba'i* (derived from the Arabic word for 4) appears over a half century after his death. The number of these attributed to him gradually grew over three centuries: over 2,000 exist in many mss. ascribed to Omar Khayyám, but modern scholarly assessment of authenticity yields from about 120 to over 170. *Rubáiyát* (the word is a plural) rhyme in a characteristic way—*aaxa* (although, very occasionally, *aaaa*)—and had Cowell not sent a transcript of the manuscript to his older friend Edward Fitzgerald, all this could hardly have mattered to English poetry. But he did, and it did. What resulted was *The Rubáiyát of Omar Khayyám*. Fitzgerald selected 75 of these from the manuscript he had and very freely translated and assembled them into his Victorian masterpiece. A unique mode of sentimental skepticism embracing a totally unchristian view of fate, time and chance emerged from the quatrains that brought new life to an older western tradition of the meditative epigram from Hellenistic times.

From *Yale Review* 86, no 3 (July 1998). © 1998 by John Hollander.

First published anonymously in 1859 (it was brought out by Bernard Quaritch, the antiquarian bookseller), with notes and a biographical and critical essay on "Omar Khayyám, the Astronomer-Poet of Persia," the poem might have sunk without trace, its 250 copies scattered, in the poet's words "to the winds like rain." But two years after—according to Swinburne almost forty years later—a friend of Rossetti's picked up the pamphlet in a sort of remainder box for a penny at Quaritch's, and gave a copy to Rossetti. Soon Swinburne, Morris, Meredith, Burne-Jones and others of their circle had read and delighted in it. Ruskin praised it, and Charles Eliot Norton wrote of it in an essay on Omar in *The North American Review* in 1869, praising Fitzgerald's poem, in its second edition, above the French prose translation from the Persian of over 460 of Omar's quatrains (from the much larger so-called Calcutta ms.) by J.B. Nicolas in 1867. Fitzgerald brought out three subsequent editions—in 1868, 1872 and 1879—expanding the number of quatrains to 110 in the first of these, and then cutting back to 101 in the last two. But as will be seen, these various editions involved continuous revision and rearrangement—something like, though on a much smaller scale—the text of Whitman's *Leaves of Grass*—and Fitzgerald's poem took on a life of its own, both privately and, as it became at first sensational and then by the turn of the century canonical, publicly as well.

It belongs to that category of literary masterpieces which, despite being possessed and acclaimed by a broad lower-middle-brow consistuency during the period of the rise of high modernism, manage to have outlasted modernism's stringent agendas. (The other obvious example is Gray's "Elegy in a Country Churchyard", whose marginalized greatness has been the study of contemporary historicist theorizing.) For the late Victorian and proto-modernist sensibility, Omar Khayyám played a role analogous to that of Hafiz and Sadi for Goethe and Emerson. Thus the young Wallace Stevens in May 29, 1906 could write in his journal that: "Modern people have never failed to crown the poet who gave them poetic thought—and modern people have had to crown Hafiz and Omar—just as the ancients [sic!-cum-giggle!] crowned Shelley, Browning and Tennyson." But the poem became through the decades a popular favorite as well, and alternate versions as well as affectionate parodies of it started appearing by the turn of the century. The young Kipling, for example, wrote an attack on an unpopular viceregal advisor in India in Fitzgerald's quatrains, even keeping to his capitalization of common nouns: it opened by announcing itself as political satire

Now the New Year, reviving last Year's Debt,
The Thoughtful Fisher casteth wide his Net;
    So with begging Dish and ready Tongue
Assail all men for all that I can get.

And for T.S. Eliot at the age of fourteen, reading the poem was—as he put it thirty years later—"like a sudden conversion; the world appeared anew, painted with bright, delicious and painful colours." (And indeed, a recent book by Vinnie-Marie D'Ambrosio, entitled *Eliot Possessed*, attempts to trace the presence of Fitzgerald throughout the later poet's work.)

The early twentieth-century humorist Gelett Burgess (author of the celebrated "I never saw a Purple Cow, / I never hope to see one. / But I can tell you, anyhow, / I'd rather see than be one") in *The Rubaiyat of Omar Cayenne* (1904) used the parody in the interests of middle-brow distrust of modernity. With reference to the portion of the poem that Fitzgerald sub-titles "*Kúza Namá*" ["Book of Pots"] in which the finished products of a potter's craft arranged on display debate teleological and moral questions. Here, books play the role of Omar's allegorical pots:

> After a literary Silence, spake
> A manuscript of Henry James' make;
>   "They sneer at me for being so occult:
> But Kipling's found such stuff is going to take."

> A book of Limericks—-Nonsense, anyhow—
> Alice in Wonderland, the Purple Cow
>   Beside me singing on Fifth Avenue—-
> Ah, this were Modern Literature enow!

And there were such others as Oliver Herford in an illustrated book of high-popular humor called *The Rubaiyat of a Persian Kitten* (1904)—each of his *rubai* was accompanied by a cute but not smarmy wash drawing:

> Wake for the Golden Cat has put to flight
> The Mouse of Darkness with his Paw of Light,
>   Which means in Plain and Simple every-day
> Unoriental Speech—the Dawn is bright.

Fitzgerald's poem was frequently published in the first part of this century in elaborate, illustrated editions: it was the sort of gift book for reading and admiring that perhaps declined, in a post-literate age, into the coffee-table one. I grew up with my parents' copy on heavy, creamy stock, with color-plates by Edmund Dulac; I kept getting them confused with Dulac's similar illustrations for a Laurence Housman translation of some of the *Arabian Nights* tales that we also had, but even more confusing was the presence of three "editions of the translation", called—still more confusingly—the first, second and "fifth". I wondered, of course, what had happened to the missing inner three. And well I might have, for there were only four (the mysterious "fifth" was in fact Fitzgerald's last version of 1879.) But more usually, reprints have been confined to one of the four versions, and there has never been an authoritative critical edition.

But a young scholar named Christopher Decker has now come forward with a splendid 258-page edition of the poem [1], containing Fitzgerald's introductory essay and notes for each. It prints all four printed versions along with ms. variants, and, most usefully indeed, appends a comparative version in which each quatrain appears in a column with its variants, keyed to their order of placement in the four editions as well as revised copy and proof texts for that of 1872. Looking through the revisions of particular quatrains allows one to see at a glance the changes within quatrains in all the editions, as well as the changes in their order of occurrence. Other appendices comment on the pronunciation of the relevant Persian words, with particular regard to syllabic stress (an important question for the characteristic rhythm of Fitzgerald's lines), and a helpful glossary. He even includes Fitzgerald's tentative Latin versions of some of the quatrains which preceded his English translation. These were in the rhymed accentual verse of medieval Latin (Fitzgerald: "to be read as Monkish Latin, like 'Dies Irae', etc." and a glance at one of them provides some amusement, but also reveals something of how the translation became an English poem. One ruba'i [109 in the Bodleian ms.] says in essence that since life doesn't last, it doesn't matter whether we die in Balkh or Babylon, whether it's bitter or sweet. Just drink on—long after us the moon will keep going through her phases. Fitzgerald's Latin already imports material from a different quatrain in its last two lines (these seem to have ended up as, with its Shakespearean echo, the well-known "Sans Wine, sans Song, sans Singer and—sans End!" of XXIII of the first edition); it changes the unfamiliar Balkh—a city in Northern Afghanistan—to a more resonant name, throws in a cup, makes the wine biting (*mordax*) rather than bitter (*amarus*) and

> Sive Babylonem, Sive Bagdad apud, Vita ruit,
> Sive suavi, sive Vino Poculum mordaci fluit:
>   Bibe, bibe: nam sub Terrâ posthâc non bibendum erit
> Sine Vino, sine Sáki; semper dormiendum erit.

But his English quatrain, unrevised in all editions, reworks the ending yet again, passing it through one potent figure in European poetry from Homer, Virgil, and Dante through Milton and Shelley, and another that seems to drift in from Keats' "To Autumn":

Whether at Naishápúr or Babylon,
Whether the Cup with sweet or bitter run,
　The Wine of Life keeps oozing drop by drop,
The Leaves of Life keep falling one by one.

(Naishápúr—Nishapur—Omar Khayyám's native city, creeps into several different translations of this quatrain.)

　　Decker's introduction is geared to a bibliographical account of the development of the poem through its editions, but it is of biographical and, particularly, of critical value as well. He gives a particularly eloquent account of his own bibliographical procedures in using all four versions of the translation as his basic copy text. But he also writes sensitively about matters of poetic—rather than merely textual—composition, as when he invokes the connection already mentioned between Fitzgerald's poem and Gray's "Elegy" in another light. Seeing *The Rubáiyát* as "one of the best poems ever written about the condition of not being a great poet, and not wanting to be." he observes that it "is affined, and affiliated with, Gray's 'Elegy Written in a Country Churchyard' that great meditation on the condition of ungreatness." But in any event, Omar's verses did indeed awaken Fitzgerald's genius (in the older sense, meaning his originality), and the poem as we have it is certainly his.

　　In a letter to Cowell the author of *The Rubáiyát* observed that "It is most ingeniously tessellated into a sort of Epicurean Eclogue in a Persian garden." He also appears to have used the word "transmogrification" of what he had done to the separate quatrains the *"Tetrastichs* "(as he designates them in Greek, "independent stanzas, consisting each of four lines of equal, though varied Prosody, sometimes all rhyming but oftener (as here attempted) the third line suspending the Cadence by which the last atones with the former Two." The structure of that Epicurean Eclogue is fairly fluid; in all four published versions the poem begins with three quatrains dealing with the dawn of a new day; throughout, some of the quatrains look back to or parallel the preceding ones, there is a pair of enjambed quatrains (LIV and LV in the first, and unrevised although in a different place throughout the editions) and there is a fixed group of nine—scattered in the Persian mss.—forming a little poem *en abîme* that Fitzgerald sub-titles "*Kúza Namá*" ["Book of Pots"] in which the finished products of a potter's craft arranged on display debate teleological and moral questions. The *carpe diem* story constantly being told in the poem, rather than unfolding in a narrative, gets turned around and around like a huge, multifaceted jewel, revealing with each new face a different angle of vision into its unchanging core. "The poem's bare outliner," as Decker puts it, "is that of a day in the life of Omar

Khayyám, beginning with the call to awaken and ending with the rising moon." The matter of wine is particularly important throughout these quatrains. Since the eighth century C.E. wine and love had been allegorically treated in Muslim Sufism as representations of the transcendent bliss of direct apprehension of God, and in the much later poetry of Hafiz and Omar, eros in the first instance and inebriation in the second are far from literal. The degree to which Omar is versifying a Sufic convention or using the trope far more in dependently continues to be a matter of the sort of scholarly debate that often surrounds poetry that can narrowly thematic reading can too easily reduce to decorated doctrine. In Fitzgerald's poem, the allegorical ramifications are widespread, and drinking can mean a variety of ways of opening up one's consciousness to Beauty:

> You know my Friends, with what a brave Carouse
> I made a Second Marriage in my House:
>   Divorced old barren Reason from my Bed
> And took the Daughter of the Vine to Spouse.
>
>   [LV, from 1872 on]

suggests a range of rotations in one's life, whether of love, or work, or thought or sensibility. For example: Fitzgerald's own intolerable, brief marriage (he preferred the company of young men) had come to an end at about the time he began to work on Omar's quatrains, and it is easy to read this as celebrating remarriage to his poem. And that poem's richness comes not from exploring the truth or consequences of the drinking, but the variety of metaphors its celebration engenders. To this degree, the poem is like a Petrarchan sonnet sequence, exploring conceits as if each were a new territory or a new state of mind. Those of *The Rubáiyát* can turn on a quibbling play on "depth", literal and figurative, in a scholastic trope which Fitzgerald himself annotated in the 1879 edition by citing Donne's image of the compasses in "A Valediction Forbidding Mourning", and one can equally imagine one of Browning's monologists coming up with it

> For "IS" and "Is-NOT" though with Rule and Line,
> And "UP-AND-DOWN" by Logic I define,
>   Of all that one should care to fathom, I
> Was never deep in anything, but—Wine.
>
>   [LVXI, from 1872 on]

Decker, too alludes to Donne in characterizing the author's devotion to perfecting the poem rhetorically and rhythmically: "For Fitzgerald, rhyme's vexation was less a dull, narcotic numbing pain than a way of taming the fierceness of boredom and loss" (*rhyme's vexation* is from "The Triple Fool"). Some of the best-known revisions are aimed at clarifying and interpreting, such as that of the celebrated *ruba'i*—II, in all editions—about the dawn (part of this apparently comes not from Omar, but from Hafiz):

> Dreaming when Dawn's left hand was in the Sky
> I heard a Voice within the Tavern cry,
>   "Awake, my Little ones, and fill the cup
> Before Life's liquor in its cup be dry."

The contrast between literal wine and the figurative liquor of life itself is perfectly good, and calling the so-called "false dawn" ("a transient light on the Horizon about an hour before the ... True Dawn; a well-known phenomenon in the East," says Fitzgerald in a note) is quite resonant. The subsequent revision, maintained throughout, changes both tropes:

> Before the phantom of False morning died,
> Methought a voice within the Tavern cried,
>   "When all the Temple is prepared within,
> Why nods the drowsy Worshipper outside?"

The celebrated quatrain form adapted by Edward Fitzgerald from the Persian *ruba'i* is, as was observed earlier, iambic pentameter rhymed *aaxa*:

> Awake, for morning in the bowl of night
> Has flung the shaft which puts the stars to flight
>   And Lo! the hunter of the East has caught
> The Sultàn's turrets in a noose of light.

James Merrill remarked in conversation once that Fitzgerald's lines characteristically sagged with a sequence of monosyllables in the third and fourth feet (as they do in ll. 1, 2,4 above. And indeed, Mr. Decker, noting this pattern as $x / x / x x x / x /$ (with / marking stressed syllables and x unstressed ones] identifies it as "the most frequent alternative to the regular iambic" in the whole poem. Like Swinburne before him (in "Laus Veneris" and "Relics"), Merrill himself used this quatrain form stanzaically, in one section of his remarkable "Lost in Translation", and in his very late poem "Home Fires", partially in response to my own Rubaiyat-like sequence, *Tesserae*. The one precursor in English poetry I can think of for the singular movement of Fitzgerald's *aaxa* stanza is one invented by Tennyson for "The

Daisy", published two years before Fitzgerald first saw the Persian ms. of
Omar Khayyam. Tennyson, incidentally, claimed that his invented stanza was
an adaptation of a classical alcaic: the feminine ending of the unrhyming line
is consistent throughout the poem:

> How richly down the rocky dell
> The torrent vineyard streaming fell
>   To meet the sun and sunny waters,
> That only heaved with summer swell.

(If Tennyson's subsequent stanza had daughters/quarters/porters as its
rhymes, the interlocking effect, analogous top that of *terza rima* would be that
used by Robert Frost in the interlocking tetrameter quatrains of his "Stopping
by Woods in a Snowy Evening.") Interestingly enough, Fitzgerald's own
observation, in his essay printed with the 1859 and subsequent editions, seems
to echo this in his description of the quatrain form as "Something as in the
Greek Alcaic, where the third lines seems to lift and suspend the Wave that
falls over in the last."

But certainly Fitzgerald's cadence is original and characteristic. A good
way to hear this is in comparison with what happens when other writers
sought to imitate it in retranslating Omar's quatrains from prose originals, or
in adapting the form for their own poetry. In the latter instance, three stanzas
of Swinburne's "Laus Veneris", written explicitly in Fitzgerald's mode, will
prove exemplary, not only for their pronounced enjambments but for the
slowed-down, many-spondeed

> Night falls like fire; the heavy lights run low,
> And as they drop, my blood and body so
>   Shake as the flame shakes, full of days and hours
> That sleep not neither weep they as they go ...

[or]   Her gateways smoke with fume of flowers and fires,
>   With loves burnt out and unassuaged desires,
>   Between her lips the steam of them is sweet,
>   The languor in her ears of many lyres.

> Her beds are all of perfume and sad sound,
> Her doors are made with music and barred round
>   With sighing and with laughter and with tears,
> With tears whereby strong souls of men are bound.

These are splendid and vigorous, but they do not sound like *The Rubáiyyát* at all.

A continuing scholarly-critical controversy surrounding Fitzgerald's poem is its inaccuracy as translation. Decker is not concerned with it, nor should he be, given that his concerns are indeed Fitzgerald's poem, not his evidently faulty knowledge of Persian which has drawn the attention of modern scholars. Even before the turn of the century, alternate English versions started appearing, usually from Nicolas' French prose text, or from Justin McCarthy's 1889 English translation of it (there was also a gnarled and mannered one by Frederick Rolfe, better known as Baron Corvo in 1903). Whether specifically aimed at some more authoritative access to the Persian originals, or simply in the interests of expansion, many of these even up until the present continued to remember Fitzgerald. Richard Le Gallienne's 1897 *A Paraphrase from Several Literal Translations* gives this version of one of Fitzgerald's most remembered quatrains

> O come, my love, the spring is in the land!
> Take wine and bread and book of verse in hand,
>   And sit with me and sing in the green shade,
> Green little home amid the desert land.

It echoes The Song of Songs and Andrew Marvell, and reflects no greater fidelity than the lines we remember

> A Book of Verses underneath the Bough,
> A Jug of Wine, a Loaf of Bread—and Thou
>   Beside me singing in the Wilderness—
> Oh, Wilderness were Paradise enow!

—as it is in the last two versions—the book of poetry having been substituted for Omar's leg of lamb and Paradise for his comparison to what a Sultan enjoys. Le Gallienne's versions are encrusted with allusions to gems of English poetry, with lines like "The thirsty earth drinks morning from a bowl" (from Cowley) or This sun that rises all too soon shall sink (from Catullus via Ben Jonson). And even the recent scholarly translation of 165 selected quatrains by Ahmad Saidi—in his *Ruba'iyat of Omar Khayyam* (Berkeley: Asian Humanities Press, 1991) resorts almost affectionately to Fitzgerald's "Ah take the Cash and let the Credit go, / Nor heed the rumble of a distant Drum" in his "Ah, take the cash and let the credit go—/Sweet sounds the drum when distant is the beat" (the last line revealing a little apothegm in the original that Fitzgerald suppresses). If one compares purportedly literal English and French translations with Fitzgerald's, he seems always to be rewriting, combining halves of two *ruba'i* (in perhaps two-thirds of the text), allowing a metaphor to takes its own course. Eben Francis Thompson's line-for line prose trot (privately printed, Boston, 1907) gives in one instance "Before that grief a night attack makes / Order that wine of rose-color they bring; / You are not gold, O heedless dolt, that thee / In the earth they hid and then bring out again." Fitzgerald's XV abandons the recurring injunction to drink for a figure that leads beautifully to the conclusion (admittedly, its syntax is dense) that dust and clay are not everlasting gold:

> And those who husbanded the golden Grain,
> And those who flung it to the Wind like Rain,
>   Alike to no Such aureate earth are turn'd
> As, buried once, men want dug up again.

The (figuratively) golden grain contrasts with the literal metallic gold that will neither spring forth in growth when buried, nor die and rot afterwards. Fitzgerald's art of poetry works in just these ways, no so much falsifying the original, as fictionalizing.

As for the questions of inauthenticity and misconstruction in relation to the original, there are several good versions, like those of A.J. Arberry, or that of Saidi mentioned above (its introductory essay is most useful for readers like myself with no Persian who want to know just what was being lost as well as gained in the translation.) Christopher Decker's achievement has been to establish an authoritative text embedded in an illuminating apparatus, allowing renewed consideration of this strangely enduring poem to begin.

NOTE

1. Edward Fitzgerald, *Rubáiyát of Omar Khayyám: A Critical Edition*, edited by Christopher Decker. University Press of Virginia, 258pp.

TRACIA LEACOCK-SEGHATOLISLAMI

The Tale of the Inimitable Rubaiyat

It is difficult to decide where to start with the Edward FitzGerald-Omar Khayyam debate, because so much has been written, it deserves its own library. Of course, most of the debate has been focused on decrying FitzGerald's liberal rendering of Khayyam. This essay is intended to give the lay reader of the *Rubaiyat* a more rounded picture of the situation.

Let it first be made clear that FitzGerald never set foot on Persian soil, or on that of any other Persophone region. He took up Persian at home in England, while in his forties, under the tutelage of his friend Edward Byles Cowell, a young scholar who was then seventeen years his junior. Shortly after FitzGerald took up his studies, Cowell was posted to Calcutta, the Indian end of the British Empire. FitzGerald corresponded with his teacher by letter (which took quite a long time in those days), and his study consisted of using a grammar book (the second edition of Sir William Jones's *Grammar of the Persian Language*) and a dictionary (Francis Johnson's *A Dictionary, Persian, Arabic & English*). He also read an 1857 travelogue by Robert B. M. Binning, *A Journal of Two Years' Travel in Persia, Ceylon, &c*, to get some feel for Persian scenery. Cowell would send him some Persian texts as practice for his studies. These studies were never very thorough, and, as many have verified, FitzGerald's understanding of the Persian language remained rudimentary at best. He did not let this 'minor' obstacle deter him, however,

From *Translation Persepctives* XI. © 2000 by the State University of New York at Binghamton.

and, as Iran Hassani Jewett puts it, 'the superficiality of his knowledge of Persian and his confidence in his superiority over the Persian poets enabled FitzGerald to compose his masterpiece in his own way, unhampered by any bothersome doubts' (143).

The manuscripts left behind in British institutions are testimony to FitzGerald's lack in understanding basic Persian. His verses are riddled with mistranslations of words. As his letters to Cowell show, he was piecing together his rendition by going through the dictionary, and, when he could not find something there, he would write to Cowell for suggestions or he would try to conjecture a meaning. In fact, at the turn of the century, some 40 years after FitzGerald's text was first printed, Edward Heron-Allen published a vehement refutation of FitzGerald and his method. Heron-Allen included letters he had himself received from FitzGerald's teacher, Cowell, who had by then become rather distressed by his student's 'translation'. After having failed to steer his protégé straight on several previous occasions, Cowell wanted no part of the situation, though it was he who had introduced FitzGerald to Khayyam in the first place. Cowell was quite embarrassed to have his reputation as a scholar of Eastern languages (he held appointments as Professor of Sanskrit and of Persian) sullied by FitzGerald's obviously inept translation of the poet.

Heron-Allen also published his own translation of the *Rubaiyat*—a more accurate but not nearly as eloquent version—which included an analysis of the sources for FitzGerald's quatrains. Heron-Allen spent more than seven years researching the sources, and published his findings in 1898:

> Of Edward FitzGerald's quatrains, forty-nine are faithful and beautiful paraphrases of single quatrains to be found in the Ouseley or Calcutta MSS., or both. Forty-four are traceable to more than one quatrain, and therefore may be termed the "composite" quatrains. Two are inspired by quatrains found by FitzGerald only in Nicolas' [French] text. Two are quatrains reflecting the whole spirit of the original poem. Two are traceable exclusively to the influence of the *Mantik ut-tair* [*Conference of the Birds*] of Ferid ud din 'Attar. Two quatrains primarily inspired by Omar were influenced by the Odes of Hafiz. And three, which appeared only in the first and second editions, and were afterwards suppressed by Edward FitzGerald himself, are not—so far as a careful search enables me to judge—attributable to any lines of the original texts. Other authors may have inspired them, but their identification is not useful in this case. (Arnot 40)

As late as 1952, the issue had not been laid to rest, and A. J. Arberry, a scholar of Eastern literature, took a turn at translating Khayyam when two new manuscripts were unearthed. In his version, each *roba'i* is put into two short stanzas, amounting to two quatrains per poem. As Arberry himself acknowledges in his 1952 introduction, this goes against 'the classical theory of Islamic poetry [which holds] that each verse should be independent in itself, and not require assistance from any previous or subsequent verse to complete its meaning' (33). Arberry's preferred format is an unfortunate choice, for it immediately distorts the visual form of the original. It does, however, allow him to give a full translation of the text, as he has more room to set out the meaning. Nonetheless, in addition to the obvious visual trauma this format causes the reader, I find that Arberry frequently stretches the Persian to make it fit his form, often resulting in epigrammatic explications of Khayyam's text. Arberry also changes the final rhyme scheme, AABA, the most recognizable trademark of the *roba'i*, to ABBA. At least FitzGerald's version is faithful to the rhyme scheme of the original.

In his introduction, Arberry is almost apologetic about offering his new version—he had already been scolded in some quarters for a first attempt (1950 Chester Beatty manuscript). By this time it was considered sacrilegious to tamper with FitzGerald's rendition. Arberry's translation could not hold a candle to FitzGerald's interpretation of Khayyam. Seven years later, in a book commemorating the centenary of the publication of FitzGerald's first edition, he too decided to join the "FitzGerald as genius" movement, professing a new enlightened appreciation for the mastery of FitzGerald's version. In his 1959 tribute, Arberry attempts to convince his reader of the marginal nature of FitzGerald's errors—being careful to point out each major one in more than a hundred pages of cross-referenced translations. The new book even included FitzGerald's letters to Cowell, detailing his difficulties with, and misreadings of, the text.

Of course, by 1959, the manuscripts Arberry had worked from were long considered to have been forgeries. As Elwell-Sutton tells us in his introduction to Dashti's 1971 book, the Persian scholar, Mojtaba Minovi even declared them to be the output of "a still active 'manuscript factory' in Tehran" (Dashti 19). This fact may explain Arberry's reverence for 'Old Fitz' in his 1959 book. In a quasi apology for his own recent versions as well as for the present undertaking, Arberry issued the following disclaimer on his 'Acknowledgments' page:

If I have anatomized the reverse side of the carpet, it is in order
that the dazzling lustre of the finished masterpiece may be more

informedly, and therefore more truly and rewardingly appreciated. Lest any misconception should remain, my object has been to enlarge and not to belittle FitzGerald's fame, secure indeed as that is against all cavilling. (7)

At least this time around Arberry reverted to the four-line format of the poems. It is from his second book that I draw samples of his translations. To date, most of the criticism is based on the following:

(a)   FitzGerald's non-immersion in the Persian language (Schopenhauer would say that he failed to grasp "the spirit of the language to be learned") and his inability to place Khayyam's work in its proper historical and literary context.

(b)   FitzGerald's abuse of the original text, which would never be tolerated for translations from Greek or Latin. (To illustrate: FitzGerald had applied his 'method' to versions of Agamemnon and *Oedipus Rex*, but condemnation and abandonment were instant in those cases.) Incidentally, FitzGerald had started out by putting Khayyam into Latin, but only managed to do about 32 quatrains in what has been called "lazy Latin." Ironically, he actually used his own Latin versions, translated back into English, in place of some of the Persian.

(c)   FitzGerald's re-ordering, paraphrasing, and cut and paste method resulted in a text so discombobulated that it is hard to trace in the Persian (when it is present at all). Sometimes, one gets a hint of a familiar-sounding phrase, but looking it up in the Persian is extremely frustrating—this line is from here, this line is inspired by this, and the rest is anyone's guess. It is a veritable wild goose chase.

There are a few samples listed at the end of this essay, but they are by no means rare or isolated occurrences. The truth of the matter is that the text of FitzGerald's *Rubaiyat* is not readily mirrored in Khayyam's. Aficionados have been struggling with this knowledge for a hundred years, mostly downplaying it. It is time, therefore, for those who cherish Khayyam to look at FitzGerald's rendering for what it is: a fabulous English poem inspired by the Persian of Khayyam, in whom FitzGerald felt he had found a kindred spirit. It has repeatedly been said that FitzGerald's *Rubaiyat* is the best and most loved 'translation' into the English language, second in popularity only to the Bible, with the *1001 Nights* holding fast in third place. (Interestingly, they all happen to be Eastern texts.) As a young girl, I simply fell in love with those poems. FitzGerald's rendering displays a sensitivity, a delicacy in the turn of phrase, which suggests that the poetic Muse was permanently encamped on his doorstep. For its sheer beauty, as whatever it is, it is a happy turn of fate that this text has come down to us.

This almost did not happen. FitzGerald rescued Khayyam's poetry (not his other writings) from obscurity, and he, in turn, had to be rescued from the same peril. As the story goes, the first edition of the book was such a dismal failure that the publisher quickly relegated it to the penny box. It was found there by Whitley Stokes, a lawyer and Celtic scholar, believed to be contributing editor of the *Saturday Review* at the time. He passed copies on to his friends—among them Dante Gabriel Rosetti, who told Algernon Swinburne and Robert Browning. When Rosetti and Swinburne (who went on to write his '*Laus Veneris*' à l'Omar) returned to purchase more copies for distribution to William Morris, George Meredith, Edward Burne-Jones, John Ruskin and the rest of the Pre-Raphaelite band, the price had been increased to twopence. They were outraged at the sudden inflation, declaring it to be "iniquitous."

At any rate, all of this fame led to the Omar Khayyam Club being founded in England, with Alfred Tennyson, George Borrow, Edmund Gosse, Thomas Hardy, and Arthur Conan Doyle listed as members. When the little text made its way across the Atlantic, thanks to Charles Eliot Norton's favorable piece in the October 1869 *North American Review*, its American readers started their own club on the East Coast, near Philadelphia. The American demand for the little book was so high that FitzGerald was forced to come out of hiding to issue third and fourth editions. Some of the changes evident in these subsequent versions altered his own originals so profoundly that it is impossible to imagine they could ever have come from the same quatrain by Khayyam. Heron-Allen asserts that FitzGerald's deeper perusal of J.B. Nicolas's French version is at play in some of the alterations made. FitzGerald even acknowledges in his introduction to the revised edition that Nicolas's version "reminded [him] of several things, and instructed [him] in others" (1868). One could say, therefore, that a good portion of the follow-up versions constitutes a reshuffling of FitzGerald's various sources.

FitzGerald's *Rubaiyat* should be labeled precisely that. But the situation is complicated, for though it is not a true translation of the original text, one could say that it frequently comes close to being an honest translation of the feel of it, in that it captures the light-hearted mood of Khayyam's sardonic phrases. Of course, FitzGerald totally omitted many of the quatrains which were too sober for his own taste. The honesty one gets out of his version, therefore, is an abbreviated and a manufactured one.

FitzGerald's reconfiguration of Khayyam's text frequently ends up perverting or obscuring the meaning of the original. By physically taking portions of the quatrains out of context, FitzGerald has all but obliterated the reader's ability to grasp the true significance of much of Khayyam's poetry, which often has a Sufistic feel to it. It should be made clear here that while Khayyam's poetry is frequently classified as Sufistic, he is not officially classified as a Sufi, because he was not part of an established Sufi order. Yet, to his readers in the original Persian and to many scholars, he was a Sufi in the truest sense of the term-shunning all 'isms' and dogmas in the pursuit of knowledge and the Divine. He often pokes fun at theologians and Sufis in his poems, he pokes fun at the pious and at religion as ritual, but he does not poke fun at the truth of religion as belief per se.

Khayyam has often been described as an agnostic, an atheist or a heretic, but I would venture to say that this is primarily a Western interpretation, the result of reading him through a Christian frame of reference. In Islam, his overt questioning of G—d would not be considered heresy. In the moments where he queries G—d he seems to believe in Him all the more (as a biblical Job). Though he questions the logic behind creation—Why is existence so transitory?—he is not an unbeliever. His questions are directed to some higher authority that he holds responsible for the perceived futility of existence. He is simply a questioner, a provocateur; he was, after all, a philosopher. Moreover, an Islamic tradition holds that the doubting or questioning believer is more prized and is nearer to G—d than the one who follows blindly. Khayyam was admired by many as one who understood the Truth, and, in some early Persian anthologies, Khayyam is referred to as *Hojjat-ol-Haqq* ("Proof of/Authority on the Truth"). This title was also given to Ibn Sina (Avicenna), and Khayyam was considered second only to him in the philosophical sciences.

Impact of FitzGerald's Khayyam:

1)   Khayyam and the touch of the Orient (or the 'exotic') made FitzGerald a household name, something he certainly would never have achieved on his own. This fame would overshadow all of his other translations, including the more serious works of Jami' (*Salaman and Absal*) and Farid ud-Din 'Attar (*Conference of the Birds or Bird Parliament*).

2)   There are a number of writers influenced by FitzGerald's Khayyam, including T.S. Eliot (who, it is said, came to writing after being inspired by Khayyam at the age of 13 or 14), Harold Lamb, and Oliver Herford (*Rubaiyat of a Persian Kitten*).

3)   FitzGerald's English translation remains the most famous, practically annihilating the French, German, etc. Irfan Shahid, then Sultanate of Oman Professor of Arabic and Islamic Literature at Georgetown University, postulated in a speech published in 1982 that the

dominance of the English version is due to the natural, linguistic affinity between English and Persian. He says this is because they are both "Indo-European" languages. I would say that this is an imagined affinity. The truth is that Persian belongs more specifically to the Indo-Aryan (whence the country's name, Iran) language group, which includes Hindi, Urdu, Sanskrit, Pashto, and Tajik. Though it is true that that group is now considered to be a subgroup of Indo-European, to this day the umbrella branch is more hypothetical than factual, and the filiation has more geographical than real justifications. Shahid states "[a] recognition of certain linguistic facts will show that English has closer affinities with Persian than either German or French or Latin or Greek.... Perhaps the most important is the fact that both English and Persian have reached a very advanced degree in the analytic process, a degree unknown to classical Greek or Latin or German" (19). Such a theory is questionable, and calls to mind Joachim du Bellay's sixteenth century manifesto, *La Défense et Illustration de la Langue française*. Moreover, as Shahid acknowledges (19–20), the argument for linguistic affinity cannot account for the relative failure of all other English versions of Khayyam.

4) Bad translations beget bad imitations. FitzGerald has been translated into almost every tongue on earth. Khayyam is known all over the world, but frequently as the result of bad translation squared.

5) Much to the chagrin of many Persian speakers, Khayyam has been held up as the epitome of their poetry, whereas for them he is broadly looked upon as a minor poet in their literary history. He is not even ranked among the top contenders of his time, and is much more famous for his writings on mathematics and physics.

6) FitzGerald brought about a new popularity of Khayyam in his native land. The impact of his fame abroad has obliged Persian scholars to (re)visit Khayyam. Tourists came to Iran looking for the Khayyam experience. This demand forced production of polyglot copies of the *Rubaiyat*. One such is my 1963 Amir-e Kabir edition. It uses FitzGerald's introduction, and lists his version with French and German beneath and Farsi (Persian) on the facing page. In such polyglot copies, the non-English versions (whose authors frequently go unnamed) are sometimes direct translations of the English, rather than translations of the Persian. The book jackets are more profusely ornamented than similar books for the domestic market, and the illustrations are often downright garish. (Elwell-Sutton also comments on this in his introduction to Dashti's work.). Sometimes, these books even include artistic depictions of mild undress.

7) The foreign interpretation of the *Rubaiyat* led to the development of a more suggestive painting style, which is sometimes referred to as Khayyamic. Of course, in Iran, this suggestive style never approached the stark nudity depicted in Western illustrations (see J. Yunge Bateman's drawings in a 1965 edition), which can be said to be yet another bad translation of Khayyam. The Western illustrations are more modest with male nudity, but women's nakedness is often depicted nearly in full. The ravishing damsel wears nothing but "a veil with tiny aster flowers," to borrow a title from Nasrin Ettehad, which floats breezily behind her, leaving her exposed. This conflicts with Persian literature, taking away the modesty, ergo, beauty, of elegantly clothed women reclining in coy poses, an omnipresent theme. To illustrate with an anecdote: even at the time of the last Shah, when Iran was at the height of Western imitation (*gharbzadegi*, to borrow a term from Jalal Al-e Ahmad), prostitutes in Tehran would wear full *chador*. They understood that even the man who consults a prostitute still wants to imagine that he is with a modest woman of noble character, who does not display the *asrar* (secrets) of her body, and the prostitute still wants to feign to be such.

8) There is no shortage of taverns, restaurants and like places of sumptuous dining, imbibing and general carousing bearing the name of Khayyam. This was also true for pre-revolution Iran. There is even an American cookbook entitled, *Dinner at Omar Khayyam's*. The food is Armenian and the restaurant was in California, but according to the author, the title comes from the Armenian story that it was one of their own who introduced the pious Khayyam to the pleasures of the Saki's cup.

9) Even his critics and subsequent translators had to resort to including FitzGerald's version in their books, thereby affording the reader an immediate opportunity to favor it. The reader was always forewarned that to compare these new texts to FitzGerald's would be to impose an undue hardship and unfair standards of excellence on the translators. Heron-Allen even went so far as to proclaim that the "excessive baldness" of his versions was "intentional" (Arnot 41). The challengers' renditions could not approach the beauty and grace of FitzGerald's and so their fate—banishment—was quickly sealed. The "Old Fitz" version has endured countless attacks from within what André Lefevere calls the "polysystem," and it has yet to be dethroned. In essence, it has been canonized, and though Lefevere assures us that "canonization is by no means final and irreversible" (55), Holbrook Jackson's hundred-year-old conjecture seems to be holding its own: "Other translators may come, but it is more probable that the *Rubaiyat* of Omar Khayyam

rendered into English verse by Edward FitzGerald will ever be the sun around which all others will revolve, lesser planets, drawing their light from him, yet paled by his greater rays. Some things are done as if by magic, with finality stamped upon them at birth" (21)

10) FitzGerald has set the standard for the translation of Classical Persian poetry, even for works by other Persian authors. This is unfair, but true. His own versions of Jamí and 'Attar were plagued by Khayyam's fame. Even today, I find that many translations of Classical Persian poetry attempt to sound like FitzGerald's work. Inevitably, it is always a case of 'Well, it isn't quite like Old Fitz's.'

FitzGerald's *Rubaiyat* lifted Khayyam's text out of what Stephen David Ross would call a "restricted economy"—national culture, literature, history, religion—and has given it a strange, yet wondrous, liberation, freeing it to "plenish the earth." Few other texts ever receive such enduring international acclaim. Still, it is a tainted freedom, which traps Khayyam and his *Roba'iyyat* in a new, imposed "restricted economy"—he is the patron saint of merry-making. On the one hand, FitzGerald has done the "Good for translation" (Ross), and Norton put it best in the Benjaminian wording of his 1869 review:

> FitzGerald is to be called 'translator' only in default of a better word, one which should express the poetic transfusion of a poetic spirit from one language to another, and the re-representation of the ideas and images of the original in a form not altogether diverse from their own, but perfectly adapted to the new conditions of time, place, custom and habit of mind in which they reappear. It is the work of a poet inspired by the work of a poet; not a copy, but a reproduction; not a translation, but the re-delivery of a poetic inspiration. (Heron-Allen 293)

On the other hand, FitzGerald is still the Pied Piper, and, sadly, the "'Messiah-like breath' of his poetic inspiration" (Arberry, *The Romance* 13) continues to paint Khayyam as the Bacchus of the East.

SAMPLE TRANSLATIONS

I.
And lately, by the Tavern Door agape,
Came stealing through the Dusk an Angel Shape,
Bearing a vessel on his Shoulder; and
He bid me taste of it; and 'twas-the Grape! EF 1, XLII

Drunken I passed by the wine-tavern last night;
I saw an old man, drunk and with a pitcher on his shoulder;
I said, 'Are you not ashamed of God, old man?'
He said: 'Generosity belongs to God; go, drink wine!' AJA 218
Sar-mast be-meikhaneh gozar kardam dush ...

The obvious irony in the Farsi quatrain is that Khayyam is also drunk. This is not evident in EF's version. Also, EF mistook the Persian word, 'piri', an old man, for 'pari', 'fairy'. Not only are these words spelt differently in Farsi, EF's error shows that he failed to recognize that the indefinite article was being used.

II.
The Moving Finger writes; and, having writ,
Moves on: nor all thy Piety nor Wit
Shall lure it back to cancel half a Line,
Nor all thy Tears wash out a Word of it. EF 1, LI

Nothing becomes different from what the Pen has once written,
and only a broken heart results from nursing grief;
though all your life through you swallow tears of blood
not one drop will be added to the existing score. AJA 126, 224
Az rafteh qaɪam hich digar-gun na-shavad ...

The characters of all creatures are on the Tablet,
The Pen always worn with writing 'Good', 'Bad':
Our grieving and striving are in vain,
Before time began all that was necessary was given. PAJHS, p. 44,
#26
Z-in pish neshan-e budaniha bud-ast ...

Oh heart, since the Reality of the world is allegory
How long will you go on nursing the grief of this prolonged anguish?
Submit the body to Fate and befriend the pain,
Since the stroke of the Pen will not return in your favor. TLS
Ay del, cho haqiqat-e jahan hast majaz ...

PAJHS has a similar version (p. 46, #32). The wording of this quatrain differs slightly in the manuscripts used by AJA and EHA. EF's version is a composite of these quatrains.

> III.
> Listen again, One Evening at the Close
> Of Ramazan, ere the better Moon arose,
> In that old Potter's Shop I stood alone
> With the clay Population round in Rows.
>
> And strange to tell, among that Earthen Lot
> Some could articulate, while others not
> And suddenly one more impatient cried—
> "Who is the Potter, pray, and who the Pot?" EF 1, LIV & IX
> (Kuza-Nama section)

Richard LeGallienne, in his version of the *Rubaiyat*, notes that FitzGerald's "kuza-nama" ("book of the pots") section is not to be found in Khayyam's Persian. Explaining why the reader will find this section missing from his own rendition, LeGallienne states: "À propos of the clay, the reader will miss that little book of the pots which is one of the triumphs of FitzGerald's version. Omar gives several hints for that quaint little miracle-play, but the development of them is so much FitzGerald's own that there was no option but to leave the pots alone" ("To The Reader").

In EF 2, 3, and 4, stanza LX was expanded into two non-sequential stanzas, each time varying greatly from EF 1, e.g.:

> Shapes of all Sorts and Sizes, great and small,
> That stood along the floor and by the wall;
> And some loquacious Vessels were; and some
> Listen'd, perhaps, but never talk'd at all.
>
> Whereat some one of the loquacious Lot—
> I think a Sufi pipkin—waxing hot—
> 'All this of Pot and Potter—Tell me, then,
> 'Who is the Potter, pray, and who the Pot?' EF 3 & 4, LXXXIII
> & LXXXVII

These were all inspired by one quatrain in the Persian, *Dar kar-gah-e kuzehgari raftam dush...*, which EBC translated as follows (AJA's is quite similar, except for 'two thousand pots', which is correct):

> I went last night into a potter's shop,
> A thousand pots did I see there, noisy and silent;
> When suddenly one of the pots raised a cry,
> 'Where is the pot-maker, the pot-buyer, the pot-seller?' EBC, in AJA, p. 228

KEY

AJA = Arthur John Arberry (1959)
EBC = Edward Byles Cowell (in Arberry, 1959)
EF = Edward FitzGerald. 1, 2, 3, 4 = FitzGerald Version
BHA = Edward Heron-Allen (1898)
PAJHS = Peter Avery & John Heath Stubbs (1979)
TLS = Tracia Leacock-Seghatolislami

WORKS CONSULTED

Arberry, Arthur J. *Omar Khayyam: A New Version Based upon Recent Discoveries*. London: John Murray, 1952.

————. *The Romance of the Rubaiyat: Edward FitzGerald's First Edition Reprinted with Introduction and Notes*. London: George Allen & Unwin Ltd., 1959.

Arnot, Robert, Ed. *The Sufistic Quatrains of Omar Khayyam, in Definitive Form including the Translations of Edward FitzGerald with Edward Heron-Allen's Analysis, E.H. Whinfield, J.B. Nicolas*. New York: M. Walter Dunne, 1903.

Benson, A. C. *Edward FitzGerald*. New York: Macmillan, 1905.

Browne, Edward Granville. *A Literary History of Persia*. 4 Volumes. Cambridge: Cambridge University Press, 1959–64.

D'Ambrosio, Vinnie-Marie. *Eliot Possessed: T. S. Eliot and FitzGerald's Rubaiyat*. New York: New York University Press, 1989.

Dashti, Ali. *In Search of Omar Khayyam*. Trans. L. P. Elwell-Sutton. London: George Allen & Unwin Ltd., 1971.

Datar, V. M. (Swami Govinda Tirtha). *The Nectar of Grace: 'Omar Khayyam's Life and Works*. Allahabad, Hyderabad: Kitabistan, 1941.

Du Bellay, Joachim. *La Défense et Illustration de la Langue française (extraits), avec oeuvres Poétiques diverses (extraits)*. Paris: Larousse, 1972.

Elwell-Sutton, L. P. "Omar Khayyam." *Persian Literature, Columbia Lectures on Iranian Studies 3*. Ed. Ehsan Yarshater. New York: Bibliotheca Persica, 1987. 147–160.

Ettehad, Nasrin. "A Veil With Tiny Aster Flowers." *Stories by Iranian Women Since the Revolution*. Trans. Soraya Paknazar Sullivan. Austin, Texas: Center for Middle Eastern Studies, The University of Texas at Austin, 1991. 173–184.

FitzGerald, Edward. *Rubaiyat of Omar Khayyam, Rendered into English Verse by Edward FitzGerald*. English-Farsi Edition. Ed. Yusef Jamshidipur. Tehran: Amir-e Kabir, S.H., 1963.1342.

———. *Rubaiyat of Omar Khayyam: The First and Fourth Editions in English verse by Edward FitzGerald*. New York: Thomas Y. Crowell Co., 1964.

———. *The Rubaiyat of Omar Khayyam: Edward FitzGerald's Translation Reprinted from the First Edition with his Preface and Notes*. Drawings by J Yunge Bateman. New York: A.S. Barnes and Co., 1965.

———. *The Rubaiyat of Omar Khayyam: Edward FitzGerald's Translation Reprinted from the First Edition with his Preface and Notes*. Drawings by J. Yunge Bateman. New York: A.S. Barnes and Co., 1965.

———. *Rubaiyat of Omar Khayyam, Rendered into English Verse by Edward FitzGerald*. New York: St. Martin's Press, 1983.

———. *Salaman and Absal. An Allegory translated from the Persian of Jami, together with A Bird's-Eye View of Farid-uddin Attar's Bird-Parliament*. Ed. Nathan Haskell Dole. Boston: L.C. Page and Co., 1899.

Heron-Allen, Edward. *The Rubaiyat of Omar Khayyam: A Facsimile of the MS in the Bodleian Library*. Second Edition. Trans. and Ed. Edward Heron-Allen. London: H.S. Nichols, Ltd., 1898.

Jackson, Holbrook. *Edward FitzGerald and Omar Khayyam: Art Essay*. London: David Nutt, 1899.

Jewett, Iran B. Hassani. *Edward FitzGerald*. Boston: Twayne Publishers, G.K. Hall & Co., 1977.

Khayyam, Omar. *Roba'yyat-e Hakim 'Omar Khayyam-e Nishapuri: Farsi, Ingilsi, Almani, Faranseh*. Third Edition. Tehran: Amir-e Kabir, S.H., 1963. 1342.

———. *The Ruba'iyat of Omar Khayyam*. Trans. Peter Avery and John Heath-Stubbs. London: Allen Lane, 1979.

———. *Roba'yyat-e Hakim 'Omar Khayyam, ba Divan-e Baba Taher 'Oryan*. Tehran, Iran: Eqbal, S.H., 1984. 1363.

Lefevere, André. "Beyond the Process: Literary Translation in Literature and Literary Theory." *Translation Spectrum: Essays in Theory and Practice*. Ed. Marilyn Gaddis Rose. Albany, NY: State University of New York Press, 1981. 52–59.

LeGallienne, Richard. *Rubaiyat of Omar Khayyam: A Paraphrase from Several Literal Translations*. New York: John Lane, 1897.

Mardikian, George. *Dinner at Omar Khayyam's*. Third Edition. New York: Viking Press, 1945.

Ross, Stephen David. "The Good for Translation." *Translation Horizons Beyond the Boundaries of Translation Spectrum, Translation Perspectives IX* (1996): 331–347.

Rypka, Jan. *History of Iranian Literature*. Dordrecht, Holland: D. Reidel Publishing Company, 1968.

Schopenhauer, Arthur. "On Language and Words." *Western Translation Theory: From Herodotus to Nietzsche*. Ed. Douglas Robinson. Manchester, UK: St. Jerome Publishing, 1997. 246–249.

Shahid, Irfan. *Omar Khayyam: The Philosopher-Poet of Medieval Islam*. Washington, DC: Georgetown University Press, 1982.

Terhune, Alfred McKinley. *The Life of Edward FitzGerald, Translator of the Rubaiyat of Omar Khayyam*. New Haven: Yale University Press, 1947.

Thonet, Jeanne-Marie H. *Etude sur Edward FitzGerald et la littérature persane, d'après les sources originales*. Liege: Imp. H. Vaillant-Carmane, 1929.

ERIK GRAY

Forgetting FitzGerald's Rubáiyát

Edward FitzGerald's *Rubáiyát of Omar Khayyám* constantly advises the reader to forget—preferably with the help of a drink: "Ah, my Beloved, fill the Cup that clears / TO-DAY of past Regret and future Fears." And again— "Oh, many a Cup of this forbidden Wine / Must drown the memory of that Insolence!"[1] Readers have not forgotten the *Rubáiyát*: by the end of the nineteenth century, it "must have been a serious contender for the title of the most popular long poem in English," and since then it has steadily continued to appear in innumerable (usually illustrated) editions.[2] Critics, on the other hand, seem to have taken FitzGerald at his word. The critical corpus is small; even major recent studies of Victorian poetry scarcely mention the poem.[3] Yet, ironically, it is the *Rubáiyát's* treatment of forgetting that marks it as a central text not only of Victorian poetry but of a rich and continuing literary tradition.

FitzGerald's poem gives a new twist to a widespread mid-Victorian preoccupation, the problem of striking an appropriate balance between memory and oblivion. Matthew Arnold, for instance, spoke out against an educational system founded upon rote memorization: "taught in such a fashion as things are now, how often must a candid and sensible man, if he were offered an art of memory to secure all that he has learned ... say with Themistocles: "teach me rather to forget!"[4] The need for forgetfulness

---

From *Studies in English Literature 1500–1900.* © 2001 by William Marsh Rice University.

continues to be a pressing issue at the end of the century for writers of the Aesthetic school; indeed, "aesthetic" literature often explicitly aspires to an *anaesthetic* condition. Consider, for instance, Dorian Gray's words, with their echo of Arnold: "[I]f you really want to console me, teach me rather to forget what has happened."[5] And the tradition has continued on into the twentieth century, most notably in the work of Jorge Luis Borges, a great reader and critic of Victorian literature.[6] Borges's heroes, in their obsession with memory, seem to be such prime candidates for Freudian analysis that it is easy to overlook the fact that they often find their closest models and analogues not in Freudian case studies but in nineteenth-century literary texts.

Among poets of the period, Alfred, Lord Tennyson and FitzGerald were the two most deeply concerned with the question of memory. I wish to begin with a brief discussion of Tennyson's poetry up to and including *In Memoriam A. H. H.*, a poem of commemoration which nevertheless seriously questions the desirability of memory. Tennyson's ambivalent feelings about "Blessèd, cursèd, Memory" date from the very start of his career; poems such as "The Lotos-Eaters" express a longing for oblivion, mingled with intense anxiety.[7] I shall argue that this anxiety stems from the important role played by memory in Tennyson's troubled conception of "dead selves"—the states a being passes through as the soul matures. Turning then to the *Rubáiyát*, which may well have been written partly as a response to Tennyson's elegy, I examine the formal means FitzGerald uses to efface his poem from the reader's memory.[8] In the concluding section, I offer a consideration of the poem's publication history, suggesting that readers have never forgotten the *Rubáiyát* paradoxically because they are unable to remember it precisely.

I

In section XLI of *In Memoriam*, Tennyson grieves over his sense of estrangement from Arthur Hallam:

> But thou art turned to something strange,
>   And I have lost the links that bound
>   Thy changes; here upon the ground,
> No more partaker of thy change.[9]

The problem is not that Tennyson has forgotten Hallam but quite contrarily that he remembers so well. A too vivid memory, rather than bringing the past nearer, tends to render it unfamiliar, in the same way that an old snapshot of a loved one can hinder one's recollections rather than revive them. This is the same problem that plagues Tennyson in section XXIV, when he begins to doubt his own memories of Hallam: they are too like "Paradise" to be compatible with the fallen world he has known since. A certain amount of forgetting is indispensable to blur the differences between past and present and give a sense of continuity; perfect memory is unforgiving.

This disturbing, even terrifying aspect of memory is best described in the twentieth century in Borges's great story, "Funes, the Memorious," the title character of which possesses an infallible memory. Borges describes him thus: "He was, let us not forget, almost incapable of general, platonic ideas. It was not only difficult for him to understand that the generic term *dog* embraced so many unlike specimens of differing sizes and different forms; he was disturbed by the fact that a dog at three-fourteen (seen in profile) should have the same name as the dog at three-fifteen (seen from the front). His own face in the mirror, his own hands, surprised him on every occasion."[10] Total recall here resembles forgetfulness, or even madness, Funes lacks the obliviousness to difference that makes life bearable. If we were incapable of forgetting, Borges suggests, every change would imply a new identity, every parting would be a death. It is only by forgetting the details that we are able to convince ourselves of continuity, that we do not mourn a lost friend with every change of hairstyle or accent. Forgetting provides what Tennyson calls the "links" that bind our "changes."

It is possible that Funes would never have needed to write *In Memoriam*, but, more importantly, it is certain that he would never have been able to write it. A perfectly memorious man could feel no great grief at a friend's death, no greater than at the infinite losses of former selves that take place every day. Hence it is that Tennyson begins his elegy by repudiating the idea that each state of existence dies to give way to the next:

> I held it truth, with him who sings
>   To one clear harp in divers tones,
>   That men may rise on stepping-stones
> Of their dead selves to higher things.
>
> But who can so forecast the years
>   And find in loss a gain to match?
>   Or reach a hand through time to catch
> The far-off interest of tears?
>
> Let Love clasp Grief lest both be drowned.

(I, 1–9)

Tennyson ascribes this rejected notion of "dead selves" to Johann Wolfgang von Goethe (the "him" of line 1), but it belongs to anyone who, like Funes, is mindful of distinct phases of development.

Yet, there is a difficulty here. Tennyson would not be Funes, or Goethe—he wishes to obliterate or forget distinctions between states of self. But, at the same time, he disowns a belief that belonged to his former self and, throughout the poem, he will continue to try to shed his current, melancholic self and to become someone new and worthy of the transformed Hallam ("following with an upward mind / The wonders that have come to thee" [XLI, 21–2]). Eric Griffiths locates this complication in the poem's very first words ("I held"): "The simple past next to 'I' immediately sets off the existence of the subject against change of state, and very sharply so, for this opening section of *In Memoriam* records altered convictions about the processes of alteration through which a self passes."[11] In its initial and continued desire to disown and forget "dead selves," and its contradictory impulse to cling to the past, *In Memoriam* writes large a conflict that reappears throughout Tennyson's poetry.[12] The paradox is present already in "Tithonus" (begun in 1833), who refers to his former self in the third person, who desires nothing more than to "forget," but who clings to memory as his only pleasure; and it continues through many of the major poems.[13]

The simplest and most complete formulation of the problem appears in "Locksley Hall" (published 1842):

> Where is comfort? in division of the records of the mind?
> Can I part her from herself, and love her, as I knew her, kind?
>
> I remember one that perished: sweetly did she speak and move:
> Such a one do I remember, whom to look at was to love.
>
> Can I think of her as dead, and love her for the love she bore?
> No—she never loved me truly: love is love for evermore.[14]

The speaker entertains the possibility of drawing a strict demarcation between past and present selves, only to dismiss the idea within six lines. Princess Ida in *The Princess* (1847), though she too will change her mind, holds out longer and more forcefully. She is the first to use the term "dead self," when she speaks to the Prince of having left behind all childish things:

> Methinks he [the Prince] seems no better than a girl;
> As girls were once, as we ourself have been:
> We had our dreams, perhaps he mixt with them:

We touch on our dead self, nor shun to do it,
Being other—[15]

That girl-self is not dead, but sleeping, as it turns out. Ida is asked in the end
to recognize that for a woman to abandon her childish self (to "lose the
child") is to risk being childless as well. The Prince advises her that she must
"nor fail in childward care, / Nor lose the childlike in the larger mind," and
although her acquiescence to such regression is not shown, it is implied.[16]
Supposedly dead selves have a way of coming back to haunt those who
claimed or sought to forget them.

   This is most painfully true in *Maud*, the speaker of which longs
explicitly for deliverance: "And ah for a man to arise in me, / That the man
I am may cease to be!"[17] The difficulty is that even when the new man
arrives, the old one refuses gracefully to quit the stage. The speaker does
change, from a melancholic, violent man into a]over, but the former self
reasserts itself the moment his childhood enemy confronts him. This is one
reason why he is so fascinated by the lovely shell on the Breton beach just
after he has killed his old rival. The shell is the dead self of some mollusk that
has now moved on, leaving the shell "Void of the little living will / That
made it stir on the shore."[18] The creature may seem to have left it behind,
but the shell is not therefore to be ignored:

   Frail, but of force to withstand,
   Year upon year, the shock
   Of cataract seas that snap
   The three decker's oaken spine
   Athwart the ledges of rock.[19]

However unassuming they may sometimes seem, dead selves are
indestructible. The wish to forget one's former self, and the impossibility of
doing so, drives the speaker of *Maud*, like that of "Locksley Hall," to the
desperate resolution of war.

   The conundrum of *In Memoriam*, however, though it concerns the
same issues, is somewhat different. Unlike his other speakers, who try to kill
off an earlier phase of existence but who soon encounter the return of the
repressed, the Tennyson of *In Memoriam* wishes to believe that there *is*
continuity from state to state. The difficulty arises when he tries to postulate
a continuity between the living Hallam and the dead Hallam. He is capable
of momentarily forgetting that any change has taken place, as when he
pictures how his friend "should strike a sudden hand in mine, / And ask a
thousand things of home."[20] Yet he is repeatedly compelled to admit that

these things are gone—that Hallam's hand and voice will never reach him
again. Physical death is too absolute a discontinuity to be treated in the same
manner as the daily deaths of former selves; the difference between Hallam
as he is now and as he used to be is simply too great to be glazed over by an
act of selective memory.

The consolation finally comes in the speaker's intimation of
immortality; yet it is a specifically Tennysonian immortality—not a
progression (like William Wordsworth's) that forgets former states of being,
but one that remembers everything:

> That each, who seems a separate whole
>   Should move his rounds, and fusing all
>   The skirts of self again, should fall
> Remerging in the general Soul,
>
> Is faith as vague as all unsweet:
>   Eternal form shall still divide
>   The eternal soul from all beside;
> And I shall know him when we meet.[21]

By conceiving an afterlife of memory, Tennyson is able to preserve the idea
of an integral self, even in the face of overwhelming change—and death.
Heaven solves the conundrum that had faced Tennyson on earth: that to
forget (Hallam) and to remember (his "change"[22]) were equally devastating.
Tennyson's distinctive heaven resembles earth in every way save one: there is
no change ("selves" is here reduced to "self"), and so no need for forgetting.
In Memoriam is a masterpiece of "negative capability": it is able and willing
to contemplate conflicting ideas without deciding between them. The poem
therefore does not propose to resolve the inherent tension between memory
and forgetfulness; but it does suggest that consolation is perhaps to be found
in the prospect of eventual changelessness. Less than a decade later, the
Rubáiyát would respond to the same problem very differently—by embracing
the inevitability of change, and hence, of oblivion.

II

The distinctive methods of the Rubáiyát are illuminated by another of
Borges's stories, which deals not with the capacity for infinite, instantaneous
memory, but with the process of memory indefinitely drawn out. "Pierre
Menard, Author of Don Quixote" concerns a young French symbolist whose
life's work is to write Don Quixote—not to transcribe it, not to transpose it to

the present, not to write an equivalent, but to write the original, which he had read once, as a boy, and of which he maintains a foggy memory, "much the same as the imprecise, anterior image of a book not yet written."[23] This extraordinary undertaking is inspired in part by a "fragment of Novalis ... which outlines the theme of *total* identification with a specific author."[24]

Herein lies much of the appeal of Borges's fantasy: his recognition that a reader who truly loves the work of an author is not satisfied merely with reading his or her works, still less with memorizing them; the dedicated reader wishes to identify with the process of actually conceiving the work. It is a commonplace that all reading is actually writing, or misreading; but Menard is not doing anything of the sort—"Any insinuation that Menard dedicated his life to the writing of a contemporary *Don Quixote* is a calumny of his illustrious memory."[25] All readers misread or rewrite, but only the truly kindred spirit does what Menard does: appropriates. Such appropriation demands a fine balance between memory and forgetting— remembering the words but forgetting their origin, obliterating the distinction between self and other.

Menard's unusual project makes him a remarkably close fictional approximation of FitzGerald, as is evident from Borges's brief, beautifully perceptive sketch, "The Enigma of Edward FitzGerald." FitzGerald is usually described simply as a "translator," but his relationship with his favorite authors, as Borges describes, was remarkably personal: "FitzGerald is aware that literature is his true destiny, and pursues it with indolence and tenacity. Over and over again he reads *Don Quixote*, which seems to him almost the greatest of books (he does not wish to be unjust to Shakespeare and 'dear old Virgil') and his passion embraces the dictionary in which he looks up words."[26] But this real-life Pierre Menard dedicated himself to the translation not of Miguel de Cervantes but of another beloved and kindred spirit, Omar Khayyám, and then "A miracle happens: from the lucky conjunction of a Persian astronomer who ventures into poetry and an English eccentric who explores Spanish and Oriental texts, without understanding them entirely, emerges an extraordinary poet who resembles neither of them."[27]

FitzGerald's *Rubáiyát* deserves all the semimystical language and veneration that Borges gives it because it is one of the oddest and most extraordinary poems in English. It is, for one thing, quite unclassifiable, thanks to FitzGerald's Menardian knack for writing someone else's poem. Borges is not alone in refusing to ascribe it either to FitzGerald or to Omar: librarians have had the same dilemma, and anyone looking for editions or references is almost invariably required to look under both names. The translation, as FitzGerald admitted, is terrifically inexact; yet FitzGerald no more wrote "a contemporary *Rubáiyát*" than Menard wrote "a contemporary *Don Quixote*." All of his liberties and his tinkering are done in good faith in the service of another: "I suppose very few people have ever taken such pains in Translation as I have."[28] The result is something selfless, yet at the same time personal: because this singular genre—the creation of another's work—is in fact peculiarly typical of FitzGerald. It was FitzGerald's habitual trick to ascribe to others his own words or images: he was a free translator, an intrusive editor, and an inveterate misquoter (that most common unacknowledged form of literary collaboration), but he never took credit for his contributions.[29] Almost all of his so-called translations appear with only the original author's name on the title page.

But, although all of FitzGerald's works show the same tendency for self-effacing collaboration as his *Rubáiyát*, none of them meant nearly as much to him as his Omar, whom he claimed as his "property."[30] Omar's verses appealed to FitzGerald for their hedonistic negligence;[31] to be sticklingly meticulous in his translation of them did not seem either necessary or proper. "Total identification" with the author required, in this case, not a perfect reconstruction of the text, but just the opposite. So when FitzGerald put forward his version of the *Rubáiyát* (anonymously, of course), the only way he could do so truly and ingenuously, with respect both to Omar and to himself, was to misremember almost every word.

The *Rubáiyát* continually exhorts us to do the very thing that Tennyson found so difficult—to forget, or at least to remember imperfectly. Forgetting is always problematic, but it is particularly so for a poet, since poetry is traditionally a mode of commemoration and preservation. It is worth examining the *Rubáiyát* in some detail, therefore, to try to understand how it achieves that very elusive state, oblivion. We might begin by noticing that there was at least one aspect of the original Persian that FitzGerald did not misremember: the all-important *aaba* rhyme scheme. This remembering is more difficult than it may seem—is, in fact, an act of memory so extraordinary as to equal an act of Menardian creativity. It is by no means self-evident that non-English verse forms should be retained in an English translation: Arnold, for instance, had to go to great lengths to make the case that Homer's hexameters are best translated by hexameters. FitzGerald's assumption of the foreign verse form is not only more successful than Arnold's, but also more daring.[32] Hexameters are not entirely uncommon in English poetry, but an *aaba* rhyme scheme is.[33] Unrhymed lines in English stanzas almost invariably come in twos (and so, though they do not rhyme with each other, at least they do-not-rhyme with each other, as it were); couple this oddity with a triple *a* rhyme, and you have something that sounds quite alien to English ears. Algernon Swinburne wrote "Laus Veneris," according to one account, within minutes of his enraptured first perusal of the *Rubáiyát*;[34] yet he was unable or unwilling to retain the unrhymed third line, but rhymed it instead with the third line of the succeeding stanza. Robert Frost's "Stopping by Woods on a Snowy Evening" also begins as a reminiscence of the *Rubáiyát* stanza (though in tetrameters), but Frost, too, recuperates the *b* rhyme, making it the rhyme word of the next stanza.

Nor was the retention of the rhyme scheme any easier for FitzGerald. His Latin translations of the quatrains for the most part retain the original scheme, but his first attempt at an English version does not:

> I long for Wine! oh Saki of my Soul
> Prepare thy Song & fill the morning Bowl;
> For this first Summer Month that brings the Rose
> Takes many a Sultan with it as it goes.[35]

The extraordinary effect of FitzGerald's brave decision to stick to the peculiar sounding original is evident when one compares the final version of this quatrain:

> Each Morn a thousand Roses brings, you say;
> Yes, but where leaves the Rose of Yesterday?
>   And this first Summer month that brings the Rose
> Shall take Jamshyd and Kaikobád away.
>
>   (IX)

This quatrain illustrates—as almost any of the quatrains might do equally well—how the form of the stanza speaks as effectively as the words. The third line proposes a new element, a change; but it is immediately, even willfully, forgotten by the fourth line. The return of the initial rhyme is like a resignation, a refusal to try to struggle with the new terms that have been introduced—as again in the next quatrain:

> Well, let it take them! What have we to do
> With Kaikobád the Great, or Kaikhosrú?
>   Let Zál and Rustum bluster as they will,
> Or Hátim call to Supper—heed not you.
>
>   (X)

If only forgetting were such an easy thing. But the fourth line, although it forgets to rhyme with the previous line, is not itself unrhymed. The "heed not you" at the end refuses to acknowledge the presence of the third line (or of Zál and Rustum); but it does look back to the sound of the opening of the quatrain. Yet this insistent triple rhyme (*do—rú—you*) is itself a sophisticated form of obliteration. It would be too simplistic to think that the narcotic, oblivious effect of the *Rubáiyát* was due only to its unrhymed lines; if this were true, blank verse would have the same effect, infinitely multiplied. The *Rubáiyát* is extraordinary not only for its unrhymes, but for its rhymes: the triple rhymes of each quatrain are themselves repeated ("rose," "wine," "dust" all reappear as the rhyming sounds of several quatrains); and the poem is also full of internal rhymes and assonance ("Rustum bluster"). This chiming is FitzGerald's way of dealing with the persistence of matter and of memory. One can make oneself forget some things by ignoring them (like the third line's *b* rhyme); others are unignorable, and must be erased by being repeated, but at the same time slightly transformed. It is therefore no contradiction of the poem's forgetful nature that the quatrain quoted above ("Each Morn a thousand Roses brings, you say") rhymes with the supposedly unrhymed line of an earlier quatrain:

> Come, fill the Cup, and in the fire of Spring
> Your Winter-garment of Repentance fling:
>   The Bird of Time has but a little way
> To flutter—and the Bird is on the Wing.
>
> (VII)

We thought we had seen the last of "way," only to find it echoed two quatrains later ("say," "Yesterday," "away"). But this reappearance, as I say, is no anomaly, because the poem is so concerned with the transformation of dead selves—how everything dies only to be reborn in different shape. Every rose was once a king, every lost friend is now grass on which we sit: and we shall soon be grass for others. Sounds likewise are constantly repeated, echoed, and transformed, and the cumulative effect of these rhymes is an impression, not of persistence, but of ephemerality. Each avatar is so brief and unremarkable as to be negligible; words and their component sounds are formed and unformed as easily as clay (and vice versa). The lush repetition of words and images is a formal means of ensuring that each individual occurrence will be forgotten. Thus the "Spring" mentioned in the quatrain above reappears near the end of the poem:

> Yet Ah, that Spring should vanish with the Rose!
> That Youth's sweet-scented manuscript should close!
>   The Nightingale that in the branches sang,
> Ah whence, and whither flown again, who knows!
>
> (XCVI)

As if to pre-empt the objection (or the consolation) that Spring does not close permanently—that it is reborn again a year later and therefore is not obliterated—FitzGerald brings it back in the very next quatrain.

> Would but the Desert of the Fountain yield
> One glimpse—if dimly, yet indeed, reveal'd,
>   To which the fainting Traveller might spring,
> As springs the trampled herbage of the field!
>
> (XCVII)

We are here offered several glimpses of "spring": not only the springing of the traveler and of the herbage, but the "Fountain" itself—"fountain" being another word for spring.[36] And yet, for all the multiplicity of "springs" in this quatrain, none of them is the same "Spring" that vanished in the quatrain before; you can not step into the same spring twice. Spring, roses, clay, both as concepts and as rhymes, keep cropping up in the poem, but always slightly changed from the previous incarnation. If they are remembered at all, they are misremembered.

At a larger structural level, the quatrains themselves are similarly forgetful. Although the separate quatrains echo each other, they do not usually pick up where the last one left off (unlike many paired or consecutive sections of *In Memoriam*). They give the impression of being at the same time cumulative and independent—as if each quatrain had a memory, but only a vague one, of what the others had said. This characteristic makes it very difficult to remember the order of the quatrains, which helps explain how such a remarkable poem can also be so utterly self-effacing. FitzGerald himself gives perhaps the best description, in a concise critique of Thomas Gray's "Elegy Written in a Country Churchyard": "I am always remembering, and always forgetting it: remembering, I mean, the several stanzas, and forgetting how they link together, partly, perhaps, because of each being so severally elaborated."[37] The *Rubáiyát*, which is even less sequential than Gray's elegy, achieves an even greater forgettability, though at the risk of lyric fragmentation. Yet, in the context of the poem's hedonism, the effect achieved is not fragmentation, but a pleasing dissolution.

III

The *Rubáiyát*'s distinctive appeal lies in the verve and sheer exuberance with which such obliteration is celebrated. The later editions of the poem make some attempt at casting it as cyclical, based on the cycle of day and night;[38] but the work is less notable as a cycle than as an example of recycling. The constant changes that bodies undergo, which had caused

Funes such surprise and Tennyson so much grief and desire for oblivion, here provide a sense of release. We discover body parts emerging in the most unusual places: the garden has a lap (XIX), the river has a lip (XX), and so does the earthen urn (XXXV), which is capable of speaking and kissing. Like the constant repetition of homonyms ("spring") or of phonemes ("earthen urn"), the reappearance of body parts destabilizes and blurs our perception of entities in the poem; dismemberment prevents remembering. As a result, repetitions that would elsewhere be infelicitous and body images that would elsewhere be grotesque here become a source of delight.

An extreme example comes in the description of the polo ball: "The Ball no question makes of Ayes and Noes / But Here or There as strikes the Player goes" (LXX). It is likely that in a poem less crammed with remembrances of human decay, a reader would not notice the "eyes and nose" peeping up out of the first line, here, by contrast, the pun is slyly insistent. Percy Shelley says that poets ought to revitalize dead language, and this is exactly what FitzGerald quite literally does (in this case with the stock collocation "ayes and noes"). The changes that bodies undergo in the text is analogous to the changes that rhymes and images and stanzas undergo. In both cases, readers are left with no choice but to do as they are told: to forget, since the endless variations of form prevent any single body or image from taking root in the memory.

One more example may serve to show how the *Rubáiyát* encourages us to rid ourselves of deep-seated memories. Consider for instance one of the poem's numerous literary allusions:

> Look to the blowing Rose about us—"Lo,
> "Laughing," she says, "into the world I blow,
>   "At once the silken tassel of my Purse
> "Tear, and its Treasure on the Garden throw."
>
> (XIV)

This quatrain contains, if not the "strongest," at least one of the most original misreadings of the final lines of Wordsworth's *Intimations Ode*: "To me the meanest flower that blows can give / Thoughts that do often lie too deep for tears."[39] Wordsworth freezes the blooming flower in the depths of imaginative memory; FitzGerald digs it back up and makes even the flower subject to change. Thoughts about flowers may lie too deep for *teers*, he suggests, but no flower can long be free from *tairs*. This whimsical misreading reminds us that from the point of view of the flower (who is here given a voice), brooding recollection is inappropriate; like everything in the *Rubáiyát*, she appears and is "at once" forgotten. FitzGerald plays on

Wordsworth's "blows" to give it a double sense: Wordsworth's flower not only blooms but blows away. Thus even Wordsworth is recalled only to be subject to immediate transformation and dissolution.

Yet, for all the forgetfulness that it both practices and preaches, the *Rubáiyát* was not forgotten, but became one of the most-read and most-remembered works in English. "In the 1953 edition of *The Oxford Book of Quotations* there are 188 excerpts from the Rubáiyát (of which 59 are complete quatrains)—this is virtually two thirds of the total work. Not even Shakespeare or the Authorized Version of the Bible are represented by such massive percentages."[40] Comparable representation appears, perhaps even more appropriately, in John Bartlett's *Familiar Quotations*. More appropriately, I say, because "familiar" is exactly the word to describe the status of quotations from the *Rubáiyát*, since the poem has this further peculiar distinction: many people can quote phrases or even whole lines that appear in it, and yet one can almost never be said entirely to have remembered a line of the *Rubáiyát*.

For what we call the *Rubáiyát* is actually four different versions of the poem, all of which, but especially the first and the fourth, are considered standard.[41] After having put forward the poem a first time, FitzGerald showed the same loving disregard for it as he showed for Omar's Persian version and retouched even those quatrains that have become the most well-known. Each successive edition has the effect of both recalling and effacing earlier versions—the poem's "dead selves." To be sure, there are other works that exist in various forms or stages.[42] But rarely do all the forms enjoy equal recognition; rarely are the variations so liberally sprinkled through the whole work; and rarely is it a work as much quoted as the *Rubáiyát*: the A, B, and C texts of *Piers Plowman*, for instance, manage two entries in Bartlett's between the three of them.

This coexistence of different versions is an essential aspect of the *Rubáiyát*, and it may very well have contributed to the poem's unexpected endurance. There is a sad truth about literature that is felt by all who delight in poetry: that a perfectly memorized poem is, to some extent, a dead poem. When one knows a poem so well that one does not even have to reflect in order to recreate it verbatim in one's mind, one gets little pleasure from remembering it. Poems and passages, on the other hand, that are only half-remembered, that need to be reconstructed, continue to haunt the memory. A line that is missing only a single word can be savored and considered, and enjoyed in a way that is denied to lines that arrive already complete. And, while searching for the perfect word, the lover of poetry can even know in part the thrill of creating a great work, merely from the fact of having forgotten it.

This thrill is characteristic of the *Rubáiyát*, and enables it to remain a living presence in the mind far beyond the usual date. When one remembers a stanza of one version of the *Rubáiyát*, even word for word, one still gets the sense of possessing only the half of it; every lover of the *Rubáiyát* is thus a miniature Pierre Menard—and a miniature FitzGerald. Indeed, we identify with FitzGerald doubly when we try to remember the poem. While we "write" the poem, we identify with him as we do with any author whose work we half-remember, and we identify with him again because this half-recollected reconstruction of the *Rubáiyát* is exactly what he undertook with Omar's version. This strong sense of identification may go some way toward explaining why FitzGerald the man has held such a great fascination for his readers—at times, indeed, has been a greater source of interest than his poem itself.[43]

For myself, I can say that I have studied the poem for years—have surely read it ten times as often as Hamlet's soliloquy or "Ozymandias": but it has been a long time since I have had the pleasure of mentally reconstructing either of these latter two. FitzGerald, on the other hand, I am never sure of having remembered, even after all those readings. And perhaps this same peculiarity that keeps the *Rubáiyát* alive in my mind explains, in part, why it continues to haunt the public in spite of its familiarity. For several generations, bits of the poem were everywhere;[44] many a person still alive probably grew up with a faded sampler in his or her bedroom that read:

> A Book of Verses underneath the Bough,
> A Jug of Wine, a Loaf of Bread—and Thou
>   Beside me singing in the Wilderness—
> Oh, Wilderness were Paradise enow!
>
> (XII)

Yet, even for that person, this stanza might not be ruined by overfamiliarity—because the same person could go downstairs and find, engraved on a plate or some other heirloom:

> Here with a Loaf of Bread beneath the Bough,
> A Flask of Wine, a book of Verse—and Thou
>   Beside me singing in the Wilderness—
> And Wilderness is Paradise enow.[45]

It is surely questionable whether the same benefit would accrue to other poems if it had been their fate to be presented to the world in such a multiplicity of forms. It would be disconcerting if *In Memoriam*, for example, existed in four equally authoritative versions; for even though *In Memoriam* does not purport to give answers, it is a poem of dwelling, of considering, and hence would only be injured, by allowing the evidence of its own piecemeal composition to become too prominent. So it is not just "benevolent destiny" that granted the *Rubáiyát* this gift of misrememberability, but something inherent in the work itself.[46] The poem is forgetful, or at least absent-minded, at every level: the rendition of the Persian, the rhymes, the quatrains, the different editions—all simultaneously recollect and efface dead selves. In its form, and in its forms, the *Rubáiyát* constantly misremembers, then demands and ensures that it should itself be richly misremembered in turn.

Tennyson and FitzGerald caught the fancy of their age by offering two poetic responses to the conflicting demands of memory and forgetting. In the early part of his career, culminating in *In Memoriam*, Tennyson revealed the importance of forgetting in allowing continuity from state to state of being—thus linking the question of memory to that other great Victorian concern, evolution. FitzGerald, in his no less enduring masterpiece, responded by creating a work which paradoxically succeeds in commemorating oblivion. The *Rubáiyát*'s peculiar authorial and textual multiplicity render it unique and hence, in the strictest sense, inimitable; but readers and poets alike seized upon it, if not as a model, yet as an inspiration.

NOTES

1. Edward FitzGerald, *The Rubáiyát of Omar Khayyám: A Critical Edition*, ed. Christopher Decker (Charlottesville and London: Univ. Press of Virginia, 1997), st. XXI, lines 1–2 and st. XXX, lines 3–4. All citations to *The Rubáiyát* will be to this volume and will refer to the fourth published edition, unless otherwise noted. Hereafter, citations will be made parenthetically in the text by stanza number.

2. Norman Page, "Larger Hopes and the New Hedonism: Tennyson and FitzGerald," in *Tennyson: Seven Essays*, ed. Philip Collins (New York: St. Martin's Press, 1992), pp. 141–59, 156. Decker's introduction notes the wide variety of audiences the poem has enjoyed: "It has been issued in illustrated editions, in pocket-sized wartime editions for servicemen in combat, in variorum editions, in limited editions, and in cheap paperbacks" (p. xiii). It is reprinted in its entirety in *The Norton Anthology of English Literature*.

3. I am thinking, for instance, of Isobel Armstrong's massive *Victorian Poetry: Poetry, Poetics, and Politics* (London and New York: Routledge, 1993), which allots the *Rubáiyát* less than a paragraph. Pauline Fletcher, *Gardens and Grim Ravines: The Language of Landscape in Victorian Poetry* (Princeton: Princeton Univ. Press, 1983), does not mention the poem at all, although Omar's Persian rose garden is arguably the most famous single garden in the poetry of the period. Other books on Victorian poetry are no more generous.

4. Matthew Arnold, "Johnson's *Lives of the Poets*," in *The Complete Prose Works of Matthew Arnold*. ed. R. H. Super, 11 vols. (Ann Arbor: Univ. of Michigan Press, 1960–77), 8:306–20, 306–7. Arnold cites Themistocles' dictum again in *The Popular Education of France and God and the Bible* (as Super points out, 8:461).

5. Oscar Wilde, *The Picture of Dorian Gray*, ed. Donald L. Lawler (New York: Norton, 1988), p. 86. Ironically, these words are addressed to Basil Hallward, whose portrait of Dorian serves as a constant reminder of "what has happened."

6. Jorge Luis Borges wrote not only the piece on FitzGerald that I mention below but also similar short essays on Robert Louis Stevenson, Wilde, G. K. Chesterton, H. G. Wells, and George Bernard Shaw.

7. Alfred, Lord Tennyson, "Memory [Ay me!]" (c. 1827), in *The Poems of Tennyson*, ed. Christopher Ricks, 2d edn., 3 vols. (Berkeley: Univ. of California Press, 1987), 1:286–8, line 5. Other early works by Tennyson on the same subject include "Memory! dear enchanter" (published 1827) and "Ode to Memory" (1830). All subsequent references to Tennyson's poems will be to the Ricks edition.

8. William Cadbury, "Fitzgerald's *Rubáiyát* as a Poem," *ELH* 34, 4 (December 1967): 541–67, notes striking verbal parallels (in addition to the clear thematic similarities); see especially pp. 554, 557.

9. "Tennyson, *In Memoriam A. H. H.*, 2:304–459, XLI, lines 5–8.

10. "Borges, "Funes, the Memorious," trans. Anthony Kerrigan, in *A Personal Anthology*, ed. Kerrigan (New York: Grove Press, 1967), pp. 35–43, 42.

11. Eric Griffiths, "Tennyson's Idle Tears," in *Tennyson: Seven Essays*, pp. 36–60, 47.

12. *Pace* James R. Kincaid, who holds that the desire to forget overwhelms the compulsion to remember; see "Forgetting to Remember: Tennyson's Happy Losses," in *Annoying the Victorians* (New York and London: Routledge, 1995), pp. 99–111.

13. Tennyson, "Tithonus," 2:605–12, line 75.

14. Tennyson, "Locksley Hall," 2:118–30, lines 69–74.

15. Tennyson, *The Princess*, 2:185–296, III, lines 202–6.

16. Tennyson, *The Princess*, VII, lines 267–8.

17. Tennyson, *Maud*, 2:513–84, I, lines 396–7.

18. Tennyson, *Maud*, II, lines 62–3.

19. Tennyson, *Maud*, II, lines 72–6.

20. Tennyson, *In Memoriam*, XIV, lines 11–2.

21. Tennyson, *In Memoriam*, XLVII, lines 1–8.

22. Tennyson, *In Memoriam*, XLI, line 8.

23. Borges, "Pierre Menard, Author of Don Quixote," trans. Anthony Bonner, ed. Anthony Kerrigan, in *Ficciones* (New York: Grove Press, 1962), pp. 45–55, 51.

24. Borges, "Pierre Menard, Author of Don Quixote," p. 48.

25. Ibid.

26. Borges, "The Enigma of Edward FitzGerald," trans. Alastair Reid, in *A Personal Anthology*, pp. 93–6, 94–5.

27. Borges, "The Enigma of Edward FitzGerald," p. 95.

28. FitzGerald, Letter of 27 April 1859 to E. B. Cowell, in *The Letters of Edward FitzGerald*, ed. Alfred McKinley and Annabelle Burdick Terhune, 4 vols. (Princeton: Princeton Univ. Press, 1980), 2:334–5, 335.

29. FitzGerald went so far as to touch up the paintings in his collection, not excluding those he ascribed to Old Masters. See Robert Bernard Martin, *With Friends Possessed: A Life of Edward FitzGerald* (London: Faber and Faber 1985), p. 227.

30. "But in truth I take old Omar rather more as my property than yours; he and I are more akin, are we not?" FitzGerald, Letter of 8 December 1857 to E. B. Cowell, in *Letters*, 2:304–6, 305.

31. FitzGerald turned to Omar specifically to help him forget: his period of most intense translation came while he was reluctantly preparing for his unhappy marriage in 1856.

32. Arnold gives tentative hexameter translations of a few passages of Homer near the end of "On Translating Homer." See *Complete Prose*, 1:160–7.

33. The rhyme scheme may, however, derive some of its effect from our familiarity with *aaba* metrical structures (the limerick is a good example); the deviation in the third element creates a suspension that is resolved in the return at the end. See Derek Attridge, *The Rhythms of English Poetry* (London and New York: Longman, 1982), pp. 94–6.

34. The story is told by George Meredith in a letter to the *Times* of 14 April 1909, reprinted as letter 2553, in C. L. Cline, ed. *The Letters of George Meredith*, 3 vols. (Oxford: Clarendon Press, 1970), 3:1691–2.

35. FitzGerald, *Letters*, 2:289. FitzGerald calls this "a poor Sir W. Jones' sort of parody," referring to a quatrain that FitzGerald saw translated into verse in Jones's Persian grammar, which can be found in the edition of the *Rubáiyát* by Dick Davis (Harmondsworth: Penguin, 1989), p. 36. Like FitzGerald's first attempt, Jones's translation abandons the Persian rhyme scheme, and rhymes *aabb*. FitzGerald's Latin versions are reprinted in Decker's edition.

36. Daniel Schenker, "Fugitive Articulation: An Introduction to *The Rubáiyát of Omar Khayyám*," *VP* 19, 1 (Spring 1981): 49–64, mentions the play on the words "spring" and "fountain" (p. 50).

37. FitzGerald, *Euphranor* (first published 1851), in *Letters and Literary Remains of Edward FitzGerald*, ed. W. A. Wright, 3 vols. (London: Macmillan, 1889), 2:1–66, 53. This passage was added in the third edition, published in 1882, by which time all four versions of the *Rubáiyát* had appeared.

38. Comparing the second edition to the first in a letter to his publisher Bernard Quaritch of 31 March 1872, FitzGerald writes of the speaker: "He begins with Dawn pretty sober and contemplative: then as he thinks and drinks, grows savage, blasphemous, etc., and then again sobers down into melancholy at nightfall" (*Letters*, 3:338–40, 339).

39. "Wordsworth, "Ode: Intimations of Immortality from Recollections of Early Childhood," in *The Poems*, ed. John O. Hayden, 2 vols. (Harmondsworth: Penguin, 1977; rprt. 1990), 1:523–9, lines 203–4.

40. From Davis's introduction to his edition, pp. 1–2. More recent editions of the *Oxford Book of Quotations* have severely cut back on quotations from the *Rubáiyát*; the entry in Bartlett, on the other hand, has not changed. It is easy to forget just how familiar the poem was until just a generation ago; as late as 1959, Hugh Kenner could begin a book on T. S. Eliot by calling "The Love Song of J. Alfred Prufrock" the "best-known English poem since the *Rubaiyat*" (*The Invisible Poet: T. S. Eliot* [New York: McDowell, Obolensky, 1959], p. 3).

41. What is often called the fifth edition is just the fourth edition with a few punctuation changes, penciled in by FitzGerald before his death.

42. Recent critical emphasis on the multiplicity of versions of even our most canonical texts makes it necessary to explain what is distinctive about the *Rubáiyát*. It is rare for multiple versions to continue to coexist, and not rather to be hidden away in publication history. Thus, although there are multiple *Hamlets* and *King Lears*, conflated versions of both plays with relatively few major variants have, until very recently, dominated classroom and stage. William Wordsworth's *The Prelude* existed in one version throughout the nineteenth century, and two through most of the twentieth; only the demands of Romantic anthologists put into circulation a third ("1799") and more recently a fourth (the "five-book *Prelude*"). Multiple versions of the *Rubáiyát*, on the other hand, have always coexisted in popular editions: the edition published in the Golden Treasury Series (1899), though it was one of the first posthumous British editions intended for a popular market (rather than for connoisseurs or enthusiasts), was a mini-variorum,

reprinting the first and fourth editions, together with an appendix showing all variants from the other editions.

43. There are far more biographies and anecdotes than studies of the verse, and a critical edition of FitzGerald's letters was available seventeen years before the first good critical edition of the *Rubáiyát* itself.

44. Any secondhand bookshop or consignment shop, in America as much as in England, bears witness to this. Paul Elmer More, writing in 1899, attests to the poem's being quoted even "in a far-away mining camp" ("Kipling and FitzGerald," in *Shelburne Essays, Second Series* [New York: Putnam's, 1907], pp. 104–25, 105). See also Barbara J. Black, *On Exhibit: Victorians and Their Museums* (Charlottesville and London: University Press of Virginia, 2000), whose second chapter (pp. 48–66) offers an account of the *Rubáiyát* as both a collection and something to be collected. Black provides an excellent analysis of just how strong a cultural presence FitzGerald's poem was; see especially pp. 59–61.

45. This version of the lines is from the first published edition, XI.

46. Thus Borges describes the mystery of the poem's composition, "The Enigma of Edward FitzGerald," p. 96.

Chronology

1809	Born Edward Purcell on March 31 at Bredfield House near Woodbridge in Suffolk, the sixth of eight children, in a well-to-do family. His father, John Purcell, was the son of a wealthy Irish doctor, who traced his descent from Cromwell. A country squire fond of hunting and shooting, as well as M.P. for Seaford, John Purcell had a penchant for impractical business schemes. His mother, Mary Frances FitzGerald Purcell, was descended from the Earls of Kildare. A very gifted and vivacious woman, she was also a good linguist and fond of poetry.
1814	Edward's father takes a house in Paris and several months are spent there in each of the next few years.
1818	FitzGerald's maternal grandfather dies. His grandfather was a man of great wealth, with estates in Ireland, Northamptonshire, Suffolk and elsewhere. FitzGerald's father, John Purcell, assumes his wife's surname, as Mary Frances is now her father's heiress.
1821	Begins studies at King Edward VI Grammar School in Bury St. Edmunds under the direction of Dr. Malkin. The school had a wonderful reputation, placing great emphasis on the writing of English. Among his school-day friends were Bodham Donne (1807–1882), the well-known historical writer; J.M. Kemble (1807–1857), the famous Anglo-Saxon

scholar; and James Spedding (1808–1881), the editor of the works of Francis Bacon and a man of great genius.

1825   The FitzGeralds leave Bredfield and move to Wherstead Lodge, a beautiful home near Ipswich. Already fond of books and devoted to the theater, FitzGerald demonstrates a talent for idealizing his friends, which will later enable him to form some very sacred friendships. Some of the eccentric personalities he encounters are Squire Jenny, a jovial old sportsman of short stature and enormous ears, who lived with open windows into which the snow was allowed to drift, and a portly old Anglo-Indian, Major Moor, who wore a huge white hat (many sizes too big) and collected images of Oriental gods, which he assembled into a mausoleum. Always happy to talk about his Eastern experiences, Moor is an important influence on Edward's interest in Oriental literature.

1826   In October, FitzGerald enters Trinity College, Cambridge, taking up residence with a Mrs. Perry at No. 19, King's Parade. The master of Trinity was Christopher Wordsworth, a younger brother of the Romantic poet William Wordsworth. Among his friends at Trinity are W. M. Thackeray, John Allen, W. H. Thompson, Frank Edgeworth, brother of the authoress, John Kemble and Charles and Alfred Tennyson.

FitzGerald is not an enthusiastic student, reading the classical authors he likes in a desultory manner and occupying himself with water-colour drawing, music, and poetry. Though he has plenty of money, he has no expensive tastes, preferring a dilapidated wardrobe.

1830   In February, Edward takes a degree without distinction.

1831   Publishes *The Meadows of Spring*, 1831, a collection of verse which appears in *Hone's Year Book*.

1832   Meets William Kenworthy Browne, sixteen-years-old, on a steamship to Tenby. They will spend many summers together fishing on the river Ouse.

1842   Attends performance of Handel's *Acis and Galatea*. The painter, Samuel Lawrence, introduces FitzGerald to the already well-know essayist and historian, Thomas Carlyle. Their friendship begins with a common interest in the battlefield at Naseby, for which Carlyle is seeking information for his biography of Cromwell. Carlyle, fifteen years older, will remain one of the FitzGerald's most famous correspondents. With FitzGerald's encouragement, a reluctant Tennyson finally publishes his *Poems* of 1842.

1844
William Kenworthy Browne is married. Around Christmas, FitzGerald is introduced to Edward Byles Cowell, while at the house of the Reverend John Charlesworth, to whose daughter, Elizabeth, FitzGerald had once thought of proposing, and whom Cowell would himself marry in 1947. Cowell was a scholarly young man seventeen years his junior with an extraordinary gift for languages. Cowell was also a more accomplished classicist. He and Edward read Latin and Greek together, and a few years later, Cowell teaches Edward Spanish.

1848
Following the failure of a mining venture, Edward's father declares bankruptcy.

1849
Edward's father separates from his mother. Bernard Barton, the Quaker poet and friend of Edward FitzGerald, dies. On his death bed Barton asks Edward to look after his daughter Lucy. At Lucy's request, FitzGerald "edits" Barton's work , selecting, rearranging, condensing, and at times rewriting nine volumes of verse into two hundred pages, including a memoir of his friend.

1850
In November, at his wife's urging and over FitzGerald's objections, Cowell leaves the management of his father's business in Suffolk to matriculate at Oxford. In December, FitzGerald visits Cowell at Oxford. Cowell starts FitzGerald's study of Persian.

1851
Publishes a philosophical dialogue, *Euphranor: A Dialogue on Youth*, the subject of which concerns education and in which FitzGerald cites Carlyle's call for national reformation of the evils of modern industrial society. By October, FitzGerald had finished Sir William Jones's book on Persian grammar (1771) and turns to Persian poetry, consulting with Cowell as necessary, and comparing notes with Tennyson for a brief time.

1852
Edward's father dies. Publishes *Polonius: A Collection of Wise Saws and Modern Instances*. Eschewing eighteenth-century

English, which he and Carlyle believed had lost its vitality, FitzGerald's preface declares his intention to the energy of the age of Elizabeth and her successors. By the fall, FitzGerald's letters express a particular fondness for the dramas of Calderón.

1853   Leaves Boulge Cottage and assumes a less settled way of life, taking rooms or staying with his friend, George Crabbe, the vicar of Bredfield and son of the poet of the same name. *Six Dramas of Calderón, Freely Translated*, from Spanish, is published in July. The dramas include *The Painter of His Own Dishonour*; *Keep Your Own Secret*; *Gil Perez, the Gallician*; *Three Judgments at a Blow*; *The Mayor of Zalamea*; and *Beware of Smooth Water*. FitzGerald admits in his preface to having taken liberties with his material. These do not receive favorable critical reception, some accusing him of rendering English imitations rather than translations. However, they are popular with the reading public. Cowell also inspires Edward FitzGerald's interest in Persian poetry.

1854   Around May, FitzGerald discovers *Salámán and Absál, An Allegory*, by the fifteenth-century poet, Jámí. Visits the Tennysons on the Isle of Wight and will pay them another visit in 1855.

1855   In the winter, FitzGerald completes his translation of *Salámán and Absál*. Edward's mother dies. Her share of the estate assures him a comfortable life. Carlyle spends ten days with FitzGerald in Suffolk.

1856   Publishes his translation of *Salámán and Absál*. On August 1, Cowell and his wife leave for India, where Cowell is to assume a professorship at Presidency College in Calcutta. Cowell's parting gift to FitzGerald is a transcript he had made from a manuscript at the Bodleian Library of one-hundred fifty-eight quatrains by the twelfth-century Perisan, Omar Khayyám. Nevertheless, Cowell's departure becomes one of many personal shocks that FitzGerald will suffer during the next several years. On November 4, at the age of forty-seven, FitzGerald marries Lucy Barton. An unhappy union, based on a promise to Lucy's father, their marriage lasts only a few months, during much of which they live apart.

1857	Crabbe dies. In August, Lucy and Edward are separated after eight months of wedlock. Though the year marks the beginning of a long retreat from his emotional life, it also marks the beginning of his literary triumph. In the winter, when he returns to his Persian studies, FitzGerald focuses on "Bird Parliament," the title he gave to Faríd al-Dín Attár's thirteenth-century allegory, and which he rendered into a "metrical abstract." However, FitzGerald's translation of Attár's allegory was not published during his lifetime. In late May, FitzGerald turns to Khayyám's quatrains as a form of "consolation." In June, Cowell sends him a manuscript of five-hundred sixteen stanzas by Khayyám found in the library of the Royal Asiatic Society at Calcutta.
1858	In January, he sends *Fraser's* magazine thirty-five quatrains that he has rendered into English. William Morris publishes his *Defence of Guenevere and Other Poems*, his title character having been accused of adultery. Morris and his colleagues, most notably Dante Gabriel Rossetti, justify their poetry on the grounds of beauty, apart from religious or moral considerations.
1859	Having received no response from the editors of *Fraser's*, FitzGerald withdraws his earlier submission, adds forty more quatrains, publishes two-hundred fifty copies and places them on sale at Bernard Quaritch's bookshop in London on April 9. The title page reads: *Rubáiyát of Omar Khayyám, the Astronomer-Poet of Persia. Translated into English Verse.* The book is published anonymously. and, priced at a shilling, it goes unnoticed for some time. W.K. Browne dies.
1860	In December, FitzGerald leaves the countryside near Woodbridge and settles into two-room lodgings on Market Hill within the town. Unlike London and the Suffolk countryside, the sea holds no painful memories for FitzGerald. FitzGerald soon advances in seamanship.
1861	FitzGerald has a sailboat made, the *Waveney*. *The Rubáiyát* is discovered by other artists and literary figures, such as Dante Gabriel Rossetti, poet and painter of the Pre-Raphaelite Brotherhood. When Rossetti and A.C. Swinburne hear of the fate of *The Rubáiyát*, they purchase several copies and distribute it among their friends, which causes the price of *The Rubáiyát* to double the following day.

1863   Another disciple of Rossetti, the painter Edward Burne-
            Jones, shows *The Rubáiyát* to John Ruskin. Ruskin is very
            impressed with the work and gives Burne-Jones a letter to
            Khayyám's anonymous translator, if his identity should ever
            be revealed. Builds a yacht, the *Scandal*, which becomes his
            summer home for the next eight years. FitzGerald loves the
            easy life of those whom make their living by the sea.
            Thackeray dies on Christmas Eve.

1864   FitzGerald becomes friendly with a herring fisherman
            named Joseph ("Posh") Fletcher, a man in whom he finds
            an ideal of active manhood complemented by a retiring
            nature.

            Browning uses another twelfth-century philosopher-
            astronomer-poet, the Spanish Jew Ibn Ezra, as his
            spokesman in "Rabbi Ben Ezra," in which he employs the
            metaphor of God as a potter, suggesting that man's
            struggles on earth shape him into a finished vessel for God's
            heavenly use.

1864   FitzGerald purchases a cottage on Pytches Road at the edge
            of Woodbridge. The Cowells return from India.

1865   Publishes anonymously *The Mighty Magician and Such Stuff
            as Dreams are Made Of: Two Plays Translated from Calderón*;
            privately prints *Agamemnon: A Tragedy Taken from Aeschylus*.

1867   Buys a herring lugger, the *Meum and Tuum*, thereby
            entering into a business partnership with Posh Fletcher.
            However, arguments over Posh's drinking and failure to
            keep accurate records as well as FitzGerald's interference,
            cause tension. The partnership will end in three years at a
            loss. With FitzGerald's assistance, Cowell is appointed
            Professor of Sanskrit at Cambridge.

            Interest in *The Rubáiyát* has grown sufficiently for Quaritch
            to suggest a second edition. A new translation of Khayyám
            is published in France by J.B. Nicolas. Nicolas maintains
            that Khayyám belonged to the sect of Moslem mystics
            known as Súfis and, accordingly, he gives the *The Rubáiyát* a
            sacred interpretation, in which wine symbolizes the love of
            God and intoxication symbolizes mystical transport. For his
            part, Cowell backs away from FitzGerald's secularized
            reading, where wine is simply wine and is used in defiance
            of Islamic law.

1868	Publishes second edition of *The Rubáiyát*, adding thirty-five more stanzas. FitzGerald explains the additional stanzas as enabling him to suggest the passage of time and shifts in the speaker's moods. In the preface to the second edition, he refutes Nicolas and argues instead that Khayyám was opposed to the Súfis.
1869	FitzGerald and Posh purchase another herring boat, the *Henrietta*. In October, Charles Eliot Norton reviews the poem in the *North American Review*, lauding it as an "original production" and rejecting the word *translation* as an apt description for FitzGerald's verses. As a result of Norton's favorable review, *The Rubáiyát* begins to gain wide popularity in American.
1870	Major critical notice of *The Rubáiyát* is given in *Fraser's*.
1872	Third edition of *The Rubáiyát* is published, shortened to one-hundred and one quatrains. When Norton arrives from the United States in the fall, Burne-Jones passes on the rumor that the author is the "Reverend Edward FitzGerald."
1873	In April, Norton repeats the rumor of the *The Rubáiyát's* authorship to Thomas Carlyle. Now that the secret is out, Ruskin's letter is delivered to FitzGerald through Norton. Norton begins his friendship with FitzGerald. FitzGerald is evicted from his Woodbridge cottage.
1874	Moves into Little Grange on Pytches Road, living in his own house for the first time in his life.
1875	In the February edition of *Lippincott's* magazine, Edward FitzGerald is publicly identified as the author of *The Rubáiyát*
1876	Tennyson visits FitzGerald with his son, Hallam. As a result of some of Omar Khayaám's American devotees, in November, FitzGerald sends Quaritch several copies to be forwarded gratis to his admirers.
1878	James Osgood brings out the first American edition of *The Rubáiyát* in Boston. Demand at home prompts Quaritch to encourage a fourth English edition. Before doing so, FitzGerald makes some minor revisions to *The Rubáiyát*, and decided to include the religious allegory *Salámán and Absál* within the same volume.

<table>
<tr><td>1879</td><td>Fourth edition of The Rubáiyát. Privately prints Readings in Crabbe: Tales of the Hall. Death of his oldest brother, John, and his youngest sister, Andalusia, leaving only him and his sister Jane the only survivors of the eight children of John Purcell and Mary Frances FitzGerald.</td></tr>
<tr><td>1880</td><td>Carlyle and James Spedding die. Anonymously publishes The Downfall and Death of King Oedipus: A Drama in Two Parts, Chieflyl Taken from the Oedipus Tyrannus and Coploneaus of Sophocles in two parts, volumes I published in 1880 and volume II in 1881.</td></tr>
<tr><td>1882</td><td>Quaritch publishes a new edition of Readings in Crabbe.</td></tr>
<tr><td>1883</td><td>In the spring, Tennyson is planning the publication of "Tiresias," and as a preface, composes a dedication in the form of a verse epistle, "To E. FitzGerald." But FitzGerald never saw this dedication. On June 14, while visiting George Crabbe, grandson of the poet whose verses he had recently decided to improve, Edward Fitzgerald dies in his sleep.</td></tr>
</table>

Contributors

HAROLD BLOOM is Sterling Professor of the Humanities at Yale University and Henry W. and Albert A. Berg Professor of English at the New York University Graduate School. He is the author of over 20 books, including *Shelley's Mythmaking* (1959), *The Visionary Company* (1961), *Blake's Apocalypse* (1963), *Yeats* (1970), *A Map of Misreading* (1975), *Kabbalah and Criticism* (1975), *Agon: Toward a Theory of Revisionism* (1982), *The American Religion* (1992), *The Western Canon* (1994), and *Omens of Millennium: The Gnosis of Angels, Dreams, and Resurrection* (1996). *The Anxiety of Influence* (1973) sets forth Professor Bloom's provocative theory of the literary relationships between the great writers and their predecessors. His most recent books include *Shakespeare: The Invention of the Human* (1998), a 1998 National Book Award finalist, *How to Read and Why* (2000), and *Genius: A Mosaic of One Hundred Exemplary Creative Minds* (2002). In 1999, Professor Bloom received the prestigious American Academy of Arts and Letters Gold Medal for Criticism, and in 2002 he received the Catalonia International Prize.

JOHN D. YOHANNAN is a widely-published Persian scholar. He is the editor of *Persian Literature in Translation* (1988) and author of *Persian Poetry in England and America: A 200-Year History* (1978).

IRAN HASSANI JEWETT has taught English literature and has written for the radio and periodicals in the United States, India and Iran. Her articles on comparative literature have appeared in such scholarly journal as *Orientalia*

Suecana and *Oriens*. She has also been the Persian editor of Twayne's World Authors Series. She is the author of *Alexander W. Kinglake* (1981).

DANIEL SCHENKER is Associate Professor in the English Department at the University of Alabama in Huntsville. He is the author of "A Samurai in the South: Cross-Cultural Disaster in T. Coraghessan Boyle's *East Is East*" (1995), "From Prophetic Vision to Willful Blindness: The Art of William Blake and Wyndham Lewis" (1988) and an editor of *Inner Space/Outer Space: Humanities, Technology and the Postmodern World* (1993).

ROBERT BERNARD MARTIN taught at Princeton, and was a Fulbright scholar at Oxford University and Professor Emeritus of English at University of Hawaii, Manoa. He is the author of *Tennyson, the Unquiet Heart* (1980), a biography of Gerard Manley Hopkins, *A Very Private Life* (1991), and *The Triumph of Wit: A Study of Victorian Comic Theory* (1974).

FREDERICK A. de ARMAS is Andrew W. Mellon Professor in Humanities at the University of Chicago. His books include: *The Invisible Mistress: Aspects of Feminism and Fantasy in the Golden Age* (1976), *The Prince in the Tower: Perspectives on "La vida es sueno"* (1993), *A Star-Crossed Golden Age: Myth and the Spanish Comedia* (1998), and *Cervantes, Raphael and the Classics* (1998).

VINNI MARIE D'AMBROSIO is the author of "'The Cat' at Wuthering Heights" (1992) and "Tzara in *The Waste Land*" (1990).

NORMAN PAGE has held the position of Professor of English Literature, Nottingham; previously he taught at the University of Alberta. He is the author of *Thomas Hardy: The Novels* (2001), "A. E. Housman and Thomas Hardy" (2000), "Art and Aesthetics" (1999), and *Auden and Isherwood: The Berlin Years* (1998).

Poet and critic JOHN HOLLANDER is Sterling Professor Emeritus of English at Yale University. His critical books include *Vision and Resonance* (1975), *The Figure of Echo* (1981), *Rhyme's Reason* (1981), [3rd expanded edition 2000], *Melodious Guile* (1988), *The Gazer's Spirit*, (1995), *The Work of Poetry* (1997), and *The Poetry of Everyday Life* (1998).

ARTHUR FREEMAN of Bernard Quaritch Ltd. is the author of "'The Report of the Illustrious Obscure': Hazlitt, Rackets, and the Coronation" (1995), *Elizabeth's Misfits: Brief Lives of English Eccentrics, Exploiters, Rogues, and Failures, 1580–1660* (1978), and co-author of "Did Halliwell Steal and Mutilate the First Quarto of Hamlet?" (2001).

TRACIA LEACOCK-SEGHATOLISLAMI has taught at the State University of New York at Binghamton. She is an editor of *Africanity Redefined: The Collected Essays of Ali A. Mazrui, Volume I.* (2002).

ERIK GRAY is Assistant Professor of English at Harvard University. He is the author of "Nostalgia, the Classics, and the Intimations Ode: Wordsworth's Forgotten Education" (2001), "Tennyson and Ulysses Becoming a Name" (2000), and "Sonnet Kisses: Sidney to Barrett Browning" (2002).

Bibliography

Alviar, Lourdes J. "A Comparison of Ecclesiastes and Rubaiyat." *Saint Louis University Research Journal* 17, no. 1 (June 1986): 109–120.

Arberry, Arthur J. *The Romance of the Rubaiyat*. London: Allen & Unwin, 1959.

———. *Rubáiyát: A New Version Based Upon Recent Discoveries*. New Haven: Yale University Press, 1952.

Bagley, F.R.C. "Omar Khayyam and FitzGerald." *Durham University Journal* LIX, 2 (N.S. XXVIII) (March 1867): 81–93.

Benson, A.C. *Edward FitzGerald*. London: Macmillan, 1905; New York: Greenwood Press, rpt. 1969.

Bentham, George. *The Variorum and Definitive Edition of the Poetical and Prose Writings Of Edward FitzGerald*, 7 volumes. New York: Doubleday, Page 1902–1903; New York: Phaeton Press, 1967.

Black, Barbara J. "Fugitive Articulation of an All-Obliterated Tongue: Fitzgerald's *Rubáiyát* and the Politics of Collecting." *On Exhibit: Victorians and Their Museums*. Charlottesville: University Press of Virginia, 2000.

Brown, Carole. "Omar Khayyam in Monto: A Reading of a Passage from James Joyce's *Ulysses*." *Neophilologus* 68, no. 4 (October 1984): 623–636.

Browne, Gerald D. "Edward FitzGerald's Revisions." *Papers of the Bibliographical Society of America* 69 (1975): 94–112.

Cadbury, William. "Fitzgerald's Rubaiyat as a Poem." *English Literary History* 34 (1967): 541–63.

Croft-Cooke, Rupert. *Feasting With Panthers: A New Consideration of Some Late Victorian Writers*. London: W.H. Allen, 1967.

Davis, Dick. *Rubaiyat of Omar Khayyam: Translated by Edward FitzGerald*. Harmondsworth: Penguin, 1989.

Elwell-Sutton, L. P. "Omar Khayyam." *Persian Literature*. Ehsan Yarshater, editor. Albany, N.Y.: Bibliotheca Persica (1988): 147–60.

———. "The Rubaiyat Revisited." *Delos* 3, (1969): 170–91.

George, Emery E. "Movable Metric, Translated Music: The Rubaiyat of Henry W. Nordmeyer." *Husbanding the Golden Grain: Studies in Honor of Henry W. Nordmeyer*. Edited by Luanne T. Frank and Emery E. George. Ann Arbor: University of Michigan Press (1973): 113–28.

Graves, Robert and Omar Ali-Shah. *The Rubaiyat of Omar Khayyam: A New Translation with Critical Commentaries*. London: Cassell, 1967.

Groome, Francis Hindes. *Edward FitzGerald: An Aftermath With Miscellanies in Verse and Prose*, 1902. Freeport, N.Y.: Books for Libraries Press, rpt. 1972.

Halbach, Helen. *Romance of the Rubaiyat: A Comprehensive Directory to the Myriad Editions of the Rubáiyát, the Ephemeron, Edward FitzGerald, Omar Khayyam and the Lesser Persian Poets*. Santa Barbara, California: Halbach, 1975.

Hammat, Abdelhalim. *Orientalism in Edward FitzGerald Seen Through His Adaptation of Omar Khayyam's Quatrains*. Algiers: University of Algiers, Institute of Foreign Languages, 1978.

Hayter, Alethea. *FitzGerald to His Friends: Selected Letters of Edward FitzGerald*. London: Scolar Press, 1979.

Helfand, Michael S. "Guide to the Year's Work in Victorian Poetry: 1985: FitzGerald and Other Minor Mid-Victorian Poets." *Victorian Poetry* 24, no. 3 (Autumn 1986): 313–316.

Lang, Cecil Y. *The Pre-Raphaelites and Their Circle. With the Rubáaiyát of Omar Khayyáam*. Boston: Houghton Mifflin, 1968.

Martin, Robert Bernard. "The Most Translatingest Man." *The American Scholar* 52, no. 4 (Autumn 1983): 540–546.

———. *Tennyson: The Unquiet Heart*. New York: Oxford University Press, 1980.

Martin, Jeffrey P. Edward FitzGerald and Bernard Barton: An Unsparing Friendship." *Syracuse University Library Associates Courier* 24, no. 2 (Fall 1989): 29–43.

Nasr, Seyyed Hossein. "Omar Kháyyám: Philosopher-Poet-Scientist." *The Islamic Intellectual Tradition in Persia*. Richmond, Surrey, England: Curzon Press, 1996.

Neuhaus, Richard John. "Eat, Drink and Be Merry." *The Eternal Pity: Reflections on Dying*. Notre Dame: University of Notre Dame Press, 2000.

Potter, Ambrose George. *A Bibliography of the Rubaiyat of Omar Khayyam, Together with Kindred Matter in Prose and Verse Pertaining Thereto*. Hildesheim; New York: Georg Olms Verlag, 1994.

Prasad, Indira. "Translation and Adaptation: Their Respective Realms." *International Journal of Translation* 2, no. 1 (January-June 1990): 37–45.

Sareen, S. K. "The Factor of Intertextuality in Translation." *International Journal of Translation* 1, no. 1 (Jan. 1989): 41–48.

Shahid, Irfan. *Omar Khayyam: The Philosopher-Poet of Medieval Islam*. Washington, D.C.: Georgetown University Press, 1982.

Terhune, Alfred McKinley. *The Life of Edward FitzGerald*. New Haven: Yale University Press, 1947.

Timko, Michael. "Edward FitzGerald." From *The Victorian Poets: A Guide to Research*, 2nd edition, edited by Frederic E. Faverty. Cambridge: Harvard University Press, 1968.

Trivedi, Harish. "Orientalism Translated: Omar Khayyam Through Persian, English and Hindi." *Colonial Transactions: English Literature and India*. Manchester; New York: Manchester University Press, 1996.

Tutin, John Ramsden. *A Concordance to FitzGerald's Translation of the Rubáiyát of Omar Khayyám*. New York: Johnson Reprint Corp., 1960.

Weber, C.J. *FitzGerald's Rubaiyat: Centennial Edition*. Waterville, Maine: Colby College Press, 1959,

———. "Preparing for the Centenary of FitzGerald's Rubaiyat." *Colby Library Quarterly*, Ser. V (March 1959): 5–14.

Yohannan, John D. *Persian Poetry in England and America: A 200-Year History*. Delmar, NY: Caravan Books, 1977.

Acknowledgments

"The Fin de Siècle Cult of FitzGerald's 'Rubaiyat' of Omar Khayyam" by John D. Yohannan. From *Review of National Literatures* 2, no. 1: 74–91. © 1971 by *Review of National Literatures*. Reprinted by permission.

"*The Rubáiyáat of Omar Khayyám*" by Iran B. Hassani Jewett. From *Edward Fitzgerald:* 73–111. © 1977 by G.K. Hall & Co. Reprinted by permission of the Gale Group.

"Fugitive Articulation: An Introduction to *The Rubáiyát of Omar Khayyám*" by Daniel Schenker. From *Victorian Poetry* 19, no. 1. © 1981 by West Virginia University. Reprinted by permission.

"The Discovery of the *Rubáiyát*" by Robert Bernard Martin. From *With Friends Possessed: A Life of Edward FitzGerald:* 211–234. © 1985 by Robert Bernard Martin. Reprinted by permission.

"The Apocalyptic Vision of La Vida es Sueño: Calderón and Edward FitzGerald" by Frederick A. de Armas. From *Comparative Literature Studies* 23, no. 2: 119–140. © 1986 Board of Trustees of the University of Illinois.

"Young Eliot's Rebellion" by Vinni Marie D'Ambrosio. From *Eliot Possessed: T. S. Eliot and FitzGerald's Rubaiyat*: 58–85. ©1989 by New York University. Reprinted by permission.

"Larger Hopes and the New Hedonism: Tennyson and FitzGerald" by Norman Page. From *Tennyson: Seven Essays*, edited by Philip Collins: 141–159. © 1992 by The Macmillan Press Ltd. Reprinted by permission.

"Bernard Quaritch and 'My Omar': The Struggle for FitzGerald's *Rubáiyát*" by Arthur Freeman. From *The Book Collector*: 60–75. © 1997 by The Collector Limited. Reprinted by permission.

"Paradise Enow" by John Hollander. From *Yale Review* 86, no. 3. © 1998 by John Hollander. Reprinted by permission.

"The Tale of the Inimitable *Rubaiyat*" by Tracia Leacock-Seghatolislami. From *Translation Persepctives* XI: 107–121. © 2000 by the State University of New York at Binghamton. Reprinted by permission.

"Forgetting FitzGerald's *Rubáiyát*" by Erik Gray. From *Studies in English Literature 1500–1900*: 765–783. © 2001 by William Marsh Rice University. Reprinted by permission.

Index